GOD'S ID

NYATHUTA

Michael Terence
Publishing

To my dear father and brother,
Wanjohi wa Mahinda and Mahinda wa Wanjoh.

Contents

Preface 1

GOD's ID 2

1: My Old Views on God 3

2: The global and Christian perception of God 5

3: Various factors have led to atheism 8

4: Why does Man need a God? 19

5: Who really is God? What is God's true identity? 20

6: A brief description of the Holy Bible and its history 28

7: Now let's see how God describes himself in the Bible 40

8: The creation 45

9: God's law 49

10: God rescues Israel from slavery 62

11: Israelites receive a discouraging report about
     the promised land 76

12: The Israelites reject leadership from Jehovah 80

13: The capture of the Ark of the Covenant by an enemy 83

14: A death casualty in the transportation of
     the Ark of the True God 89

15: God rescues Jerusalem from capture by the Assyrians 93

16: Three Israelites challenge the mighty king of Babylon 99

17: Jesus Christ 113

18: A Prologue of the Life of Jesus Christ 119

19: Now let's get to the key question. What proof is
     there that Jesus Christ was the son of God? 127

20: The miracles performed by Jesus Christ 142

21: How big were the crowds, that followed Jesus? 148

22: Moses the prophet mentioned Christ 151

23: How does Jesus take away the sins of the world? 155

24: What led to the death of Jesus Christ? 164

25: Conspiracy to kill Jesus Christ 169

26: The Last Supper 173

27: The death of Jesus Christ 183

28: The resurrection of Jesus Christ 197

29: The reception of The Holy Spirit 205

**30: What did Jesus accomplish through his
      mission on earth?** 210

31: God is there to benefit man 227

32: Miscellaneous 229

**33: Psychedelics, new cures for drug addiction
      and mental disorders** 297

Preface

Why have I chosen to write about God's identity? Many people today do not really know who God is and there is a lot of confusion regarding God's identity; that is why I decided to write on this subject. For many years I did not have a correct concept of God. I am a Christian and I am writing about God from a Christian point of view. However, the perception of God is an individual matter, relating to one's religious teachings but much more important, to an individual's personal experience with God.

Why is it important to know who God really is? That is His identity, as far as the human mind can grasp. This knowledge is vital for all human beings because of the enormous benefits we get throughout our lives from knowing the true God and relying on Him. Secondly, this knowledge of God leads to eternal life. On the other hand, if we get the wrong concept of God, then our relationship with Him, if we have any, might be awkward, compromised and could even be a source of great distress or fear; for example, if you believe God is ready to throw you into a burning fire from which you have no escape. Wrong beliefs could create an aversion to God; this is why it is important to have an accurate knowledge of Him.

Unfortunately, people who do not know God at all, are bound to miss out on His vital support throughout life. I hope that this book will serve as a platform, from which we can begin our personal search for God. For those who believe there is a God simply because they were taught so, this book could help them re-assess their belief and come up with their own, personal conviction that God really does exist.

GOD's ID

Before I delve deeper into the subject of God's identity, I will start by outlining some important background information.

- A survey of why people, in general, do not believe in God.
- I will outline the concept of God in Christianity, based on the Bible; it can be quite a divisive topic among Christians.
- Who created the Bible? Is it a valid book, a book that I can rely on?
- What information is required for an ID? What is God's ID, based on this format?

Then I will explore what other means we can use to understand God's Identity.

There are five important clues to God's identity:

1. The creation/nature
2. How God describes Himself in the Bible
3. God's Law from the Bible
4. God's interactions with the Israelite people, from the Bible
5. The life and teachings of Jesus Christ, from the Bible

After that, I will explore what Jesus had to say on some controversial topics.

In the last chapter, I will give examples of relying on God's support to solve some important problems.

1

My Old Views on God

As a Christian, Catholic child I was given a very conflicting view of God; first, as a caring loving God who provides for all our needs and second, as a very vindictive being, who if you died in sin, would throw you into a place called Hell, where you would burn forever in a fire that does not extinguish. One gets the impression that God is coercing man into obeying Him and this generates resentment and rebellion.

For many years, I had never really made a great effort to understand the Bible. If you believe God is a "Vindictive Being" you will not want to read the Bible, as you have already acquired a bias against it.

The first commandment in **Exodus 20: 3,** where God says, *"You must not have any other gods besides me,"* only served to increase my resentment towards God; it seemed to me that God was forcing me to worship Him. I also perceived this Law to be an act of intimidation because if I did not worship God, I might end up in Hell. I wondered, why would God want me, practically a nobody, to worship Him. He, God has everything. He owns the whole universe, knows everything and is very powerful; He never dies etc. Is He not content with that? Why also, does He have the pretext that I should worship Him?

Then one day, after my very long existence on this earth, I reviewed this first commandment and it occurred to me that perhaps I had misunderstood the definition of the word "God." So, I decided to investigate the meaning of that word. How did I go about it? I Googled the word "God" to find out how God is identified by different people all over the world and then I decided to see from the Bible how God identifies Himself.

Why the Bible? I had always had serious doubts about the credibility of the first part of the Bible; I had often wondered who was present when God created the world, to be able to write down what happened during creation. I believed, however, that most of the Bible, in general, was inspired by God, but first, just to be sure, I decided to do some research on its origin and its authenticity. First let us see how God is identified in the world, in general.

2

The global and Christian

perception of God

Atheism is the belief that a God or gods do not exist. Agnosticism is the view that the existence of a God or a supernatural being is unknown or unknowable. Theism, in philosophy, is the view that there is a God who is the creator and sustainer of the universe and is unlimited regarding knowledge (omniscience), power (omnipotence), extension (omnipresence) and moral perfection (omnibenevolence). This God as described here, is the principal object of faith and worship in monotheistic religions.

Generally, Christians have the same concept of God, as that expressed in theism. In most religions, God is perceived as a superhuman being or spirit worshipped as having power over nature and human fortunes.

Let's look in more detail at the concept of God, as perceived in Christianity. In Christianity and according to the Bible, God has the following characteristics:

1. **The Creator:** He created the universe and everything in it.
2. All merciful: feeling or showing sympathy and concern for others.
3. Omnibenevolence: infinitely good or all-loving.
4. Omniscient: all-knowing i.e., has perfect knowledge of everything, hence also a source of moral authority, a source of justice and righteousness.
5. Omnipotent: all-powerful, all-mighty, supreme.

6. Omnipresent: was present in the past; is now present and will be present in the future; eternally present and has knowledge of what is happening everywhere simultaneously.

7. One Unique Being: there is no other similar being in existence and He does not change with time.

I believe the above seven definitions summarize almost all the other different definitions given to God in general. In Christianity, however, one very important manner of defining God is constantly left out i.e. "Our Father" or in other words, one who lovingly takes care of us, human beings and takes care of the entire universe, through His constant, positive and dynamic energy. "My Father" or "Our Father," was used repeatedly by Jesus Christ to address God.

Please note, the "Our" before the word "Father," means that all human beings are brothers since we all originate from the one source, from the one and only Creator, God.

The omission of this very important definition of God as "Our Father" has alienated man from his Creator. Although God is a super-genius in all, if He had no relationship with us human beings, what use would all His knowledge and other benevolent properties be to man? None at all.

These super qualities of God seem to create a huge inferiority complex in many individuals. I too felt kind of intimidated by all these super qualities. However, once I realised that these same qualities could be used for my support if requested and when required, my intimidation disappeared. Today, I feel comforted by the knowledge that God uses his qualities, also for the benefit of all mankind and the entire universe.

Before the 20th century, there were practically no people living freely in this world, who did not have a God and/or religion, but from the 20th century onwards, atheism has continued to flourish. Why? Never before in man's history, has the existence of God been more challenged than it is today. Atheism, i.e., not believing in the existence of any God, is at its highest peak ever. Why is this so?

3

Various factors

have led to atheism

Lack of religious teachings and incorrect religious teachings

Nowadays in society, whether at school or in most homes, there is no religious teaching; even the basics such as the existence of God or the fact that He created the universe, including man. Instead, new scientific ideas regarding the origin of man and the origin of creation have emerged and these ideas, such as evolution and the Big Bang theory, are the ones that are taught in schools and transmitted by the mass media. Therefore, as a result, a large majority of people now believe in evolution, but do not believe in "creation."

So, you end up with no religious education in schools and no religious education at home. However, some Christian Churches do have catechism or some other form of religious teachings from the clergy or members of the congregation. The problem is, many of these religious teachings are not accurate and a lot of emphasis is given to human doctrines that have little to do with the Bible.

Quite frequently, one discovers later **ON IN LIFE**, that the religious teachings given to you as a child were not correct. This can create mistrust and repulsion towards the church as an institution and a sense of revulsion for religion in general, at least temporarily. However, for some, this could also be an incentive to look for "the true religion" or to look for the true God, elsewhere.

Living in wealthy nations means that almost all your needs are catered for and therefore, one does not really feel the need for a God for his survival, until something drastic or unexplained happens, for example, a close encounter with death or the occurrence of natural disasters like earthquakes, hurricanes etc. These events make "modern" man realize how terribly vulnerable he is and that he has no control at all over what happens to him; then, he starts to ask questions and seek answers.

Hiding the dead, the human corpses from young people

It is quite easy nowadays to find people aged twenty years or more, who have never seen a human corpse. In some cultures, children and young people are shielded by society, especially their parents, from seeing dead people, even when they were part of the family or very close members of the family. This, in my opinion, is a missed opportunity for any human being, even young children, to start seeking crucial answers to their origin, their purpose in life and their final destiny. Such questions would most probably lead one to question if there exists a God and the purpose of this God.

Children are able to cope a lot better with death than adults and this is especially true if they get to know that the dead do not suffer. Knowing where the dead go will depend on their culture or religion.

May I say that young people who might end up believing that they are somehow immortal might get very shocked the day they realise they too will die, eventually? Some could even end up with psychiatric problems. Therefore, hiding the dead from young people is doing them a great disservice.

Man's direct contact with nature, has been greatly reduced

Nature is the most prominent expression of God; everything in nature carries the signature of the Creator, from the invisible viruses and bacteria to ants, trees, animals and up to the heavenly bodies. If one observes nature attentively, whether under a microscope or with the naked eye, one is bound to conclude that there must be "a Creator" because of its complexity, intelligence, beauty, harmony and how its characteristics adapt extremely well for its survival. It is difficult to believe that such order and complexity were derived from "chaos" i.e., "the Big Bang."

Lack of free time

This precious item has been greatly reduced and targeted by many industries as a great source of income. Here are a few examples: watching television programmes; excessive use of smartphones and their Apps; Facebook, Tik-Tok, and YouTube; games etc; play stations; computers; the excessive practice of sport; hanging out frequently with friends in pubs etc. so that one ends up having little or no time to reflect. The result is that many people exist without really reflecting deeply on their lives.

The doctrine of self-reliance

Many teachings of modern society encourage people to be self-sufficient, to rely mainly on themselves and that "being independent" is something to be sought after. Anyone who believes in a God is clearly not self-sufficient but relies on God to sustain him in all ways. By acknowledging God, one makes make it clear to all, that you are not independent. When it comes to the public image, pride is an obstacle to God because most of us would like others to believe that we rely only upon ourselves.

God is out of fashion

It is not fashionable to talk about God because it could be a source of embarrassment to people who are ignorant about God, as their ignorance would become evident to all if they can't join in the discussion. Talking about God in public could be a source of conflict for those who perceive God differently from you in a multicultural and multi-ethnic society, or it could irritate those such as atheists who contest the very existence of God. Therefore, this topic is constantly avoided.

God is blamed for the presence of evil on earth

Many people ask: **"If there is a God, why is there so much evil in the world?"** Another question that closely follows is: **"If He is all-powerful, why does he not do something about it?"** The people who ask such questions, clearly do not know God or the Bible because evil really is the absence of God.

Man tends to forget that the existence of the Devil is real and man by himself, without God, is easy prey for the Devil. The Devil prefers to remain incognito and many people, myself included, tend to forget that he is real. Jesus instead, acknowledged the existence of evil spirits.

See **Luke 10:17-20**: The seventy-two disciples of Jesus Christ returned after preaching with joy and said, "Lord, even the demons submit to us in your name."

Man has free will; if he decides he wants to live in evil, as some people opt to worship Satan to get rich, he is free to do so. If one reads the Bible, there are very many occasions in which God has intervened to destroy evil: Sodom and Gomorrah; flooding the earth during Noah's time and according to the Bible, the destruction of very many cities and civilizations, to purge evil and restore God's righteousness.

God intervenes in his own time, mainly when evil has reached a very high level. God will always protect and guide righteous people even when surrounded by evil. For example, before the destruction of Sodom and Gomorrah, Abraham, a righteous man, enquired, "Will you really sweep away the righteous with the wicked?" Abraham then goes on to enquire, "Suppose only ten righteous men are found there in Sodom and Gomorrah, will you destroy these ten righteous men together with the wicked people?" The reply given was, "I will not destroy Sodom and Gomorrah, for the sake of the ten." **Genesis 18:32.**

The practice of baptizing infants

A large number of Christian Churches perform baptism on infants and this has been another source of the decline of Christianity. First, let's see the definition of baptism. Baptism is a Christian rite of publicly accepting the teachings of Jesus Christ, publicly admitting your faith in Jesus Christ and an act of dedication to live according to God's Law. It is also an act of being officially admitted into the Christian Church. It is symbolized by pouring or sprinkling water on the head, or by immersing, either partially or completely, in water. This act symbolises purification from sins and renewal or rebirth into a new life of dedication to God. Christening is another name for baptism when associated also with the naming of an infant. Not all Christians baptize with water e.g., Quakers and Salvation Army.

In the colonial era and even to the present day, Christening done during baptism in some countries is associated with acquiring a foreign name, generally that of a foreign saint. These saints are supposed to protect the individual being baptized. I have heard some Europeans ask how come an African has a European name. I personally, do not believe any saint can protect you, once **THEY** die; only God can. Nowadays, you are not obliged to acquire a foreign name during baptism.

Nowadays, some Christian Churches baptize only adults or people who have reached an age where they fully understand the significance of baptism. This practice is called, **credobaptism or believer's baptism**. These Christian churches believe that baptism is such a serious issue that you should be fully aware of what you are committing yourself to when you accept to get baptized.

In **infant baptism**, also called **paedo-baptism**, the child has no capacity to understand and therefore to dedicate their life to God or even to a specific Christian Church. This fact is brushed aside by the churches practising it, by saying God claims the child with divine grace. Most of the Churches practising paedo-baptism also give these infants "a godfather" or "a godmother", **THAT IS**, a practising Christian adult who takes on the responsibility of ensuring the infant grows up "dedicated to God." Most paedo-baptized people have absolutely no idea who their godfather or godmother is, therefore these "guiding figures" are completely absent from their lives.

Paedo-baptism **deprives the individual of knowing about God** and of deciding if they would like to dedicate their lives to Him because someone else makes decisions for them without their consent and makes these infants into "Christians." Some of these paedo-baptised individuals will eventually enquire and search for God, but for others, "religion," and "God," will remain a blind spot in their lives.

Note; Jesus Christ was baptized as an adult: **John 1: 29-34** and **Matthew 3:13-17**; all the baptism done by the early Christians was done to adults only.

Unchristian life supported by the media

The clergy of many Christian Churches today will not preach against subjects like sexual immorality, people being obsessed with their physical appearance and other uncomfortable subjects very present in society today and promoted by the media, they just turn a blind eye. These Christian clergy probably do not want to offend or lose some members of their congregation. Also, they too could be subjected to bad publicity by the media. It is the duty of all Christians to uphold God's laws, but the clergy of many Christian Churches seem more afraid of the media and humans than of God.

Misleading rituals and man-made doctrines present in certain Christian Churches

The Doctrine of the Trinity

Some Christian Churches do not have a clear definition of who God really is. They teach that God exists as the Holy Trinity, that He is one but at the same time, made of three distinct Gods. If one seeks an explanation from the clergy regarding this Holy Trinity, you are advised to have faith. The word Trinity or Holy Trinity is completely absent from the Bible. This problem of uncertainty when it comes to defining God, is very disorienting because one does not even know who they are addressing their prayers to.

One day, I happened to hear someone preaching to the public and he made the following statement: *"Jesus is God and Jesus is also the Holy Spirit."* I asked this guy, *"If Jesus is God, who was he praying to?"* He did not have an answer to this question. A religion cannot afford to have a wrong concept of God.

The Doctrine of Transubstantiation of the Eucharist

During his last meal with his disciples, after Jesus had taken the bread and broken it, he gave thanks and then made this statement, "This is my body given for you; **do this in remembrance of me.**" **(Luke 22: 19)**. Many Christian Churches repeat this ritual performed by Jesus Christ during his Last Supper, by giving the **Eucharist also called the Holy Communion** to their congregation. In his last supper, Jesus requested his disciples to use the bread and the wine **as a symbol**, mainly to commemorate his death, **but** some Christian Churches claim otherwise and have introduced the concept of transubstantiation.

The concept of transubstantiation, according to the teaching of some Christian Churches, is the change of the whole substance of bread which is used as the Eucharist, into the **real** Body of Christ and the change of the wine taken with the Eucharist, into the **real**

Blood of Christ. This change is perceived to be real and brought about by the efficacy of prayer and by the action of the Holy Spirit.

However, the outward characteristics of bread and wine remain unaltered.

I have taken the Eucharist and the wine of the Holy Communion, several times. I can confirm that the bread retains the taste and texture of bread and the wine also retains the taste and texture of wine and not of blood.

Can man transform any earthly materials into a "Godly substance?" Do you believe that this is possible? If something is "Godly," then it should have "Godly" power/s.

If the apostles had actually eaten "the body of Jesus" or drunk "the blood of Jesus," when Jesus instituted the Eucharist/The Holy Communion, it would surely have been noted by them with reactions of surprise and horror, if not of disgust. As none of these reactions took place, it can only mean one thing, **no transubstantiation took place, when Jesus instituted the first Holy Communion.**

Jesus Christ was a Jew and practised Judaism; cannibalism is not permitted in Judaism; this is why Jesus could not have literally transformed bread into his own flesh.

I believe this "literal change" of the bread and wine, might be justified by a biblical verse: **John 6: 53-56**: So, Jesus said to them, *"Truly, truly, I say to you, unless you eat the flesh of the Son of Man and drink His blood, you have no life in yourselves. He who eats my flesh and drinks my blood has eternal life, and I will raise him up on the last day. <u>For my flesh is true food, and my blood is true drink.</u> He who eats my flesh and drinks my blood abides in me, and I in him."*

Jesus concluded the above preaching by saying; **John 6: 63**: *"It is the spirit that is life-giving; the flesh is of no use at all. The sayings that I have spoken to you are spirit and are life."*

The frequent reception of The Eucharist /The Holy Communion, if perceived to be the real body of Jesus Christ means that, whoever receives it will obviously be under the impression that they have a passport to Heaven. They will not be concerned about knowing the scriptures, and therefore the word of God; furthermore, who will ever go to Hell, if they have internalized the body of Christ? **It is very painful for me to acknowledge that this false conviction is equivalent to idolatry because one perceives a piece of "man-made bread" and "man-made wine" to have Godly powers**. This particular ritual keeps man away from God by creating false assurances, that the Eucharist will somehow protect him because it is the real body of Christ.

The institution of the Eucharist was done **as part of the Passover meal.** In Judaism, the Passover meal is done once a year. How then did this Remembrance Meal end up being done, in some Christian Churches so frequently, sometimes several times daily, despite the fact that when something is done frequently, it loses its importance?

Perhaps it is time to review some practices present in various Christian Churches and update them.

Scandals in the Institution of the Christian Churches

As a child, or even as an adult, one is taught to have complete confidence in the Christian Church and its clergy. If this trust is broken, one loses trust in the institutions of the Christian Church, but it could also seriously affect one's faith in God. These Christian institutions are meant to promote the Christian faith, not destroy it.

The scandals regarding sexual abuse by the Christian clergy have made it very clear that the institutions of the Christian Churches are managed by human beings, with all their weaknesses **AND ALSO THAT**, it is not correct to have blind faith in these institutions and it is okay to ask questions about the clergy and take legal action when necessary.

Hierarchy in the Christian Churches

Before officially ordaining priests, certain Christian Churches require Oaths of Canonical Obedience, whereby the people being ordained make an oath of submission to the canons of a church and an oath of submission to their bishop and their higher-ranking clergy. Other religious orders, Nuns, Monks etc are also required to make an oath of obedience, of submission to their superiors.

Should an ordained priest discover his superiors are practising something criminal or contrary to the teachings of the Bible or contrary to the law of the country he lives in, he will be obliged to report it to "the superiors of his superior." If his superiors have requested him not to go to the police when a crime is committed and no action is taken to address his complaints, what should he do?

Up until the recent past, it would have been useless to go to the police, because, for many years, the power of many Christian Churches has been able to block almost all prosecutions of its clergy. It seems like things have changed in recent years; many Christian Churches have declared that they will no longer seek to protect any of their clergy when accused of child abuse if there is enough evidence to convict them. It all remains to be seen if things have actually changed.

I believe these "professional" oaths present in Christian Churches, are an important factor that has led to the successful cover-up, of child abuse over many years by the Christian clergy. These abuse scandals by the Christian clergy created disillusion and atheism among their congregation and especially among young people. Let's hope, however, that many Christians have discovered that the true God is quite different from the institutions of the Christian Church itself.

These oaths of obedience are contrary to the teaching of Jesus, because, if you have to obey someone unconditionally, this implies that they are superior to you.

The scriptures say: **Matthew 23:8-11;** *"But you, do not you be called Rabbi, for one is your Teacher, **and all of you are brothers;** Moreover, do not call anyone on earth, your father, for one is your Father, The Heavenly One. Neither be called leaders, for your leader is one, the Christ/ the Messiah."*

In some countries, there are oaths of obedience imposed on the clergy to the political system, e.g., that of obedience to a monarchy. Such oaths mean that the clergy cannot speak up and condemn anything bad or let's say unchristian, done by the political systems of these countries. Jesus Christ was apolitical; he did not engage in politics and therefore the Church, if it claims to follow Christ, should practise autonomy as far as possible from politics and political systems.

I believe all Christian Churches should update themselves regularly, if they are to survive, because, all kinds of information is now easily accessible to the public and Christian Churches are open to public scrutiny more than ever.

4

Why does Man need a God?

From time immemorial man has always been conscious of his own limits. As a human being, he cannot foresee the future, **he** is susceptible to death; he cannot control natural disasters like earthquakes, tsunamis, famine, flooding and hurricanes; his enemies could be stronger than him; sometimes he doesn't even know who his enemies really are. On the other hand, man has always perceived that someone or something out there, much more powerful than him could or will assist him to overcome his obstacles in life; a God.

I believe man was created with an innate capacity to perceive and communicate with God. Without this communication, God would be of no benefit to man. Man needs God to help him resolve his problems, especially when he finds that he cannot resolve them; and for this reason, God/gods have been held in high regard by all peoples. One just needs to see the magnificent temples, churches and mosques constructed as places of worship, all over the world and the magnificent natural sites reserved as "Holy sites" by the people living nearby; for example, the Himalayas, Mt Kilimanjaro, Mt Kenya, etc.

In the past and right up to the present day, there has been a tendency to worship objects in nature, on which man relies heavily for his survival, for example, the sun and great rivers like the Nile or River Ganges. From the natural sites and places of worship associated with God/gods, it is clear that man has always perceived God or gods mainly as benefactors.

5

Who really is God?

What is God's true identity?

If you look at any identification document or ID, it has four to five pieces of information/data, that are essential to identify any individual; but it could also have more information.

In the Developing and Third World countries, many homes have no street names or numbers, therefore, addresses are not obtainable. The use of biometrics indexes is essential to making an ID specific to one person. Nowadays, in more advanced countries, iris biometric data is used in the creation of ID documents.

Biometric index definition is a physical characteristic drawn from one part of the human body which is specific to that one individual, e.g. fingerprints, iris, facial image etc. and which is used for automated recognition/automated authentication of the individual.

The following is what is required of any ID:

1) The name of a particular individual

2) An image of the individual, generally in the form of a photo

3) The date of birth

4) An address

5) Biometric index e.g. a fingerprint or an image of your iris

It would be impossible for any two or more individuals to have in common all the above five pieces of data; even identical twins, have different biometric indexes.

Using the information above, let's see if we can get to know God's identity as far as our human mind can grasp.

Does God have a name?

The Bible confirms that God actually has a name that identifies Him and Him alone, in other words, a unique name.

According to MyNameStatistics.com, a database in the United States of America which is used to check the frequency of various names in the US Census Bureau, one out of ten million Americans is called Jehovah. Then a "prophet" in Western Kenya calls himself Jehovah. Apparently, the real Jehovah, that is God, has permitted these people to be alive today.

If the children receive names from their parents, what can they do about it? Or if someone is suffering from a delusion, a psychiatric illness, whereby one becomes irreversibly convinced of something, generally of an abnormal idea of being God, what can be done about it? What I do know is Jehovah represents justice and is extremely merciful.

Yes, God has a name; as revealed to the prophet Moses, as four Hebrew consonants, YHWH, called the Tetragrammaton, Greek for four-letter word and pronounced, Yahweh.

Latin does not have the letter Y, therefore the Christian Latin-speaking scholars translating the Hebrew texts into Latin substituted the Y of the Tetragrammaton with the letter J and therefore God's name came to be written as JeHoWAH and pronounced "Jehovah".

Moses in **Exodus 3: 13,** enquires of God: "*Suppose I go to the sons of Israel and say to them, 'The God of your fathers has sent me to you,' and they ask me, 'What is His Name?' What should I say to them?*" In **Exodus 3: 14-15**, God answered Moses, "**I am who I am.**" Then He said, "*You are to say to the sons of Israel, 'I am' has sent me to you. This is what you are to say to the Israelites, YAHWEH the God of your forefathers, the God of Abraham, the God of Isaac, and the*

God of Jacob, has sent me to you.' This is my name forever, and this is how I am to be remembered from generation to generation."

God's name in Judaism, Yahweh, is considered too holy by practising Jews to be written or pronounced. Jews also avoid using it, so as not to break the third commandment: *"You must not take up the name of* **Yahweh/Jehovah your God** *in a worthless way, for Yahweh/Jehovah will not leave unpunished the one who takes up His name in a worthless way."* The Jews therefore, have substituted God's real name with six other names and these too, are considered holy.

What is the significance of this name: **I am who I am?**

I interpret, **I am** as equivalent to 'I do exist', and **I am who I am** as 'You cannot define me, but I do exist.' I find it unimaginably overwhelming to try to define someone who can create the whole universe and everything in it; what words would suffice to define such a Supreme Being? However, one must have a concept of God, to address him in prayer.

God also mentions his name several times in the hearing of all the Israelites gathered below Mount Sinai, receiving the Ten Commandments, **Because God spoke out aloud to the Israelites**; see: **Exodus 20: 1** and **Exodus 20: 22** and read out all the Ten Commandments in their hearing. Jehovah then inscribed on a slate of stone, the Ten Commandments for the Israelites.

The Third Commandment is**: "**You must not take up the name of Jehovah your God in a worthless way, for Jehovah will not leave unpunished the one who takes up His name in a worthless way." This Third Commandment would not make sense if Jehovah did not have a specific and unique name.

Jehovah has made provisions to protect his unique and holy name and to punish those who misuse it. A more precise interpretation of this law is: Jehovah hears and answers you, when you call on his name, (from any part of the universe), but do not abuse this privilege by disturbing Him for nothing.

Christ, who was sent as God's representative, did not dispute God's name, instead, he confirmed it by quoting scriptures from the Torah, (the Hebrew scripture that contains The Law, equivalent to the first five books of the Bible, as written by the prophet Moses), on more than one occasion, see below:

Deuteronomy 8: 3/ Matthew 4: 4; But he answered: "*It is written: 'Man must live, not on bread alone, but on every word that comes from **Jehovah's** mouth.*"

Deuteronomy 6: 16/ Matthew 4: 7; Jesus said to him: "*Again it is written: 'You must not put **Jehovah** your God to the test.'*"

Deuteronomy 5: 9/ Matthew 4: 10; Then Jesus said to him*: "Get away from me, Satan! For it is written: 'It is **Jehovah** your God you must worship, and it is to **Him alone** you must render sacred service.*"

All the information above, confirms that God does have a name.

The term "**the Lord**," used in very many Bible versions to represent the name of God, is simply a title, such as King, Duke, Ayatollah etc. and cannot be considered to represent God's name. The omission of God's name in these Bibles is a scandal because it is clear that **God would like people to know that he is real and that having a name makes him more real**. In King James' newest Bible version, **the Divine Name King James Bible** (2011) God's name has been restored and now appears six thousand, nine hundred and seventy-two (**6,972**) times.

God's image

You cannot identify a person from his name only, you need an image, generally in the form of a photo as it gives the most easily-recognizable representation of the person. In **Exodus 33: 20,** God said to Moses; "No living being can see God and live."

In the Bible, all the prophets who have had a close encounter with God, have instinctively covered their faces when in the presence of God. Examples: Moses: **Exodus 3:6** and Elijah: **1 Kings 19: 11-13.** Also, God himself took the precaution of screening prophets' faces away from Him, to preserve them alive, if he appeared to them in a vision; **Exodus 33: 21-23.**

Generally, people who do not worship idols perceive God to exist in the form of a spirit. According to Jesus Christ, God exists in the form of a spirit; **John 4: 24**: *"God is a Spirit, and those worshipping him must worship with spirit and truth."* A spirit is immaterial, therefore it's impossible for man to represent God in any form or image or photo and it is impossible to have any biometric index from God, as he does not have a body.

I have not heard anyone today or in the past, claim to have seen God, **except Jesus Christ.** See the scriptures: **John 6: 46**; *"Not that any man has seen the Father, except the one who is from God; this one has seen the Father."*

Michelangelo and other artists have drawn images of God, but these images are simply the fruit of their imagination. Never did any of these artists claim to have seen God.

The Bible, however, says that man is actually made in the image of God. "Then God said: *"Let us make man in our image, according to our likeness..."* **Genesis 1: 26.** Most probably this statement regards God's qualities, not his physical appearance because as Jesus tells his apostles in **John 14: 9**, "Have I been with you so long, and you still do not know me, Philip? Whoever has seen me has seen the Father. How can you say, 'Show us the Father'?

If God is a Spirit our human eyes are not able to perceive spirits.

I feel confident to conclude that God's image remains unknown to man.

What is God's address?

Quoting **Isaiah 66: 1**; This is what Jehovah says:

> *"The heavens are my throne, and the earth is my footstool.*
>
> *Where, then, is the house that you could build for me,*
>
> *And where is my resting place?"*

Quoting Jesus Christ, **"***Our Father, who is in the Heavens, let your name* be *sanctified."* I believe, therefore, that The Heavens are the official residence of God.

In the past, God chose to reside among the Israelites, that is He was present among them; **Exodus 29: 43-46.** Also, He chose to reside in the Temple of Jerusalem: **2 Chronicles 7: 16.** This shows that God can decide to be present in certain places which then become holy.

Wherever God chooses to reside, he is always aware of all that goes on elsewhere in the universe; see **1 King 19: 17-18. "***Yet I reserve seven thousand in Israel--all whose knees have not bowed down to Baal and whose mouths have not kissed him."*

Although the nation of Israel had abandoned Jehovah, not everyone was worshipping the foreign god Baal: an idol, and Jehovah knew exactly who these faithful Israelites were.

To conclude, no living being knows exactly where God's residence is located, therefore, God's address remains unknown to man. However, God remains accessible to man from any place on earth because it is His will that man should access him.

What is God's date of birth?

The Bible starts with the following phrase: **Genesis 1: 1**; "In the beginning, God created the heavens and the earth." According to the most recent scientific data, of 2019, the **universe is 13.7 billion years and the earth is 4.54 billion years.** Eventually, with new discoveries over the years, this data is bound to change. It is my sincere belief that no man knows or will ever know, the age of the earth or the universe; the scientific data will keep changing periodically, as it always does, to accommodate new discoveries.

In the Bible, God says many times, that He, Himself, created the universe; this means that God Himself is older than the universe.

Isaiah 45: 12; "I made the earth and created man on it. I stretched out the heavens with my own hands, and I give orders to all their army/hosts/bodies."

Isaiah 48:13; My own hand laid the foundation of the earth, and my right hand spread out the heavens. I marshalled their starry hosts.

The truth is God has made it known to man that he doesn't have a date of birth; He is ageless and He has always existed. See in **Revelation 1: 8;** "*I am the Alpha and the Omega, the beginning and the end*" says Jehovah God, "*the One who is and who was and who is coming, the Almighty.*"

Now, resuming God's true identity;

- God has a unique name
- has no image
- his residence is unknown
- his is ageless
- and has no biometric index; He is a spirit

I believe you are not able to identify someone with a name only, even if he/she has a unique name. Now, imagine you are a detective and a hideous crime has been committed and the only information given to you is: "A masked man committed the crime." How would you go about creating the suspect's profile? To start with, you must also consider that the masked man might have been a woman and exclude this fact.

I am sure, as a detective, you would first go onto the site of the crime and collect any clues you think might be useful in identifying the culprit; cigarette butts, fingerprints, or any objects left by the criminal. You would also interrogate anyone who was on or near the crime scene when it happened. Then you would comb all the CCTV cameras nearby, if present, and you'd look for clues that might lead you to identify the culprit.

Now, the same thing goes for God; one is forced to look for clues, to identify Him better.

God has left numerous clues for mankind, for us to gain insight into who He is. The most important ones are:

- His creation
- He describes himself very well in the Bible
- His Laws; from the Bible
- His numerous interactions with different peoples and especially with the Israelites, as recorded in the Old Testament of the Bible
- Jesus Christ's life and his teachings; from the Bible

All these clues help man gain insight into the true nature of God.

If you really want to know someone's identity, you are bound to ask him or her, "*Who are you and what do you do for a living?*" Then, you must have a means to verify this information. This is why it is important for us to know how God identifies himself in the Bible.

Most of the information I have used to reveal God's identity is taken from the Bible. The Bible is a book made up of different "books" or scriptures and is used by Christians as their main book of worship. First, I had to do my private research, regarding the authnticity of the Christian Bible.

6

A brief description of the

Holy Bible and its history

As written previously, I had always questioned the authenticity of the first part of the Bible, Genesis; because it talked about The Creation even before man was created. How was it known what had happened before man was created?

When I learnt that **the first five books** of the Bible, in the Old Testament, had been written down by the prophet Moses, my doubts disappeared. I knew very well that Moses spent a lot of time on Mt Sinai, in God's presence and this removed any doubts I might have had on the validity of the initial part of the Bible. Then on reading the New Testament, I found that Jesus himself actually quoted some phrases from the initial part of the Old Testament and this further confirmed its validity.

Luke 17: 26-27; *"Moreover, just as it occurred in the days of Noah, so it will be in the days of the Son of man: they were eating, they were drinking, men were marrying, women were being given in marriage until that day when Noah entered into the ark, and the Flood came and destroyed them all."*

Matthew 11: 24; But I tell you that it will be more tolerable for Sodom on the Day of Judgment than for you.

See **Matthew 19: 3-6;** And Pharisees came to him intent on testing him and they asked: "Is it lawful for a man to divorce his wife on every sort of grounds?" In reply, he said: *"Have you not read that the one who created them from the beginning made them male and female and said: 'For this reason, a man will leave his father and his mother and will stick to his wife, and the two will be one flesh'? So* *that they are no longer two, but one flesh. Therefore, what God has yoked together, let no man put apart."*

Description of the Bible

The name Bible comes from Latin, Biblia, which means book or books and this word comes from the Greek, Ta Biblia, the books.

The Bible is made up of two parts:

The Old Testament is the first part of the Christian Bible; it makes up about 75% of the entire Bible and it was written by prophets from the Jewish nation. It is derived from the Jewish/Hebrew Bible, the Tanakh/Tanach. It regards God's Law and his relationship with the Jewish Nation from its formation up until the death of Jesus Christ, as narrated by different Jewish prophets.

Why up until the death of Christ? A few years after the death of Jesus Christ and precisely in **70 AD**, Jerusalem, the core of the Jewish nation, was destroyed by the Roman military forces for rebelling against Rome. There followed other Jewish revolts against Rome which ended in defeat and the dispersion of the Jews as a nation, worldwide, until 1948, when a new nation of Israel came into existence. There was no Jewish nation for almost 2000 years.

The New Testament is the second part of the Bible. It makes up about 25% of the entire Bible. It regards mainly the events and teachings of Jesus Christ and is written from the direct testimony of some apostles/companions of Jesus Christ. It also includes the life events of some of Christ's apostles and the first Christian converts after the death of Jesus. The last part of the New Testament, Revelation, writes of prophesies regarding the events that will lead to the end of the present world, the universal judgement and the restoration of a new permanent world which will last forever.

The New Testament was written from about **50 CE** to **100 CE;** it is formed of twenty seven books.

The first part of the New Testament is made up of the **four Canonical Gospels**; it narrates mainly the different events regarding the active life of Jesus Christ, from when he started his active mission on earth, to his death. The Canonical Gospels were written by or from the direct testimony of four of Christ's apostles/companions, Matthew, Mark, Luke and John. The scriptures of Matthew, Mark and Luke are very similar and are called synoptic gospels, but that of the apostle John is quite different.

The scriptures that follow the Canonical Gospels, regard events after the death of Jesus Christ. Here is a brief description of these scriptures:

We have the **Book of Acts**, written by the apostle Luke. It regards the rapid and miraculous spread of Christianity. Then we have **Twenty-one Epistles** which are letters written by apostles and first Christian converts; these letters were addressed to distant Christian communities in various regions of the Mediterranean. Paul, who was a Pharisee but then became a Christian convert, **wrote thirteen or fourteen books** of these Epistles; practically half of the New Testament. Nowadays, there is a dispute as to who wrote the Epistle to the Hebrews; it is no longer attributed to Paul. The other seven epistles are James (1), Peter (2), John (3) and Jude (1). It is said, James and Jude were both brothers of Jesus Christ. The last book of the New Testament is called **Revelation** and is based on a vision of events leading to The End of Times or End of the World, as revealed to John, one of Christ's apostles.

The Tanakh

The Tanakh, the Jewish Bible, is the origin of the Old Testament and is made up of three parts. **The Torah/**The Law/The instructions contain the five books_of Moses; Genesis, Exodus, Leviticus, Numbers and Deuteronomy. **The Nevi'im** /book of the prophets which contains writings by different prophets; eight books_and **the Ketuvim** (writings): eleven books: Ruth, Psalms,

Job, Proverbs, Ecclesiastes, Song of Solomon, Lamentations, Daniel, Esther, Ezra which includes Nehemiah, and I and II Chronicles.

The term **Torah** is also used to designate the entire Hebrew Bible.

The term **Miqra** is also used to refer to the Tanakh.

How authentic is the Jewish Bible?

To start with, let's just verify the authenticity of **only** the Torah, which is the oldest part of both the Tanakh and the Old Testament of the Bible. It contains the five books written by the prophet Moses: Genesis, Exodus, Leviticus, Numbers and Deuteronomy. These **Five Books of Moses** are also referred to as **Pentateuch**, a Greek word which means five books.

The current belief is The Torah was originally dictated to Moses by God.

Please note: The Samaritan people who claim to be Israelites and descendants of the ancient nation of Israel, northern Judah also have their own Torah called a Samaritan Torah. It has about six thousand differences from the Jewish Torah. In ancient times, perhaps even today, the Jews did not acknowledge the Samaritan people to be part of the Jewish nation. However, today they are part of the nation of Israel.

The Jewish Torah in use today **does not have other versions** and is called the Masoretic Torah. The Old Testament of the Christian Bible, is derived from the Masoretic Torah, not the Samaritan one and this is the one I will be referring to here.

How do we know that the Torah we have today reflects accurately, the one written by Moses?

The Jews had highly-trained professionals, **the Scribes**, whose job was that of transcribing documents. Transcription was necessary because there were no photocopying machines or paper in ancient Israel. The scriptures were hand-written on material of organic origin that degenerated with time and therefore before the scrolls of scriptures could get completely destroyed due to decay; they were transcribed onto new materials. Transcription was also required for the creation of new Tanakhs which would cater for Israelites living far away in foreign territories.

The transcription done by the scribes was ridiculously accurate; it involved copying the form of the letters and the exact spacing between the words and letters, a kind of hand-photocopying. If a letter touched another in any spot, it invalidated the entire Torah; this and other rules safeguarded the transcription process from any errors.

You can view how meticulously the Torah text was transcribed and all the rules regarding its transcription, from Google; digit: Accuracy of the Torah Text - Aish.com and other internet sites.

One Torah scroll is about 126 feet or 38.4m long and 20 inches or 0.48m wide; invalidating it for a minor error would have been extremely painful and expensive, therefore accuracy was essential.

In 2014, research was done by the Hebrew University in Israel, whereby **all the Torahs in the world, (not the Tanakh), were compared**, word for word. The result was astonishing; they were all practically identical, but the Yemenite Torah differed from the others; it differed in the spelling of nine words. These words had the same meaning and pronunciation.

See: "**The Dead Sea Scrolls** confirm the accuracy of the present-day Torah," from: jewishbelief.com/is-the-torahs-text-accurate/.

The Dead Sea Scrolls were found in the Judean desert in 1947 and following years. Among the treasure trove of artefacts and scrolls dating back more than 2,000 years, an almost complete

Torah scroll was found. The Dead Sea Scrolls Torah was found to be 95% similar to the Masoretic version we have today. The differences were primarily spelling variations and obvious pen slips.

This extremely high level of accuracy in transcribing the Torah gives us confidence that we can fully trust **in the present-day Torah to be accurately transmitting the Torah written by God's prophet, Moses.**

It is said that before his death, Moses wrote Thirteen Torah Scrolls. Twelve of these were distributed to each of the 12 Tribes of Israel. The thirteenth one was placed in the Ark of the Covenant, with the Tablets on which were inscribed the Ten Commandments. If anyone attempted to falsify the Torah, the other distributed copies would testify against him and also the one in the Ark would testify against him.

Today, there exists only one version of the Masoretic Torah and this text has been preserved practically unchanged over the centuries since it was first written by the Prophet Moses. The extremely high precision of its transcription and the very high level of security given to the Torah by the Jewish community and above all by God, has made this possible.

Today, we can also be confident that the rest of the Tanakh/Jewish Bible has the same degree of accuracy as the Torah because it was written by the same professionals that transcribed the Torah; also, it contains the word of the same God who dictated the Torah to Moses.

The creation of the Bible

Who put in place all the scriptures, to create the Holy Bible? The Bible is regarded as holy because it contains the word of God, which is holy.

The Bible as it is today was **officially** put together by The Third Canonical Council of Carthage, also called **Synod 397,** by them selecting scriptures from Judaism and scriptures originally written by, or from, narration from Christ's apostles and disciples; to form the present-day Bible. In this particular meeting, various Church authorities of the day, came together with the **foremost result being the official recognition of a list of the biblical canons, (a collection or list of sacred books accepted as genuine), as the accepted books of the Bible. The canons listed were the 27 books of the New Testament, as well as the 39 books of the Old Testament.**

Note: Before this Synod 397, bibles were already in existence: the **Codex Vaticanus**, discovered in**1475**, in the library of the Vatican and **Codex Sinaiticus,** discovered in **1844** in St Catherin's Monastery at the foot of Mt Sinai are Bibles, both written in Greek and both were written in the fourth century; before the creation of the official Latin Vulgate Bible.

Pope Damasus in 382 A.D. had commissioned Jerome, the leading biblical scholar of his day, to produce an acceptable Latin version of the Bible from the various translations then being used. This task was accomplished between A.D. 383 and 404. Jerome was fluent in Greek and Hebrew. He translated the Old Testament from the original Hebrew Scriptures directly into Latin, though there already existed a Greek translation, the Septuagint. He also revised the New Testament from the existing older Vetus Latin into a more accurate, uptodate Latin. The St Jerome's Latin Vulgate (from the Latin vulgata, meaning 'common' or 'popular'), employs the everyday written Latin style of the fourth century. The Versio Vulgate Latin Bible, became the standard Latin version of the Bible for the Western Latin-speaking Church.

Some books were not included as part of the Bible because they were not considered to be inspired texts e.g., Maccabees and Esdras and came to form the Apocrypha. In Judaism, the Apocrypha books were never accepted as part of the Hebrew Bible but were treated with respect.

The scriptures of the Bible are the inspired word of God **but** were put together **by man**, by the Christian authority of the time.

The 397 Synod also discredited various texts. These "false texts" were written by the so-called "Heretics." Heretics are people who practise heresy, a belief contrary to the orthodox or official religion and the generally accepted belief. In the early Christian Church, people who disagreed with the main Catholic teachings, even though their motives were very valid, ended up being ostracized and labelled as heretics, forbidden to practise or teach their beliefs.

Important controversies existed in the early Christian Church right from its formation and are still present today. The two most important ones are: the validity or not, of the concept that God exists as a Trinity, introduced as a concept into the Christian Church after the first council of Nicaea in 325 A.D. and the second one is: the nature of Jesus; is Jesus God?

How reliable is the Bible today?

Today, there are very many different versions of the Holy Bible, reflecting the fragmentation of Christians and also because the entire Bible has been translated into over 700 languages and the New Testament alone into over 1,600. However, the Bible is still valid. This means that what is written in the Bible is not some fanciful stories, but proven and documented facts that really did happen. Many of the biblical facts, especially those of the Old Testament, are well documented in various historical monuments.

Note: The entire Old Testament is derived from the Jewish Bible, the Tanakh. Today, various Bible versions differ slightly in wording when reporting a fact, but the substance is the same. For instance, some Christians say Jesus was crucified on a stake or a wooden post, while others say on a cross. The fact is that Jesus was executed on a piece of wood.

The reliability of the New Testament has been scrutinized many times in our time and has stood up to the test, despite numerous transcriptions and translations over the centuries.

Many websites offer online Bible scriptures from the most common versions of Christian Bibles. A few examples of these websites are: www.biblehub.com; which offers over **twenty-six versions of Bibles** and www.wol.jw.org, which offers **seven different versions of Bibles.** So, if you wish, you could always compare how one particular verse is expressed in the different Bibles.

Generally, the variations in the different Bibles can be traced to when and why they came into existence. For example, some time back, I happened to be listening to a BBC programme on the radio, I believe on Radio Four, regarding the creation of the first King James Bible and this comment was made: *"King James had the Bible written in such a way, that his subjects would understand that he had God-given authority to rule them i.e., divine right to govern them"* and the speaker gave a few examples of where the King had the Bible modified.

The original Jewish scriptures that form the Old Testament were first written in Hebrew and only two parts, Daniel and Ezra, were in Aramaic, (a language commonly spoken in Babylon, where Daniel and Ezra had been exiled). The very first translation of the Hebrew scripture was into Koine Greek.

After the extensive conquests of Alexander the Great, in **322 B.C.**, Greek became the dominant language in the Mediterranean region, including Egypt. The Hebrew Bible was translated at the request of the then Egyptian Pharaoh, of Greek origin, Ptolemy II Philadelphus, **285-247BCE**, for the Great Library of Alexandria. This first translation of the entire Tanakh was called **the Septuagint**, from the Latin, 'septuaginta' which means seventy. This translation of the Hebrew Scriptures into Koine Greek was done by 72 Hebrew Scholars, six scholars from each of the Tribes of Israel. It is said that each group independently produced identical translations from the Hebrew Scriptures.

The Hebrew Scriptures were now made accessible to the resident Jewish community of Alexandria, many of whom were no longer fluent in Hebrew but in Greek. These same scriptures became accessible also to non-Jewish people. The Septuagint was written from the 3rd through to the 1st centuries BCE and it is this Greek translation that was used by the early Christian Churches to write the Old Testament.

Note 1: The Septuagint does not have The New Testament, only the Old Testament. It was written before the birth of Jesus Christ.

Note 2: Christianity came into existence when Greek dominance had ceased in the Mediterranean region and had been replaced by the Roman Empire; however, Greek was still the main written language in many areas of the Mediterranean. This explains why most of the New Testament scriptures were first written in Greek.

The fact that the Old Testament comes from the Jewish Bible, the Tanakh, is very comforting to us Christians because if in doubt about a specific scripture, we can always consult the Tanakh, which has remained practically unchanged since it was first written. For example, any change or changes made to the first five books of the Old Testament which originate from the Torah, will be easily identified if one refers to the Jewish Torah for a second opinion.

In Christendom today, there exist two different sets of the Ten Commandments; those of the Catholic Church and Lutheran Church differ from those of the other Christians Churches. I had to verify from the Torah which of the two Commandments was valid and concluded that the Catholic Church had deleted The Second Commandment. This is the second, most important alteration, I have found in the Bible to date; the first being the removal of God's name, Jehovah, from the Bible.

The Second Commandment **from the Torah is**: "You must not make for yourself a carved image or a form like anything that is in the heavens above or on the earth below or in the waters under the earth."

The Second Commandment from the Bibles used by Catholics and Lutherans, says: "You must not take up the name of the Lord your God in a worthless way," **which is the Third Commandment in the Torah** and also in the majority of Christian Bibles.

The question is, why would the Catholic Church have deleted the Second Commandment? I believe the answer could be traced way back to the era of the brutal persecution of Christians in the Roman Empire.

The spread of Christianity in the early Christian Church was based on preaching the moving testimonies of Christians tolerating severe persecution and even accepting martyrdom. It is reported that there were many miraculous events accompanying these brutal persecutions and martyrdom, which made many pagans convert to Christianity.

I believe it would have been much more difficult to convert pagans, for example, Romans, Greeks and others, if they were obliged to get rid of all the numerous statues present in their community, in the public squares, their offices, their homes and in their temples. In my opinion, the Second Commandment was deleted to make Christianity more acceptable to the pagan authorities and their population. Just imagine what would have happened if Emperor Constantine, who was the first Roman emperor to convert to Christianity, in 312 A.D, had been requested to demolish his own statue, which stood twelve metres or forty feet high, simply because he had become a Christian.

Deleting the Second Commandment meant that the new converts could keep their much-loved statues and at the same time be Christians. Also, the Catholic Church itself, at that time the only Christian Church, absorbed this pagan habit of keeping statues in its churches and its community.

Note: Before the invention of the printing process, the Bibles were very few and **inaccessible to the public**, therefore, Christians had no grounds to challenge the Catholic Church on any unchristian attitudes or behaviour.

After the Printing Revolution, from 1440 onwards, the Bible became more accessible to the literate people and any doctrine or way of life or behaviour which did not conform to the writings of the Bible did not go unnoticed and unchallenged, creating division and even wars, among Christians.

The Bible is still a very reliable book and Christians, myself included, believe it to be the inspired word of God. This is why I have used it as a basis for investigating God's identity. The authors of the Bible wrote it for the benefit of all mankind.

7

Now let's see how God describes himself in the Bible

Moses had made this request to Jehovah: "Please show me your glory," in **Exodus 33:18**.

Glory means high renown, famous or honour won by notable achievement; it also means magnificence, impressive or having great beauty.

Jehovah informed Moses that: "You cannot see my face, for no man can see me and live." See **Exodus 33:20**. Jehovah said further: "Here is a place near me. Station yourself on the rock. When my glory is passing by, I will place you in a crevice of the rock, and I will shield you with my hand until I have passed by. After that, I will take my hand away, and you will see my back. But my face may not be seen."

The next day on Mt Sinai, Jehovah comes down in a cloud (**Exodus 34: 6-7**) and is passing before Moses, declaring: *"Jehovah, Jehovah, a God merciful and compassionate, slow to anger and abundant in loyal love and truth, showing loyal love to thousands, pardoning error and transgression and sin, but he will by no means leave the guilty unpunished bringing punishment for the error of fathers upon sons and upon grandsons, upon the third generation and upon the fourth generation."*

Note that Jehovah does not define Himself as: *"all powerful, all knowledgeable, everlasting etc."* His main interest is in the bond He has with mankind and specifically, with each individual. This is what His mercy serves; to forgive whatever wrong you have done, by breaking His Law, if you really repent, to preserve or let's say, re-establish your relationship with Him.

God is compassionate; He is concerned about people, especially those with negative events in their lives. If you turn to Him for help, he will surely assist you; if you have faith and full confidence in Him.

God cannot ignore sin once it is committed. "He will by no means leave the guilty unpunished", this is in line with His eternal justice; laws are made to be respected, if no punishment is incurred on transgression, of what use would they be? We have to remember that when Jehovah describes Himself, he starts by saying that He is merciful and goes on to say that He is slow to anger, therefore, we can abandon ourselves to His mercy and have confidence in His judgement, if we repent.

When we look at God's way of dealing with man, we see His generosity is far superior to his punishment; in fact, it seems to cancel His punishment. Let's see the Second Commandment in **Exodus 20: 5-6:** "You must not make for yourself a carved image or a form like anything that is in the heavens above or on the earth below or in the waters under the earth. You must not bow down to them nor be enticed to serve them. For I, Jehovah your God, am a God who requires exclusive devotion, bringing punishment for the error of fathers upon sons, upon the third generation and upon the fourth generation of those who hate me, **but showing loyal love to the thousandth generation** of those who love me and keep my commandments."

There are many places in the Bible where God defines Himself, but I have chosen to highlight a few descriptions from just one book, that of the prophet Isaiah, in the Old Testament of the Bible.

Isaiah:

41: 10; *"Do not be afraid, for I am with you. Do not be anxious, for I am your God. I will fortify you, yes, I will help you, I will really hold on to you with my right hand of righteousness."*

41:13; *"For I, Jehovah your God, am grasping your right hand, The One saying to you, 'Do not be afraid, I myself will help you."*

42: 8; *"I am Jehovah. That is my name; I give my glory to no one else, Nor my praise to graven images."*

42: 9: *"The first things, here they have come, but new things, here I am telling out before they begin to spring up, I cause you people to hear them."*

43:11; *"I—I am Jehovah, and besides me, there is no saviour/deliverer/rescuer."*

43:13; *"From eternity to eternity, I am God; And no one can snatch anything out of my hand. When I act, who can prevent it?"*

44: 6; This is what Jehovah says, The King of Israel and his Repurchaser, Jehovah of armies: *"I am the first and I am the last.* ***There is no God but me."***

44:24; This is what Jehovah says, your Repurchaser, who formed you since you were in the womb: *"I am Jehovah, who made everything. I stretched out the heavens **by myself**, And I spread out the earth. **Who was with me?"***

45: 12; *"I made the earth and created man on it. I stretched out the heavens with my own hands. All their hosts, are at my command."*

45: 19;*" I did not speak in a concealed place, in a land of darkness; I did not say to the offspring of Jacob, "Seek me simply for nothing." I am Jehovah, who speaks the truth and declares what is righteous."*

45:21; *"Make your report, present your case. Let them consult together in unity. Who foretold this long ago; And declared it from* times past? Is it not I, Jehovah? **There is no other God but me**; A righteous God and a Saviour, there is none besides me."

45: 22; "Turn to me and be saved, all you ends of the earth, For I am God, and **there is no other."**

48:13; "My own hand laid the foundation of the earth, and my right hand spread out the heavens. When I call to them, they stand up together."

48:12; "Listen to me, O Jacob, and Israel, whom I have called. **I alone am God;** I am the first and I am the last."

48: 17-18; This is what Jehovah says, your Repurchaser, the Holy One of Israel: "I, Jehovah, am your God, The One teaching you to benefit yourself, The One guiding you in the way you should walk. If only you would pay attention to my commandments! Then your peace would become just like a river. And your righteousness like the waves of the sea."

I would like to rewrite a summary of the above verses.

Do not be afraid or anxious. Why? Because I will help you**. Please take note; I am God! That is 100% reliable and cannot fail in any task I take on.** Whatever your problem is; I am The Absolute Saviour. I can protect you from any danger and help you overcome whatever difficulties you have. Do you know of anyone else who is capable of doing all this? There is no one else because **I am the only God in existence.** What I teach you, is for your own benefit; to guide you on how you should live. **If only you could pay attention to my Law**, you'd have a life of immense peace and righteousness.

From how Jehovah describes Himself in the above phrases of the Old Testament, it is clear that He is a compassionate, caring, unique, ageless and powerful God, The Creator. "There is no other God, but me," is repeated throughout the Bible, meaning that it is **very important** to Jehovah that the Israelite nation understands and acknowledges that there is no other God, except Him. A righteous, morally right God who sustains man, helps, foretells events, comforts, teaches, protects, defends and is there to benefit all those who obey his Law and trust in Him.

Do you yourself know of any other God or gods, with the above characteristics? Does God define Himself as made of three units, the **Trinity**?

Jehovah repeatedly got very angry with the Israelites when they abandoned him from time to time in favour of idols, lifeless objects, which they themselves as mortal men had crafted from earthly materials. It infuriated Him that even though the Israelites had experienced many huge benefits from Him, they chose to ignore these positive events and preferred to worship their idols. Clearly, these idols were of no benefit to them and frankly, there is nothing more stupid than this.

8

The creation

The first verse of the Bible is: "In the beginning, God created the heavens and the earth." This identifies God as the supreme authority of the entire universe. No one in the whole world, as far as I know, has ever made a claim to having created the universe, the world, a mountain, a tree or an ant. Many different people all over the world, including many scientists, believe that God created the world. The most commonly accepted scientific idea on the origin of the universe is: The Big Bang Theory. This theory states that the universe started from an extremely hot spot that exploded, creating matter and propelling it outward to form billions of Galaxies that are present in the universe today. This expansion of the universe is deemed to be still happening today. **This theory contradicts a basic science theory: you cannot form energy or material from nothing.**

God repeatedly declares in the Bible that He created the universe and all that is in it. **Isaiah 45: 12** "*I made the earth and created man on it. My own hands stretched out the heavens, and I command all the heavenly hosts.*" This is just one of the many verses in the Bible where God declares that He, Himself, created the Universe.

What does the creation tell us about God? If you observe any living creature or plant, you are left very impressed by its structure, its capabilities and how everything in it makes sense, in that, it has adapted for its own survival in that particular environment. This is what evolutionists call adaptation; the better you adapt to an environment, the better your chances are for survival.

Some of these adaptations are extremely complex: one is bound to ask how does a bee know its way home? Or how do the migratory birds or fish know their migratory routes, thousands of kilometres across continents? Who taught the birds how to make their nests? Who taught spiders how to make their complex webs? Is it due to evolution?

All creation carries the signature of The Creator, from the invisible viruses and bacteria to the stars in the sky, they all proclaim God's endless knowledge, His majestic glory, His supreme power, His perfection, His splendour and above all His immense love for man, for creating him such a beautiful planet. If you look attentively at images of various places on planet Earth, you will not find any ugly place, except where man has been and left a mess.

God identifies Himself with his creation, in fact "The Creator" is another name given to God, because He only has succeeded in creating life. Man's creations use something already in existence; man cannot create material from nothing and most importantly, man cannot create life. This profession of Creator and Sustainer of the Universe is unique to God. This does not exclude God from having other important roles, for example regarding the spiritual realm.

Man has never, ever created anything living from scratch. Creation is an activity God has reserved exclusively for Himself and does not want man even to copy his creations. The Second Commandment says, *"You must not make for yourself a carved image or a form like anything that is in the heavens above or on the earth below or in the waters under the earth. You must not bow down to them nor be enticed to serve them, for I, Jehovah your God, I **am a God who requires exclusive devotion."***

Why should man not try to copy God's creations? This has been forbidden by God, in anticipation of man's reaction regarding "his" creation/s. God created man and therefore, knows him very well.

I believe the biggest issue about man creating is that man tends to adore what he has created; not only does he take great pride in his creation, just look at fashion, but often man makes his creations into a real god, due to the attention given to them, for example, the statues and paintings of famous artists like Michelangelo, Van Gogh, Picasso, Monet, Da Vinci, etc.

In history, many different peoples have had practices of worshipping idols or statues that represent someone or something but God forbids it, even if they represent someone supposedly holy like a saint or Mary the mother of Jesus.

- "You **shall not make** for yourself an image in the form of anything.
  "**Exodus 20:4**

- "**You shall not bow down to them or worship them;"**
  Exodus 20:5

And he tells us why: ***"I am a God who requires exclusive*** (entire, undivided, absolute and total), ***devotion*** *and religious worship."*

In **Isaiah 42:8**; *"I am Jehovah. That is my name; I give my glory to* ***no one else****,* ***nor my praise to graven images."***

Although man has been to the moon and beyond, he has not had such success when it comes to **creating life**. A cell, the basic unit of life, is a micro-cosmic world, another microscopic universe which eluded man for centuries. The invention of the electron microscope in 1939, gave an insight into the complexity of a cell.

Just to get an idea of how complex this unit of life is, ask Google, "Has any scientist succeeded in creating a living cell?" The answer I got was, "Yes" a synthetic cell by Craig Venter; **it took his team 15 years to make it. On further investigation, I found this information was not true;** see the website: from Google: "The Mysterious Thing about a Marvellous, New Synthetic Cell," by Ed Yong; March 2016 and Scientist: "We didn't create life from scratch." CNN.COM, "Have scientists created a living cell?"

The reality today is that scientists say only 2% of the human DNA encodes for proteins and therefore the scientist can understand its function. However, the remaining 75-90% of the human genome/DNA that does not encode proteins is sometimes called junk DNA, **because scientists do not understand its function.** See: "Junk DNA debunked" from Google. So, man still has to go a very long way before fully understanding all the functions of the DNA.

To create life means great knowledge and responsibility which man does not have. Man can modify organisms, such as plants, animals, fungi, bacteria and viruses by adding, subtracting and modifying the genetic material. Some of this genetic manipulation has been very useful to man, for example, the synthesis of penicillin, but this is done in a controlled environment in laboratories. When genetic manipulation is done on a large scale, such as having huge plantations of genetically modified plants or GMO crops, man never really knows how his new creations will influence the ecosystem, meaning the surrounding community of living organisms such as plants and animals and their physical, non-living environment, of water, air and soil. See: "Weighing the GMOs arguments against FAO" from the United Nations' Food and Agriculture Organization (FAO) website and also from: livingnongmo.org/2017/10/10/the-buzz-about-cross-pollination. There are many more websites and other sources of information on this subject, so one can investigate further if one chooses to.

In all the genetic manipulation, man is just modifying the living organism, **not** creating a new organism.

If God commands man not to copy his creations, He knows what He is doing because He created man and is able to foresee man's actions. Creation is an activity reserved exclusively for The Creator because only He can take full responsibility for his creation; only He knows all the properties of the creations and the consequences they have on the environment.

9

God's law

It is well known that God is perfect, if this is so, then His Law is also perfect. Also, one is able to perceive God's personality through his Law. The Law used by Christians has its origin in Judaism, so let's have a look at who made this Law and a summary of its contents.

Where did Israelites acquire their Law from? Their Law was given to the prophet Moses, by God himself on Mount Sinai. The first Ten Commandments were spoken out by Jehovah in the hearing of all the Israelites (**Exodus 20: 01 and Deut. 4: 33**) and were later inscribed on stone slabs by God Himself. The other 603 laws were made known to Moses, while on Mt Sinai, by God Himself. Altogether, Judaism has a total of 613 laws; this includes also the Ten Commandments. These laws were given specifically to the Israelite nation, as part of a covenant, or an official agreement, between them and Jehovah their God, on their way from Egypt to the Promised Land. Many of the 613 laws apply even to this day, but some could no longer be practised after the destruction of the second temple of Jerusalem.

The Ten Commandments have been adapted by Christians and are considered relevant to the Christian faith, today. I do not know most of the other laws in Judaism but I have had to look up what their Law says concerning various topics, such as property, commerce, slavery, foreigners, sexual behaviour and so on. I noted that God's Law starts by addressing the rights of the most vulnerable people in society, who generally, do not have anyone to uphold their Rights; the slaves. One of the most fantastic laws is in **Deuteronomy 23: 15-16**; *"You should not hand over a slave to his master when he escapes from his master and comes to you. He may dwell among you in whatever place he chooses, in one of your cities,* *wherever he likes. You must not mistreat him."* If this Law was respected, it would protect slaves from mistreatment.

Exodus 21: 16: Whoever kidnaps someone and sells him, and anyone found in possession of him, shall be put to death.

Exodus 21:20; If a man **strikes** his manservant or maidservant with a rod, and the servant dies by his hand, he shall surely be punished. Some Bibles have changed the word strike to beat, which means to hit someone hard, repeatedly. In Judaism, this verse is, **"If a man strikes..."**

Note, that God does acknowledge the existence of slavery, but is appalled by any mistreatment of slaves. Slavery has always been part of many cultures in various forms. In my opinion, there will always be slavery in one form or another, as part of man's activities, that of over-exploiting the less fortunate. The presence of wars, political dominance, debt bondage, natural disasters like famine etc. has generally been a constant source of slavery in human society. What is important is to treat others well and to limit the level of exploitation, to permit others to live a reasonably comfortable life, even if they are your slaves.

I was shocked to learn from the Bible that some slaves would refuse their liberty because they had come to love and respect their master and his family. Therefore, when freedom was offered to them, they chose to remain enslaved to their master. **Deuteronomy 15: 16-17**: *But if he says to you, 'I will not go out from you,' because he loves you and your household, since he is well-off with you, then you shall take an awl, (a tool which resembles a pointed screwdriver, used to make holes in leather), and put it through his ear into the door, and he shall be your slave forever. And to your female slave, you shall do the same.*

Now, one might not agree with some of God's Laws, to start with. I, too have found myself questioning some of them, but in the end, when I fully understood them, I had to admit that they made a lot of sense. I don't claim to know or understand all of

God's Laws; one has to ponder over some of them, for quite a while, to understand them.

It is not a sin to question God's Laws. When a teacher talks about a certain topic in a classroom, generally, there are a few hands that go up after the teacher has finished his or her talk, and students will start to query what they did not understand, saying: *"I did not understand that." "Why did you say this?" "Why did you say that?"* It is only natural to question because one is trying to understand; questioning is part of the learning process and God knows it. If instead, one does not agree with God's Law, it would be a lot better to think deeply about the Law and to pray to God Himself to illuminate your mind and give you understanding. Alternatively, you could search the Web or discuss it with others and you will discover that **God is always right.** Do not forget that God is the source of all knowledge and would like man to know His Law and is, therefore, willing to give a hand to anyone who requests it.

God does not want man to follow His Law blindly, because everyone is following it or for fear of going to Hell. He would like man to reflect and meditate on His Law so that one can fully understand it. It is only when you have clearly understood God's Law that you can fully appreciate it and follow it wholeheartedly.

Regarding foreigners who were residing with the Israelites, God commands that his Law should be applied equally both to foreigners and to the Israelites. See **Numbers 15: 15-16**; "You, who are of the congregation and the foreigner who is residing with you will have one statute. It will be a lasting statute for all your generations. The foreign resident should be the same as you before Jehovah. There should be one law and one judicial decision for you and for the foreigner who is residing with you." This makes sense; we are all equal, in front of the Law.

Laws are a basic necessity for any society; they set up boundaries regarding people's actions towards public and private property, towards God, towards public institutions and each other, without which, no society could survive. Every caring parent provides his children with some basic teaching and discipline, without which life might prove very difficult, especially outside the home.

God had taken charge of the Israelite nation once it was freed from slavery in Egypt and therefore, just like a parent, had to teach it how to behave by providing it with His Law. Therefore, Jehovah's Law is an act of loving-kindness, an act of taking care of the Israelites. He is more qualified than anyone else to decide what is right and what is wrong. He is the source of righteousness; therefore, it was a huge privilege for the Israelites to receive their Law directly from Jehovah Himself.

Please note that before handing the Law to the Israelites, Jehovah sent Moses to enquire if the Israelites would be willing to abide by his Law; it was not enforced on them. The Israelites accepted to live according to Jehovah's Law: **Exodus 19: 3-9**; an official agreement/a covenant was made, between God and the Israelites; the Israelites were to live according to Jehovah's Law and Jehovah would be their God and He would take care of them.

Let's see briefly the first Ten Commandments, given directly to the Israelites, by the voice of Jehovah Himself; **Exodus 20: 1-17 and Deuteronomy 5: 6-21**.

The First Commandment

"I am Jehovah your God, who brought you out of the land of Egypt, out of the house of slavery. You must not have any other gods besides me."

I find it rather humiliating to keep on reminding the Israelites of their previous state of slavery in Egypt, but God does it with a purpose, to bring to their minds the mighty miracles he performed there, in Egypt; emphasizing His capabilities and His reliability. Who else is more capable than Him? Jehovah tells the Israelites, that they should have **only** Him as a God and no one and nothing else.

As you can see from above, Jehovah is taking full responsibility for the Israelites through this first commandment. What he is saying is, "I am responsible for your well-being, you people; it is I who takes care of you. D**o not go looking elsewhere for help.** It was and is a great privilege for the Israelites to have Jehovah as their God. **Who else is more capable or more reliable than Him?**

The Second Commandment

*"You must not make for yourself a carved image or a form like anything that is in the heavens, above or on the earth, below or in the waters under the earth. You must not bow down to them nor be enticed to serve them, for I, Jehovah your God, am a God who requires **exclusive** devotion,* entire, **undivided**, absolute and total devotion." In other words, all your worship should be reserved for me, **only; no trinity.**

Therefore, God forbids man to use intermediates, such as saints or Mary the mother of Jesus, when praying to Him. Your prayers and worship should be for God only.

God acts preventively, to protect the Israelites from idol worship, because if they worshipped lifeless objects, they would be the losers; they would get no benefit from their idols and they will lose all the benefits they might have had from God.

The Third Commandment

"You must not take up the name of Jehovah your God in a worthless way, for Jehovah will not leave unpunished the one who takes up His name in a worthless way," Jehovah has made provisions to protect his unique and holy name and to punish those who misuse it.

How should God's name be used?

Jehovah is alive; He is the most alive being in the whole universe. This means if you call Him, if you cry out to Him or just whisper from anywhere, He will hear you, but you should call Him only if you need Him when seeking His assistance. He, The

Sovereign Lord of the Universe, has made Himself easily accessible to man; **if you trust Him and you live according to His laws**, just call on His name, wherever you happen to be, and He will assist you from your trouble. Remember, you are not alone, in this world.

The Fourth Commandment

"Remember the Sabbath day to keep it sacred/holy."

Sacred means associated with God and deserving veneration and great respect. You are to labour and do all your work for six days, but the seventh day is a Sabbath to Jehovah your God. You must not do any work, neither you nor your son nor your daughter nor your slave man nor your slave girl nor your domestic animal nor your foreign resident who is inside your settlements. For in six days, Jehovah made the heavens and the earth, the sea and all that is in them, and he began to rest on the seventh day. That is why Jehovah blessed the Sabbath day and made it sacred.

Please note: If Jehovah claims that He made the world in six days, why should anyone doubt this capability?

In **Deuteronomy 5:14**, Moses further explains the additional benefits of this commandment: it means that your slave man and your slave girl may rest the same as you. This law protects also the other workers, including animals like ploughing bulls, from extreme exploitation as rest is imposed on the entire Jewish community.

In **Exodus 35: 1-3**, Moses later gathered the entire assembly of the Israelites together and said to them: *"These are the things that Jehovah has commanded to be done: Work may be done for six days, but the seventh day will become something holy to you, a Sabbath of complete rest to Jehovah. Anybody doing work on it will be put to death. You must not light a fire in any of your dwelling places on the Sabbath day."*

This day is sacred; the Israelites were supposed to pray and offer sacred service to Jehovah; they were to re-connect spiritually to their God, acknowledge their reliance on Him, acknowledge all the benefits they have received from Him the preceding week/s and request Jehovah's support in the week/s to come.

In the scriptures: **Numbers 15: 32-36,** an Israelite man was stoned to death for working on the Sabbath. It might seem very brutal to kill a man for working on the Sabbath, but when you reason over his actions, you are bound to say, "He asked for it." First, every Israelite should have been informed of Jehovah's Ten Commandments as the basis of Jehovah's Law. Therefore, an act of deliberately disobeying Jehovah is equivalent to challenging His authority and breaking the Covenant established with Him; this in itself deserves death. Second, what is the purpose of your working? Is it not to maintain your livelihood? It is God who really maintains your livelihood. This act of profaning the Sabbath might encourage others to do the same. There really should have been no excuse for disobeying Jehovah.

This fourth commandment is another act of loving kindness from Jehovah to the Israelites because if they were to spend all their lives running after their jobs and other earthly pursuits, they were bound to abandon Jehovah, the source of all their benefits. The Sabbath obliges the Israelites to reflect on their lives and not to live a life of just existence.

The first four commandments regard God's relationship with man. The other commandments, from the fifth to the tenth, regard man, his private affairs, his relationship with his family and his relationship with the rest of society. They are found in **Exodus 20: 12-17.**

The Fifth Commandment

"Honour your father and your mother, that your days may be long in the land that the Lord your God is giving you."

In this commandment, God acknowledges your parents as a source of authority. In **Exodus 21:15**; *One who strikes his father or* *mother, must be put to death* and in **Exodus 21: 17**; "Anyone who curses his father or his mother must be put to death," Jehovah takes provision to protect parenthood. The authority of parents is associated with various serious responsibilities, but I would say, the most important responsibility is that of teaching their children, about Jehovah and His Law. In **Deut. 6: 4-9**: Moses explains:

"Listen, O Israel: Jehovah our God is one Jehovah. You must love Jehovah your God with all your heart and all your soul and all your strength. These words that I am commanding you today must be in your heart, and you must inculcate them in your sons and speak of them when you sit in your house and when you walk on the road and when you lie down and when you get up. Tie them as a reminder on your hand, and they must be like a headband on your forehead /and they shall be for ornaments between your eyes. Write them on the doorposts of your house and on your gates,"

Therefore, according to God, religious education should be taught first of all at your own home, before anywhere else.

Please note: I must say that some parents abuse their God-given authority by doing things like forcing their children to get married to people whom they clearly dislike. Authority is there to serve the needs of others, especially those of your own family and not to coerce and oppress them.

The Sixth Commandment
You shall not murder.

The Seventh Commandment
You shall not commit adultery.

The Eighth Commandment
You shall not steal.

The Ninth Commandment

You shall not bear false witness against your neighbour.

The Tenth Commandment

You shall not covet, nor strongly desire your neighbour's house; you shall not covet your neighbour's wife, or his male servant, or his female servant, or his ox, or his donkey, or anything that is your neighbour's. **This Tenth Commandment is special because it is your own conscience that will judge you. Nobody knows your thoughts, except God. Also, this law acts preventively, to stop you from progressing into more evil territory**. This means that you should monitor where your thoughts are leading, to avoid progressing into forbidden territory. If you find that you cannot control your thoughts, appeal for God's help and He will help you overcome wrong thoughts.

The above Ten Commandments were still valid in Christ's day and are still considered valid in Judaism and Christianity, today.

It is good to know that all the laws given to the Israelite nation, all 613 of them, can be reduced to two basic laws. We deduce this from a discussion between Jesus Christ and some Pharisees. This discussion takes place in **Mathew 22: 35-40** as written below.

Mathew 22:35-36; One of them, an expert in the Law, a Pharisee, tested Jesus Christ with this question, "Teacher, which is the greatest commandment in the Law?"

Mathew 22: 37-38; He said to him, *"You must love Jehovah your God with your whole heart and with your whole soul and with your whole mind. This is the greatest and first commandment."*

Mathew 22:38-40. *"And the second is like it: Love your neighbour as yourself.* **All the law and the prophets hang on these two laws."**

The Old Testament is divided into two major divisions: The Law of Moses, five books written by Moses, and the other part, The

Prophets which Moses did not write, but was written by other prophets.

The reply above, given by Christ summarizes all the Laws in Judaism and also in Christianity; it clearly shows that whoever claims to be a believer and hence to live according to God's Law, should know who God really is, because you cannot love or worship something you do not know. Now God is a super-genius, all-powerful, all-knowledgeable, fully reliable and cannot fail in any task He pursues. He is the True God and is also willing to support man, free of charge. Why? God cares for man that is why He is willing to support anyone who requests it from Him. Why should any intelligent being look anywhere else for support?

The second law obliges anyone who claims to believe in God to have great consideration for other people and to treat everyone regardless of his or her nationality, religious background or social status, as they would like to be treated. Christ further explains who our neighbour really is, through the story of the **Good Samaritan**: **Luke 10: 25-37.** One cannot claim to love God or be Christian, if they do not treat others, whoever they happen to be, with consideration.

All of God's Laws are based on love, on God's caring affection for mankind. In the English language, the word love is used to express many types of affection; this could generate some uncertainty when using it in reference to God. The word love used in the Bible actually means loving-kindness.

In Greek, for example, the word love is subdivided into seven types of love: **philia,** deep friendship, brotherly love, shared goodwill; **eros,** sexual, passionate love; **ludus,** playful love such as among children or flirting, uncommitted with no strings attached; **pragma** is mature love, founded on reason or duty, on one's long-term interests, such as that which develops in long-married couples, about making compromises to help the relationship work over time, and showing patience and tolerance; **Storge,** the love that exists between parents and their children; **Philautia**, love of yourself, looking after yourself physically, emotionally and spiritually, because in the first place, this is your personal responsibility. **Health is a gift from God, do not neglect it**, also, you will need to be in form to do God's will in the best manner possible; **Agape,** is a Greco-Christian term referring to unconditional love, the highest form of love, charity, self-less love, extended to everybody, family, non-family members and also to foreigners. It is a universal love for everyone. Therefore, in the Greek Bible, Agape would be the word used to express God's love for mankind.

I interpret "God is love" to mean God shows caring concern or loving kindness to mankind. We are a product of His creation and He is our Heavenly Father. This caring nature is also part of God's personality. It comes naturally for us to love our parents because they take good care of us. Why then should we not love God if He too takes good care of us with loving kindness? Why should we want to offend Him by breaking His Law if he is so kind to us? The truth is most people do not even know that it is God who takes care of us because they have the wrong concept of God. Many people believe God is in Heaven and very far away from us all.

Christ provided a very important input regarding God's Law; He explained that one should use reason to interpret it and not follow it blindly. He explained that the Law was made for man's benefit and not the other way around; man was not made or created to benefit the Law. In Christ's time, the Sabbath had been converted from what should have been a pleasant and relaxing day in honour of Jehovah, to the most distressful day of the week. This is because there existed many man-made regulations regarding what should not be done on the Sabbath, called Melachots in Judaism, and they still exist today. These man-made laws were a source of distress for the Israelites who would spend the Sabbath "on tip-toe" in order not to break any of these numerous man-made laws imposed on them. Here is just one example:

In **Exodus 35:3**, Moses commands the Israelites, "*You shall not light a fire at home on the Sabbath day.*" This is interpreted to mean making a fire or causing anything to burn. Electricity has the same status as fire regarding the Sabbath for Orthodox Jews. Therefore, on the Sabbath, all strictly observant Orthodox Jews avoid turning any electrical appliance on or off and they cannot switch on or off lights, switch on a car or use lifts etc. They cannot use a telephone if it involves using electricity or even striking a match. This is just one regulation and I have not covered all the other thirty-eight prohibitions or Melachots regarding the Sabbath.

Jehovah has provided His Laws as an act of loving kindness, instructions for man's own benefit, not for His benefit. If you do not follow Jehovah's Law, you are only hurting yourself and not Jehovah. Sin acts as a barrier between you and Jehovah and also between your fellow man. No God-fearing man would like to be associating with someone who acts contrary to what his own God recommends. The importance of Jehovah to mankind is the benefit we gain from Him if we live according to His Law. Sin, not living according to Jehovah's Law, acts as a barrier to your relationship with God and to your benefitting from God.

God in His wisdom has created man and has inscribed his own Law into man's heart. This is evident from the fact that the fifth to the tenth commandments are very present as laws in almost all if not all, people throughout the world. Any developed or let's say refined human being, will always sympathise with other people when things go wrong for them. A typical example is if people are watching a film and there happen to be some very tragic scenes, you will find that all those watching will feel sad too, some may even cry; this is called empathy, created by our Heavenly Father. The definition of **Empathy** is the ability to understand and share the feelings of one another.

With or without a reward, the important thing is to do what is right according to God's law.

To summarize, God provided the Israelites with his Law as a gift, informing them where to get help when in need and instructing them how to live in harmony with each other. As God is the source of knowledge, righteousness and justice, His law should reflect these qualities. The Law can be reduced to, Jehovah is a caring God and wanted the Israelites to have a caring attitude towards each other.

10

God rescues Israel from slavery

God has interacted with different peoples all over the world and there are numerous testimonies from different peoples of these events. However, I have chosen to write what I know from the Old Testament of the Bible, about God's interactions with the Israelite nation. These experiences give us a real insight into the true nature of God and His identity.

The rescue of the Israelites from slavery in Egypt

God's numerous interactions with the Israelite nation are registered in the Jewish Bible, the Tanakh and also in the Old Testament of the Bible which is derived from the Tanakh. As the most significant of all the interactions that the Israelite nation had with their God, Jehovah, I have selected God's rescue of the Israelites from Egypt, where they had fallen into slavery. I say fallen, because when the Israelites arrived in Egypt, they lived comfortably as free men for very many years.

When the Israelites migrated to Egypt because of severe famine, they found that through God's intervention, Joseph, the very first Israelite to settle in Egypt, had become the highest-ranking official in the court of the Egyptian king, the Pharaoh. Joseph had become known to the Pharaoh by interpreting his dream, which had caused him great distress and which no one else in Egypt could interpret. God revealed this dream and its correct interpretation to Joseph, that a severe famine lasting up to seven years, would strike Egypt, and all the surrounding countries, but before the famine struck, there would be seven years of abundant harvest. Joseph had been given a very high-ranking position, second in command to the Pharaoh, for successfully interpreting this dream. The Pharaoh also became convinced that Joseph had godly powers, due to the correct interpretation of his dream and which consequently had safeguarded the Egyptian nation from death by famine. This revelation permitted Egypt to be the only country that had prepared itself for the famine by storing great quantities of food. Egypt and especially the Pharaoh, became extremely wealthy by selling its food for seven years, to all the surrounding nations and peoples who had none.

Many years back, when Joseph was seventeen years old, his eleven brothers conspired and sold him into slavery. Why? Out of envy because of his father's affection for him; he was the favourite son. They presented their father with Joseph's coat covered in blood and had then lied to him saying that Joseph was dead, probably killed by a wild animal, although no corpse was found. See **Genesis chapter 37**.

Joseph's father's name was Jacob, also called Israel, and his grandfather was Isaac, the son of the Jewish patriarch, Abraham. When the famine set in, in the land of Canaan, Joseph's land of origin, Jacob his father sent some of his sons to Egypt to buy food for his family. Jacob had twelve sons, but he believed one of them, Joseph, was dead.

When Joseph's brothers arrived in Egypt, God led them to Joseph, who was now a high-ranking Egyptian and dressed as one, he recognized them but they did not. Joseph had a very dramatic encounter with his brothers before revealing his true identity to them. Eventually, Joseph forgave his brothers for their betrayal, brought all his family to Egypt and settled them in the very best parts of Egypt, as commanded by the Pharaoh. See **Gen 47: 6** and he also gave them a lot of support, supplying them with free food during the famine in Egypt. After the famine was over, he helped them settle with his continuing support. The Israelites started their life in Egypt in a very privileged position and prospered in this country. Also, God was with them as He had promised Jacob their father. See **Genesis 46: 1-4**.

On arrival in Egypt, the Israelites had been made to feel very welcome, especially by the Pharaoh and lived as free men for many years. God gives the following law to the Israelites: "*You must not hate an Egyptian, for you became a foreign resident in his country. The third generation of children born to them may enter the congregation of Jehovah.*" See **Deuteronomy 23: 7-8**.

In time, however, there arose over Egypt a new King, a Pharaoh who did not know Joseph. So, he said to his people: "*Look! The people of Israel are more numerous and mightier than we are. Let us deal shrewdly with them, otherwise, they will continue to multiply, and if a war breaks out, they will join our enemies and fight against us and leave the country.*" (**Exodus 1: 8-10**).

So, they put slave masters over them to oppress them with forced labour, and they built Pithom and Rameses as store cities for Pharaoh. (**Exodus 1:11**). Thus, Israelites became slaves in Egypt, by orders of the Pharaoh.

It was God's plan that the Israelites should excel in Egypt and become a great nation and also that they should suffer the consequences; **Genesis 15:12-14 and Genesis 46: 3-4**. Even in slavery, the Israelite population continued to increase rapidly. Pharaoh called the Israelite mid-wives and ordered them **to kill** every male child who was born, but they did not do it. When asked by the Pharaoh why they did not follow his instruction, the midwives replied, "The Hebrew women are not like the Egyptian women. They are lively and have already given birth before the midwife can come to them."

Then Pharaoh gave this order to **all his people**, "Every Hebrew boy that is born you must throw into the Nile, but let every girl live." See **Exodus 1:22.**

The Israelites found themselves in such a disastrous situation and had practically no chance of overcoming it; slaves to the most powerful nation on earth. It was during this period that a great prophet, Moses, was born. His mother hid him indoors until three months of age, as all Israelite males had to be thrown into the Nile, by orders of the Pharaoh. Then she put him into a papyrus basket made impermeable with bitumen, a tar from petroleum, and pitch made from tree resins and transferred him onto the banks of the river Nile, among the reeds. She requested her daughter to watch over this basket from a distance.

One day, Pharaoh's daughter came down to bathe in the Nile. She and her female attendants were walking by the side of the Nile when she caught sight of the basket in the middle of the reeds. She immediately sent her slave girl to get it. When she opened it, she saw a child, a baby boy who was crying. She felt compassion for him but said, "This is one of the children of the Hebrews." Then, the child's sister who had been watching the basket from a distance, came near and said to Pharaoh's daughter, "Shall I go and call a nursing woman from the Hebrews to nurse the child for you?" Pharaoh's daughter said to her, "Go!" At once the girl went and called the child's mother. Pharaoh's daughter then said to her, "Take this child with you and nurse him for me, and I will pay you." So, the woman took the child and nursed him. When the child grew older, she brought him to Pharaoh's daughter, and he became a son to her. She named him Moses and said, "It is because I have drawn him out of the water."

Moses lived a princely life in the Pharaoh's court until he became an adult, but he knew he was an Israelite and that his people were under harsh slavery; his own mother, who had nursed him as a child must have told him.

One day, while out, he saw an Egyptian man beating an Israelite slave. He intervened and when he thought that no one was in sight, he killed the Egyptian man and hid him in the sand. This criminal act of killing an Egyptian man to protect an Israelite slave leaked and when Pharaoh heard of it, he tried to kill Moses. Moses had to run far away from Egypt to save his life and he ended up in the land of Median, a territory north-west of present-day Saudi Arabia. To cut a long story short, he got married and ended up becoming employed as a shepherd by his father-in-law, Jethro, or Ruel, who was also a priest in the land of Midian.

One day, while out shepherding Jethro's flock, Moses observed a strange sight, a thorn bush was burning without being consumed. Moses moved closer to have a look, then he was called from within this burning thorn bush, "Moses! Moses!" to which he answered, "Here I am." Then the voice said, "Do not come any nearer. Remove your sandals from your feet because the place on which you are standing is holy ground." Moses removed his sandals.

The voice went on to say, "*I am the God of your father, the God of Abraham, the God of Isaac, and the God of Jacob.*" Then Moses hid his face because he was afraid to look at the true God. Jehovah added, "*I have certainly seen the affliction of my people who are in Egypt, and I have heard their outcry because of those who force them to work; I well know the pains they suffer.*

God made a request to Moses; if he would be willing to go on a mission to Egypt, this would serve to:

a) Inform the elders of the Israelites that God has decided to free them from their bondage and to lead them to a good and spacious land, flowing with milk and honey.

b) Go to the Pharaoh, accompanied by the elders of the Israelites to make the following request: "*the God of the Hebrews has communicated with us. So, please, let us make a three-day journey into the wilderness so that we may sacrifice to Jehovah our God.*" **Exodus 3: 18.**

God also warned Moses that this would not be an easy task. See: **Exodus 3: 19-20;** "*But I myself well know that the king of Egypt will not give you permission to go unless a mighty hand compels him. So, I will have to stretch out my hand and strike Egypt with all my extraordinary acts that I will do in it, and after that, he will send you out.*"

Moses needed answers to some important questions and reassurance before accepting this mission. The first question he asks God is: *"Who am I that I should go to Pharaoh and bring the Israelites out of Egypt?"* Moses clearly knew his limits and that the pharaoh had unlimited power to do all he wished. To this, Jehovah said, *"I will prove to be with you, and this is the sign for you that it was I who sent you: after you have brought the people out of Egypt, you people will serve the true god on this mountain."*

Then Moses said to God, "Suppose I go to the Israelites and say to them, the God of your forefathers has sent me to you, and they say to me, **what is his name? What should I say to them?"** So, God said to Moses, **"I am who I am."** And he added, "This is what you are to say to the Israelites, **I am** has sent me to you. Then God said once more to Moses, "This is what you are to say to the Israelites, **Yahweh/Jehovah,** the God of your forefathers, the God of Abraham, the God of Isaac, and the God of Jacob, has sent me to you. This is my name forever and this is how I am to be remembered from generation to generation." **Exodus 3:15**.

Some interpret the name Yahweh to mean, **I will be what I will be;** this implies that God changes and contradicts the scriptures which say that God is always the same; He doesn't change.

Moses and the Israelites of that period had never had any personal experience with God. I believe therefore, they did not know God at all, neither did they trust in Him. God understood Moses' reluctance to be sent by Him. However, Moses answered, "But suppose they do not believe me and do not listen to my voice, for they will say, Jehovah did not appear to you." Then God gave Moses three ways to convince the Israelites, that he had actually been sent by Him:

1. The rod Moses carried while shepherding would change into a serpent, if thrown to the ground and would become a rod again if he picked up "the serpent" by its tail.

2. If he put his hand inside his upper garment and pulled it out it would be white with leprosy, but if he put it inside his upper

garments again, it would be completely healed. Leprosy was an incurable disease then. Leprosy is a disease where your body parts rot and fall off. In ancient Israel, anyone who had leprosy was required to self-isolate, by living far off from his society. If the sick person left his area of residence, when anyone approached him or her, he was required to shout so as to make people aware of his or her presence, so that the people could keep their distance to avoid being contaminated. It was a real curse to have this disease.

3. Lastly, God informed Moses that if he took some water from the Nile and poured it on dry land, this water would change into blood.

Moses, however, did not feel confident to accept this task and he complained to God, "*Pardon me, Jehovah, but I have never been a fluent speaker, neither in the past nor since you have spoken to your servant, for I am slow of speech and slow of tongue.*" It is said Moses had a stammer; see **Exodus 4:10.**

Jehovah replied to Moses, "Who made a mouth for man, or who makes them speechless, deaf, clear-sighted, or blind? Is it, not I, Jehovah? So go now, and I will be with you as you speak, and I will teach you what you should say."

It is very clear that Moses had no idea of God's capabilities, this was his very first encounter with God. If Jehovah gave him a job to do, it is obvious that He would also have provided the required means to do it. **Moses refused to accept this mission; he felt too intimidated by the task ahead of him and ended up saying**, "*Pardon me, Jehovah, please send anyone whom you want to send,*" see **Exodus 4:13**.

At that point, Jehovah accommodated Moses' level of understanding and said to Moses, **Exodus 4: 14-16,** "*What about your brother Aaron the Levite? I know that he can speak very well. And he is now on his way here to meet you. When he sees you, his heart will rejoice. So, you must speak to him and put the words in his mouth, and I will be with you and him as you speak, and I will teach you men* what to do. He will speak for you to the people, and he will be your spokesman, and you will serve as God to him." Moses was now content and accepted his mission.

Please note, regarding God's reaction to Moses' refusal to accept His request, He could have threatened, punished or killed Moses, but Jehovah did not.

Jehovah also foretold before Moses' first encounter with the Pharaoh, that he would kill all the firstborns of the Egyptians, if Pharaoh refused to send the Israelites away; in fact, He requests Moses to say this exact phrase to the Pharaoh; **Exodus 4: 22-23.** "You must say to Pharaoh, this is what Jehovah says, Israel is my son, my firstborn. I say to you, send my son away so that he may serve me. But if you refuse to send him away, I am going to kill your son, your firstborn."

Moses went to the Israelites but had to perform all the three signs that Jehovah had given him before they could believe him.

Then Moses and Aaron went to meet the Pharaoh. They said, *"Jehovah, the God of the Israelites has communicated with us. Please, we want to make a three-day journey into the wilderness and sacrifice to Jehovah our God; otherwise, he will strike us with disease or with the sword."*

But Pharaoh said, *"Who is Jehovah, that I should obey his voice to send Israel away? I do not know Jehovah at all, and what is more, I will not send Israel away."*

Following that first encounter between Pharaoh and Moses, the Egyptian king increased greatly the labour for all the Israelites and accused Moses and Aaron of distracting the Israelites from their work, with fanciful ideas of, *"going to sacrifice to their God."* The Israelites in turn accused Moses and Aaron of bringing evil upon them, and then Moses and Aaron got angry with God. See **Exodus 5:22-23**.

The Israelites were so greatly discouraged by their increase in forced labour, that they did not want to listen to Moses and Aaron any more. Then for a second time, Jehovah persuaded Moses to go with his brother Aaron to Pharaoh, to request him again to free the Israelites. This time, Pharaoh asked Moses to perform a miracle to prove that he was sent by God. God had foreseen this request from Pharaoh and told Moses exactly what to do; **Exodus 7: 8**. Aaron threw his rod on the ground and it turned into a big snake. However, the King's magicians were also able to do this same thing, but Moses' snake ate up all the snakes produced from the rods of Pharaoh's magicians. Pharaoh, however, refused to send the Israelites away.

From that time onwards, Jehovah sent Moses and Aaron repeatedly to request the Pharaoh to let the Israelites go free. Each request was accompanied by a different "miraculous event" but these miracles were not positive events, on the contrary, they were aimed at causing absolute misery to the Egyptians, to put pressure on Pharaoh to set the Israelites free. These miracles are also called plagues, due to their negative effects, of causing misery to the Egyptians.

After a few days of suffering damage and misery from these plagues, Pharaoh would sent for Moses and would inform him that he had finally decided to let the Israelites go free and would also promise to do so. Pharaoh would then request Moses to plead to Jehovah and ask Him to stop the plague in process. Moses would then raise his hands up to Jehovah and the plague would stop, but the Pharaoh never respected his promises and did not free the Israelites.

Jehovah foretold to Moses several times; **Exodus 7: 3, Exodus 10: 1-2, Exodus 11: 9-10, that** Pharaoh would never have respected his promises, in fact, Jehovah claimed that it was He Himself who made Pharaoh's heart stubborn. Why would Jehovah do such a thing? It seems like He would be acting against His own interests. Jehovah says that Pharaoh's refusal to set the Israelites free meant that He would be forced to use a heavy hand on the

Egyptians and to multiply His signs, His acts and His miracles against them, leading to His name being declared in all the earth; Jehovah was using Pharaoh for His own cause. These signs, miracles and plagues from Jehovah were also meant to prove to the Israelites that he was The True God, one capable of challenging Pharaoh and all the gods of Egypt, single-handed and winning His cause.

Please note, while the Israelite slaves had a single God, the Egyptians had many gods and each god had specific duties: Horus was the guardian of the Egyptian nation; Heka, the god of magic and medicine; Ra, the sun god, was the king of deities and the father of all creation, patron of the sun, heavens and kingship etc. Each of Jehovah's miracles discredited the functions of a god or a group of Egyptian gods. For example, in the first miracle, when the Nile's water was converted into blood, where were all the Egyptian gods responsible for protecting the Nile? Jehovah, all by Himself, proved superior to all the different Egyptian gods responsible for protecting the Nile.

I will mention briefly the ten "miracles," also called the ten "plagues" performed against the Egyptians, by Jehovah, the God of the Israelites.

The first plague: all water sources in Egypt, including the river Nile, were turned into blood for seven days and had the fish in the Nile rotting and also created a serious water shortage everywhere.

The second plague: frogs came up from the Nile, swarmed everywhere, invading all corners of Egyptian homes.

Note; the magic practising priests of Egypt were able to replicate the first two miracles done by Jehovah, but failed to replicate all the others. They informed Pharaoh that the miracles performed by Jehovah proved that He was a real God, but Pharaoh ignored this information.

Note: The Goshen area in Egypt was inhabited by the Israelite slaves. From the third plague onwards, this area was protected from the plagues aimed at the Egyptians.

The third plague: Aaron struck the ground with his rod and all the dust of the earth became gnats in all the land of Egypt and there was a massive invasion by this two-winged, biting fly, causing misery to both man and domestic animals.

The Torah says that when Aaron struck the dust with his rod, "bugs crawled forth from the dust to cover the land" which are said to be lice. Whatever these bugs were, they caused extreme misery to both man and beast.

Fourth plague: a massive invasion of all Egypt by gadflies. These flies generally bite livestock. Also, according to the Torah, hordes of wild animals, destroying everything in their path, were sent to terrorize the Egyptians.

Fifth plague: pestilence on all Egyptian livestock, resulting in their death.

Sixth plague: a serious epidemic of festering boils, open, oozing, itching, wounds on man and beast.

Seventh plague: a hailstorm that destroyed all the crops and killed any man or livestock out in the field; the Egyptians had been warned not to let out their animals and to keep themselves indoors.

Eighth plague: a multitude of locusts invaded all the land, consuming any plant that had survived the hailstorm.

Ninth plague: for three days, all of Egypt was enveloped in a thick and impenetrable veil of darkness; it was so thick that it could be felt and it extinguished all lights kindled. The Egyptians were gripped with fear and remained glued to their places wherever they stood or sat.

The tenth and last plague: all the firstborns of all Egyptians, including Pharaoh and also all the firstborns of the Egyptians' servants and the firstborn of their livestock died overnight, precisely at midnight.

Pharaoh got up that night along with all his servants and all the other Egyptians and there was a great outcry of wailing among the Egyptians because there was not a house where someone was not dead. See **Exodus 12:30**.

The tenth miracle finally worked; with the death of his firstborn, Pharaoh practically kicked out all the Israelites from Egypt. He had finally realized that he and all of Egypt were extremely vulnerable to the God of the Hebrew slaves; this God could do to them practically anything he chose and they would be completely defenceless; you cannot fight an invisible enemy.

Never has there been recorded in history, to date, such huge miracles, as those that were performed in the land of Egypt in a bid to free the Israelites from slavery. Never has there been recorded a battle, where one army suffered 100% casualties; all Egyptians had a death in the family, while the other had 0% casualties; the people God was fighting for, the Israelites, had no causalities at all. All these events in Egypt clearly proved to the Israelites and prove to us today, that Jehovah is a real and true God. Jehovah, all by Himself defeated the most powerful nation on earth.

Did I rightly hear someone say, that they, mortal man, are fighting for God, the Creator of all the universe? Just the idea that mortal man can fight for God is equivalent to blasphemy because it implies that God is not capable of doing this task Himself, he needs help from man. **God does not need help from anyone nor to be defended by anyone.**

When the Israelites witnessed all the mighty miracles performed by Jehovah, they gradually put faith in Him and started listening to what Moses and Aaron had to say. They must have felt awe towards their God; after years of hardship and exploitation, finally, here was someone who could help them.

A few days before Jehovah sent the last plague to the Egyptians, He requested every one of the Israelites, through Moses and Aaron, to kill a lamb and paint the doorposts of their external doors in the sheep's blood. Jehovah said that this sign would be recognized by "The Angel of Death" sent to kill the firstborns of the Egyptians, he would then "pass over" the Israelites' homes, hence no death would come to their firstborns. No Israelite family suffered any death on that particular night.

God gave a command to the Israelites that they should always celebrate to time indefinite, the day they were freed from slavery in the land of Egypt. This is done every year by those who practise Judaism, a few days before the Christian Easter celebration; this solemn Jewish celebration is called The Passover, Pesach in Judaism.

The state of slavery reduces man to doing only the basic things in life, wash, eat and sleep. Why? One lacks time, money and other resources because one spends most of the day doing hard work without pay. At the end of the day, one needs just food and rest and lacks the energy and resources to do other things. After many years of slavery, the Israelites were bound to have become an extremely ignorant people, due to their extremely deprived state. God eventually provided them with His Law to instruct them to remedy this state of ignorance and to protect them from evil.

God delivered the Israelites from slavery, for the following reasons:

- He had pity on them
- In order to fulfil his promise to Abraham, Isaac and Jacob
- So that they could serve him **freely**

Note, the term, "so that they could serve God freely" could be misinterpreted to mean "work for God." Before they were serving the Egyptians and were under the Egyptian authority, but now they would be serving God and they would be under His authority. When the Israelites served the Egyptians, they benefitted the Egyptians, to their disadvantage. When the Israelites served God, by living according to His Law, only they themselves benefited, not God who was taking care of them.

All these miracles done in the land of Egypt to free the Israelites were recorded by Moses in the Torah and therefore made accessible to all humankind, so that we too may acknowledge The True God.

Now the function of a God is to protect and sustain in all ways. The Israelites had just been freed and had a long way to go before arriving at their final destination, The Promised Land. Jehovah fulfilled all His duties as a God throughout this eventful journey, but the nation of Israel rebelled several times against Moses, their guide, who had been chosen by Jehovah Himself and hence against God.

11

Israelites receive a discouraging report about the promised land

I would like to write of one particular rebellion of the Israelites that caused very heavy, but justified punishment from Jehovah. The Israelites arrived in sight of their destination, The Promised Land, after travelling for a little less than one year from Egypt, but before going on to take the territories that God had promised them, Moses sent out into these lands twelve spies, representing the twelve tribes of Israel. This request made to Moses to send out spies came from the Israelites; **Deuteronomy 1: 21-23,** because they did not feel confident enough, did not have faith in God, to go and seize The Promised Land; they hesitated.

Moses requested these twelve spies to scout the land for forty days in order to gather information regarding the people living there, who they were; their level of organization, how productive the land was, what kind of landscape was present etc. After forty days, all the twelve spies returned to give their respective reports to Moses. They all agreed on one fact, the land was indeed flowing with milk and honey. This land was extremely fertile; a bunch of grapes was brought in; it was so large and heavy that it required two men to carry it; pomegranates and figs were also brought in to prove how fertile the land was. Of the twelve spies sent by Moses, ten of them gave a negative report. They said that the cities were extremely well-fortified, the inhabitants of these lands were huge, strong and well-built individuals; they said that it would have been practically impossible for the Israelites to conquer these cities.

Two of the twelve spies sent by Moses disagreed with the negative reports provided by the other ten spies; their names were Joshua and Caleb. They told the Israelites that, with God's help, they would surely conquer these inhabitants and they encouraged the Israelites to go forward in battle to seize these lands.

The Israelite nation chose to believe the negative reports from the ten spies. On the day these reports were delivered, there was a lot of distress and anguish in Israel; **Numbers 14: 1-4.** Then, **all** the assembly raised their voices and the people continued crying out and weeping all through that night. **The whole assembly** grumbled against Moses and Aaron and said to them, *"If only we had died in Egypt or even here, in the wilderness, why did Jehovah bring us to this land only to fall by the sword? Our wives and little ones will be carried off as plunder. Wouldn't it be better for us to return to Egypt?"* Then they plotted amongst themselves: *"Let's choose a new leader and go back to Egypt."*

Moses and Aaron fell face down on the ground in front of the whole Israelite assembly gathered there. Caleb and Joshua tore their garments, a sign of extreme distress and despair among the Israelites. They tried to encourage the people, saying that they should have no fear because Jehovah would be with them and they should not fear the inhabitants of these lands, but **the whole assembly** talked about stoning them. **Numbers 14: 10**

Then the glory of Jehovah appeared to all the Israelites at the Tent of Meeting; this tent was the official headquarters where Jehovah communicated to Moses and where Moses exercised the function of judging the people. Despite all the numerous miracles that Jehovah had performed among the Israelites throughout their journey to the Promised Land, they still did not have confidence or faith in Him. Jehovah was furious with the Israelites; He threatened to strike them down with a plague and destroy them all. Moses had to plead with Jehovah for mercy.

"Please, now, Jehovah, let your power be great, as you promised when you said: 'Jehovah is slow to anger and abundant in loyal love,

pardoning error and transgression, but he will by no means leave the guilty unpunished, bringing punishment for the error of fathers upon sons, upon the third generation and upon the fourth generation.' Forgive, please, the error of this people according to your great loyal love, just as you have pardoned this people from Egypt until now."

To cut the story short, Jehovah forgave them but not without punishing them. The ten spies who brought back a negative report died shortly after of plague.

Jehovah said he would grant the Israelites what they had requested: ***"If only we had died in Egypt or in the wilderness."*** Everyone above twenty years of age who had rebelled against Jehovah, (practically everyone), except Caleb, son of Jephunneh and Joshua, son of Nun; would not live to see the Promised Land, they would all die in the wilderness of the desert. Only Caleb and Joshua would live to see and enter the Promised Land.

"And I will bring in your children, who you said would become plunder, and they will get to know the land that you have rejected. But your own corpses will fall in this wilderness. Now your sons will become shepherds in the wilderness for 40 years, and they will have to answer for your acts of unfaithfulness until the last one of your corpses falls in the wilderness. According to the number of the days that you spied out the land, 40 days, a day for a year, a day for a year, you will answer for your errors 40 years, for you will know what it means to oppose me." **Numbers 14: 30-34**.

The whole assembly was ordered to turn around and go back into the desert where they roamed and lived for the following forty years. Against the advice of Moses, some Israelites decided to go ahead and fight their way through to the Promised Land. They were all killed in battle by the inhabitants of these lands. By the end of forty years, all those who had rebelled against Moses were dead. Jehovah sustained the Israelites for all these forty years with protection, His laws, food, water and their garments did not wear out. He did not abandon them but proved again to be their true God.

The native inhabitants of the lands which were to become the property of the Israelites, were evil practising people. These evil practices originated from the worship of their god, Baal, which is why Jehovah, judged them and used Israel to wipe them out. See **Deuteronomy 20: 17-18;** Completely destroy them, the Hittites, Amorites, Canaanites, Perizzites, Hivites and Jebusites, as Jehovah has commanded you. Otherwise, they will teach you to follow all the detestable things they do in worshipping their god, such as freeing male prostitution in their temple and sacrificing their children by burning them alive in fire to their God, Baal etc and you will sin against Jehovah your God.

When the Israelites had lived in the Promised Land for some time, they eventually abandoned Jehovah. **Judges 1:27-36**, says Israel, some tribes of Israel, did not obey God's commandment to wipe out all the Canaanites. They let them live beside and among them. Eventually, Israel was ensnared by the gods of Canaanites and forgot their own God; they worshipped idols.

Israel took up the evil practices of the neighbouring nations, including burning their children alive in fire as a sacrifice to the god, Baal; see **Jeremiah 19: 3-5**. The Israelites too got kicked out of the land that God had given them. God used the Assyrians to destroy the northern part of the Israeli territory and much later on, Babylon, to destroy Judah in the South.

12

The Israelites reject leadership from Jehovah

Jehovah had chosen Israel out of all nations of the earth, as "a model nation." What does "model" really mean? Let's see: **Exodus 19: 5-6**; "*Now if you will strictly obey my voice and keep my covenant, you will certainly become my special property, out of all peoples, for the whole earth belongs to me. You will become to me a kingdom of priests and a holy nation. These are the words that you are to speak to the Israelites.*"

As you can see, God is concerned mainly with the moral aspect of the Israelite nation, not giving it excessive wealth and power, through conquering other nations. Further protection from Jehovah to the Israelites was, see **Exodus 34: 24;** as long as they kept Jehovah's Law, no nation would desire their land.

The Israelites agreed to obey God and to keep His Law. See **Exodus 19: 7-8;** So Moses went and summoned the elders of the people and declared to them all these words that Jehovah had commanded him. After that, all the people answered unanimously: "*All that Jehovah has spoken, we are willing to do.*" Moses immediately took the people's response to Jehovah.

When the Israelite nation left Egypt, they were ruled by Jehovah, through His prophets; first through Moses, then through Joshua and then through Judges who were leaders chosen by God. At a certain period of the Israelites' history, when they had already settled in their Promised Land and when Samuel was Jehovah's main prophet, the Israelites decided that they no longer wanted Jehovah as their political leader; they wanted to be ruled by man and precisely by kings; "Just like the other nations surrounding them," see **1 Samuel 8: 4-7**.

Samuel warned the Israelites of the consequences of being ruled by "earthly kings," but they would not listen; on the contrary, they insisted on having kings rule them. See **1 Samuel 8: 9-18**.

See **1 Samuel 8: 19-20:** But the people refused to listen to Samuel. *"No!"* they said. *"We want a king over us. Then we will be like all the other nations, with a king to lead us and to go out before us and fight our battles."*

The Israelites, actually desired a man, in place of God, to lead them in battle! Jehovah granted them what they desired: to be ruled by kings and not Him.

I have written this particular biblical episode, to show that **Jehovah does not force Himself onto anybody who does not want him.** If one decides to move away from God, it is he who will be a loser and not God. Jehovah was saddened when the Israelites rejected his leadership because He already knew the difficulties they would face; they and their property would become the "personal property," of their kings and then, worst of all, they would be induced by these very kings to leave Jehovah and to worship idols.

Here are some of the difficulties the Israelite nation suffered as a consequence of being ruled by kings:

1 Kings 5: 13-16, 1 Kings 12:1-14, 28-30 etc. All of chapter **21 of 2 Kings** tells of one of the darkest kingships in the history of Israel, regarding idol worship promoted by Manasseh, King of Judah.

Please note that Jehovah did not punish anybody following the decision to substitute Him with human kings, He just accepted their very unwise decision; he even warned them of the consequences of their decision. **God respects man's free will, which He has given to him.**

The Israelites removed God from their leadership and substituted him with a mortal man; furthermore, they wanted to be: "just like the other nations." They were tired of being "a special property of Jehovah."

How did the Israelites become so enticed by this idea of "kings?" Was it not due to them being already involved with the nations surrounding them? From the above request, forwarded to the prophet Samuel, of having kings to govern Israel, it was very clear that Israel had already left Jehovah.

13

The capture of the Ark
of the Covenant by an enemy

Let's see another event written in the Bible which gives insight into The True God. The following event proves again that Jehovah does not need man to fight for Him, because He is capable of fighting His own battles, all by Himself. This is an event written in **1 Samuel chapters 4-5.**

During this period, Israel was governed by kings and precisely by **K**ing David, son of Jesse and the second king of the nation of Israel. By this time, Jehovah had already permitted Israel to be ruled by kings. Israel went to war with their neighbour, the Philistines, but was defeated in battle, losing **about four thousand men.** This defeat came as a total shock to Israel. The Israelites forgot that Jehovah had promised to sustain them in battle, on condition that they kept His Covenant, that is they should live according to His Law; see **Deuteronomy chapter 28:7**.

1 Samuel 4: 3; When the people returned to the camp, the elders of Israel said: *"Why did Jehovah allow us to be defeated today by the Philistines?"*

It was obvious to the Israelites that Jehovah had not sustained them in that particular battle, because it is impossible to lose any battle if Jehovah is on your side. The elders of Israel did not think of enquiring why Jehovah had not backed them and did not even bother to seek Jehovah's support in their forthcoming battles, instead, they came up with "a brilliant idea," of how to get Jehovah to go back into battle with them.

The elders of Israel said: *"Let us take the ark of Jehovah's covenant with us from Shiloh, so that IT may be with us and save us from the hand of our enemies."* Please note: *"so that IT may save us"* and not, *"so that Jehovah may save us."*

Some members of the Israelite army went to the High Priest, Eli and requested him for the Ark of the Covenant. The Ark of the Covenant also called The Ark of the True God or The Ark of the Testimony, was an elaborate gold-covered, wooden box and it contained, among other items, the two stone tablets with the Ten Commandments, inscribed by Jehovah Himself; see **Deuteronomy 10: 1-5**. This Ark represented God's physical presence among the Israelites; it also represented the covenant, an official agreement between the Israelites and their God, Jehovah, that Jehovah alone would be their God and they, in turn, would be His special or chosen People, in that, they would live according to His Law.

The Ark was built by the Israelites but the instruction on how to build it came directly from Jehovah, through His prophet, Moses. **It was the property of Jehovah.** Eli, the High Priest, agreed to give The Ark to them to be carried into battle; also, two of those carrying the Ark into battle were actually his sons, Hophni and Phinehas. According to the Talmud, The Ark of the Covenant had remained in Shiloh for a period of 369 years, before being captured by the Philistines. The Talmud means study or learning; it is a compilation of ancient teachings, based on rabbinic comments and reasoning and debates on the teachings of the Torah.

The Ark of the Covenant had been stationed in Shiloh from when the Israelites first came into The Promised Land. The Bible describes Shiloh as an assembly place for the people of Israel from the time of Joshua. Sacrifices were brought there by the Israelites during the period of judges, and it was also the site of various religious celebrations and festivals, as such it was the major site for worship in Israel before the construction of the first temple in Jerusalem.

From the scriptures, we know that Shiloh was eventually destroyed, see: **Jeremiah 7:12**; "But go now to My place which was in Shiloh, where I set My name at the first, and see what I did to it because of the wickedness of My people Israel."

See **Jeremiah 26:5-6**; "and if you do not listen to the words of my servants the prophets, whom I have sent to you again and again (though you have not listened), **then I will make this house like Shiloh** and this city a curse among all the nations of the earth."

It is clear that Jehovah destroyed and burned down the area where the Ark first resided in Shiloh, probably through conquest by the Philistines, because the prophet Jeremiah lived in the period when Jerusalem was destroyed by being burned down by the Babylonians.

Israel went into battle against the Philistines again, but this time they took with them the Ark of the True God. Before the start of the battle, the Israelite army gave such a mighty shout, that the earth resounded; this time fully confident of winning the battle. The Philistines, on the other hand, were extremely distressed and intimidated by the idea of fighting a battle where there was a presence of a God; they had heard of the miracles performed by Jehovah in Egypt to free the Israelites. The Philistines, however, decided to go ahead with the battle.

The Israelites were defeated for a second time and the Ark of the True God was captured by the enemy! The Israelite army fled from the battle, both of Eli's sons were killed and the number of the Israelite soldiers killed this time was **thirty thousand,** a total disaster. When the news got back home of the capture of the Ark and the heavy defeat of the Israelites, there was real despair in Israel; the whole nation sent up a cry. When Eli the High Priest heard that the Ark had been captured, he fell backwards from his chair and broke his neck, he was a heavy man, and he died.

Samuel, a young man, under Eli's care, and destined to be a great prophet, had received a revelation from Jehovah some time back. From this revelation, Eli learnt that his sons would be punished for very serious errors they had committed against Jehovah and that he too, would not be spared because he had failed to reprimand them. **1 Samuel 2:12-17** and **1 Samuel 3: 10-18.**

The Philistines took The Ark to the city of Ashdod, and then to the temple of their God, Dagon. The Philistines had the insight to treat godly items with respect! The next morning, when they went into their temple, they found the statue of their god Dagon had fallen upon his face to the earth before The Ark. Dagon's statue was placed back in its original place in the temple.

On the second day of the Ark's stay in Dagon's temple, the Ashdodites found that Dagon had been decapitated and his hands too had been amputated; both the hands and the head were at the threshold of the temple. The remaining stump of Dagon had fallen face down before the Ark. Consequently, in Ashdod there came to be an epidemic of piles, that is, haemorrhoids among the men. The Ashdodites did not want to keep this Ark any more in their city, because they felt it was responsible for the epidemic of piles and also, they themselves and their god Dagon had been seriously humiliated. Cutting off Dagon's head and hands clearly showed that Dagon was inferior to Jehovah and as such would not manage to protect them from any actions taken by Jehovah. This Ark proved to be a source of distress, hence an enemy, right inside their city. The Lords of the Philistines met and decided to transfer it to another of their cities, Gath.

In Gath, the arrival of the Ark was accompanied by a sense of great panic everywhere and a serious epidemic of haemorrhoids broke out among men of all ages, so it was decided to transfer The Ark of the God of Israel to Ekron.

The Ark was transferred to Ekron amid resistance from the Ekronites, who were already nervous, due to what had happened in the other cities that hosted it. The city was in panic due to a strange sense of doom; it was perceived that the presence of this

Ark would cause them death. There was an epidemic of piles also in this city, furthermore, mice appeared everywhere and were bringing their land to ruin. The Ark of the God of Israel had been with the Philistines now for seven months and had brought them great distress.

It was decided by the Lords of the Philistines to consult their priests and diviners as to what should be done with the Ark. They decided to send it back to Israel. The Lords of the Philistines were informed that the Ark was not to be sent back empty-handed, but the God of Israel was to be honoured. The Ark was to be accompanied by a guilt offering from the Philistines, which would comprise models of five golden piles and five golden mice, according to the number of the Lords of the Philistines. The Diviners advised that this guilt offering might permit them and their land to be healed. These images reflected the scourge that had afflicted all of them. See **1 Samuel 6:4-9**.

The Lords of the Philistines were advised not to harden their hearts like the Egyptians. They then were to take the Ark and put it on a new wagon, drawn by two cows that had never ploughed. Their guilt offering was to be placed in a box **beside** the Ark. Then they were to lead the wagon onto the road and watch where it was heading. If the wagon went towards Bethshemesh, its own territory, the Israelite territory, then Jehovah was responsible for bringing all the misery to the Philistines, but if the wagon took another road, then all their misfortunes were just a coincidence.

The Lords of the Philistines did all that had been suggested to them by their priests and diviners; then they followed the wagon carrying the Ark. It took the road leading to Bethshemesh, Israel. The cows were mooing and did not turn right or left, but went straight on. On the boundary of Bethshemesh, the Lords of the Philistine turned back and went home.

The wagon went straight back to the field of Joshua, the Bethshemite, and stopped there near a large stone. The Israelites who were in the fields reaping the wheat were overjoyed when they raised their eyes and saw The Ark on the wagon. **The Levites took down the ark of Jehovah together with the chest containing the gold objects and placed them on the large rock.** On that day, the people of Bethshemesh offered burnt offerings and made sacrifices to Jehovah. **They chopped up the wagon** and offered the cows as a burned offering to Jehovah.

God, however, struck down the men of Bethshemesh, because they had looked irreverently upon the Ark of Jehovah. **He struck down 50,070** among the people, and the people began mourning because Jehovah had struck them down with a great slaughter. They asked, *"Who will be able to stand before Jehovah, this holy God and to whom will he go away from us?"*

The priests in Bethshemesh had failed to carry out their duty, to cover The Ark, bringing heavy judgement upon the population there who had gazed irreverently at the Ark of the True God. The Israelites knew, however, that it was forbidden to look upon the uncovered Ark and anyone doing so would be struck dead; **Numbers 4: 15 - 20. *"They must not come in and see the holy things even for an instant, or they will die."***

So, the Bethshemites sent messengers to the inhabitants of Kiriathjearim, saying: *"The Philistines have returned the Ark of Jehovah. Come down and take it up with you."* So, the Ark was taken to Kiriathjearim in Judah and stayed there until King David of Israel went to pick it up.

Please note that no death came to the Philistine for gazing at the Ark of The True God, when they captured it.

From the above episode, we see that Jehovah is very capable of looking after His own property. His Ark was meant to be kept by the Israelites as a constant reminder of their covenant with Him, so he manoeuvred the Philistines until they took it back to where it should have been, in Israel.

14

A death casualty in the transportation of the Ark of the True God

This chapter tells of an event where King David of Israel, the second king of the nation of Israel, goes to Kiriathjearim, (see **1 Samuel 7:1-2**), to bring the Ark of the Covenant to Jerusalem. It had been in this place for twenty years. This event shows, again, that Jehovah is capable of looking after his own affairs. This event is written in **1 Chronicles chapter 13.**

King David consulted with the chiefs of the thousands and of the hundreds and with every leader. Then David said to all the congregation of Israel: *"If it seems good to you and it is acceptable to Jehovah our God, let us send word to our remaining brothers in all regions of Israel and also to the priests and the Levites in their cities with pastures to come and join us. And let us bring back the Ark of our God."*

So, David congregated all of Israel and they went out to Kiriathjearim, a part of Judah, to bring back the Ark of the True God to Jerusalem. They went to Abinadab, the man who had The Ark in custody. King David put The Ark on a new wagon drawn by cows. The sons of Abinadab, Uzzah and Ahio were leading the wagon. King David and all of Israel were celebrating before the true God with all their might, accompanied by songs, harps, other stringed instruments, tambourines, cymbals, and trumpets. But when they came to the threshing floor of Chidon, Uzzah, Abinadab's son, thrust his hand out and grabbed hold of the Ark, for the cattle nearly upset it. At that, Jehovah's anger blazed against Uzzah and

He struck him down because he had thrust his hand out to the Ark and he died there before God.

But King David became angry because Jehovah's wrath had broken through against Uzzah. He decided not to carry The Ark further and left it in a nearby place in the house of Obededom, the Gittite. The Ark of the True God was with the household of Obededom, remaining at his house for three months, and Jehovah kept blessing the household of Obededom and all he had.

I too got angry when I read this episode. After all, Uzzah was just trying to be helpful. However, when I thought it over and investigated the Ark's transportation regulations, I concluded that Uzzah's death might have been an act of mercy on King David and all those who were near The Ark, during the transportation.

Let's look at this episode a bit more closely. Uzzah did something he should never have done; he touched The Ark of the God of Israel, but Jehovah clearly states that only the Levites are authorized to touch His Ark, anybody else breaching this rule will die. **Numbers 4: 15:** "After Aaron and his sons (Levites) have finished covering the holy furnishings and all the holy articles, and when the camp is ready to move, only then are the Kohathites (another class of Levite) to come and do the carrying. **but they must not touch the holy place or they will die.** The Kohathites are to carry those things that are in the tent /tabernacle of meeting."

Aaron's sons also assigned other groups of Levites, sons of Gershon, Gershonites and sons of Merari, Merarites, different roles in the transportation of other items used in The Ark of The Covenant. **The Ark was to be transported by the Levites on their shoulders, holding onto poles.**

I have wondered if trying to assist God is not in itself an act of blasphemy, in that a mortal man believes he could assist a God, by propping up His Ark. What kind of God is this that needs man to assist Him? Uzzah most probably acted instinctively and unconsciously, when he tried to prop up the Ark. First, I believe that The Ark would never have fallen off the wagon because of God's protection. However, supposing it did, the people nearby would have run instinctively to pick it up, and any other objects that might have fallen out of the Ark. The result is all of them would have been struck down dead.

The death of Uzzah brought to focus one thing, the correct procedure of moving and transporting the Ark, which had been provided by Jehovah Himself, had been totally ignored. See the rules of transporting The Ark in **Numbers chapter 4**. This is The Ark of the Sovereign Lord of the Universe; you just cannot load it and handle it as you please.

To understand the cause of Uzzah's death, let's consider the following example. Now if Queen Elizabeth left you her dog to look after for a while, while away for one reason or another, you would try and get all the information regarding what that particular dog likes and requires. However, I am sure the Queen herself, would have provided all the information she thought might make the life of her dog comfortable while she was away. Now, if the Queen had forgotten to provide you with a piece of information that you considered important, you yourself would have had to request it from someone you were confident could provide correct information on the matter. Looking after the Queen's dog is an honour and you surely would not like any harm to befall the Queen's dog while it is in your care.

Now, Jehovah did not strike dead the people transporting The Ark wrongly, although they did not follow the correct transportation procedure, but touching The Ark was real ignorance and had to be dealt with appropriately. Uzzah and his family had been keeping The Ark in custody, since its arrival from Bethshemesh and to be precise, **for twenty years**, yet it seems they had not got acquainted with how to handle the Ark of The True God. This kind of ignorance can only be equated to a lack of reverence for Jehovah.

King David later admitted to his error and his responsibility, regarding the death of Uzzah; he himself, had breached Jehovah's rules and procedures involved in the transportation of His Ark: **1 Chronicles 15: 13-15.**

When King David had cooled down and reflected, he summoned the Levite priests and the rest of his fellow citizens and collected The Ark, following the correct procedure prescribed by Jehovah and brought it to Jerusalem, accompanied by a huge ceremony and celebration.

What do you make of the 1981 film: "Raiders of the Lost Ark"?

Aaron's sons die fulminated by Jehovah

There is another episode in the Bible that shows how important it is to follow accurately what God instructs. If one is not attentive to what God says, this is a sure sign of disrespect to God.

Leviticus 10:1-3: Later Aaron's sons Nadab and Abihu each took his fire holder and put fire in it and placed incense on it. Then they began offering before Jehovah unauthorized fire, which he had not commanded them to do. At this, a fire came out from before Jehovah and consumed them, so that they died before Jehovah. Then Moses said to Aaron, "This is what Jehovah has said, 'I will be made holy among those near to me, and I will be glorified before all the people." And Aaron kept silent.

To be chosen to serve God, as Aaron and his family were, is an honour and one is required to do it diligently. Aaron's sons, Nadab and Abihu invented their own homemade procedures, without God's consent and went to impose them on God, a sure sign of disrespect, because they did not follow the prescribed procedures and God had not requested any service from them.

15

God rescues Jerusalem from capture by the Assyrians

Now, let's see another event in the Bible regarding Jehovah's interaction with the Israelites. This is a story of an Israelite king who finds his capital and home city, Jerusalem, surrounded by a very powerful enemy. This king realizes that he and his people do not have the military capability to defeat this enemy. He, therefore, appeals to Jehovah for help; this happened about the year, **701 BC**.

At an earlier date, about **930 BC**, the nation of Israel, which had, up to that point, always existed as a single nation, broke up into two kingdoms; one nation in the north, which retained the name Israel and the other in the south, which was known as Judah. Ten of the twelve tribes of Israel came to form the nation of Israel in the north, while only two of the twelve tribes, Benjamin and Judah, formed the nation of Judah in the south. The capital of the Northern kingdom, Israel, was called Samaria and that of the Southern kingdom of Judah remained Jerusalem.

During the period of **740 to 722 BCE,** all the kingdom of Israel in the north was captured by the Assyrian kings; first Tiglath-Pileser III (Pul), then Shalmaneser V, then Sargon II and this job was finally finished by his successor, Sennacherib. The then defeated Israelites were deported, that is, exiled into other regions of the Assyrian empire. The Assyrian king then brought people, non-Israelites, from other nations and settled them in the territory of Israel north of Judah, in the territory previously occupied by the ten tribes of Israel.

According to the Bible, **2 Kings 17: 5-18**, Jehovah removed the nation of Israel from His sight because it had become an extremely wicked nation and unwilling to listen to His prophets. The identity of the place, where these Ten Tribes of Israel went to, remained and remains unknown today; apparently, they were assimilated into the vast Assyrian Empire. These ten tribes of Israel that seemed to have just disappeared; are referred to as: "The Ten Lost Tribes of Israel." Lately, however, the increased rate of globalization in the transport and tourism industry has finally made it possible to trace many distant and isolated groups of people, all over the world, who claim to be of Jewish origin; (maybe the Lost Tribes of Israel) and to reconnect them with their ancestral home, Israel.

After the fall of Samaria in the North, the then-reigning Assyrian king, Sennacherib, turned his attention to Judah in the South. He attacked the fortified cities of Judah and captured them, that is the cities outside Jerusalem, for example, Lachish which was second in importance to Jerusalem. He then came against Jerusalem and at that time it was ruled by King Hezekiah. This was a king who did what was right in Jehovah's eyes. He came to power at the age of twenty-five and destroyed all the idols that were in his territory. At first, King Hezekiah tried to stop the fall of Jerusalem, by offering to pay taxes to Sennacherib, the Assyrian king. An extremely heavy tax was imposed on Hezekiah by Sennacherib; however, he paid it all. Hezekiah went up to the point of removing precious items from Jehovah's temple, to pay this tax. See **2 Kings 18: 13-16.**

Despite having received all his due taxes, the Assyrian king, Sennacherib, decided to conquer Jerusalem. Why should he accept "a few pennies" from Jerusalem, when he could have the whole city? He sent a vast army and his envoys, the Tartan, Commander in Chief, the Rabsaris or Chief of Officers and the Rabshaken, Chief of Princes, who had the duty of negotiating a peaceful surrender, through threats and intimidation, to Hezekiah the then reigning king of Judah.

In those days, the Assyrians, who were the dominant power in the Middle East, preferred negotiating surrender through intimidation, rather than attacking and destroying cities, most of which had huge defensive walls and were quite difficult to conquer. Furthermore, it is better to have functional cities added to your empire, than ruined cities, that is, if the inhabitants choose to fight the Assyrians, rather than to surrender.

The diplomats of Sennacherib and a vast army stationed themselves outside the walls of the city of Jerusalem and then they sent for King Hezekiah. The king sent three trusted men to represent him, but he had ordered the rest of the public not to reply to the Assyrians. Now King Hezekiah's envoys requested the Assyrian envoys, to speak in the Aramaic language and not in the Jewish language, because the crowd might panic if they understood the contents of the speech; but this request really annoyed the Assyrian envoys, who then decided to shout out all their message in the Jewish language, starting with an insult: *"Was it only to your lord (the king) and to you, (the king's representatives) that my lord sent me to speak these words? Is it not also to the men who sit on the wall, those who will eat their own excrement and drink their own urine along with you?"* See **2 Kings 18:27**

Rabshaken then shouted out: **2 Kings 18: 28-36;** *"Hear the words of the great king, the king of Assyria. Do not listen to Hezekiah, for this is what the king of Assyria says: Do not let Hezekiah deceive you, for he is not able to rescue you, out of my hand. And do not let Hezekiah cause you to trust in Jehovah by saying: "Jehovah will surely rescue us and this city will not be given into the hand of the king of Assyria." Do not listen to Hezekiah, for this is what the king of Assyria says: "Make peace with me and surrender, and each of you will eat from his own vine and from his own fig tree and will drink water from his own cistern, until I come and take you to a land like your own, a land of grain and new wine, a land of bread and vineyards, a land of olive trees and honey. Then you will live and not die. Do not listen to Hezekiah, for he misleads you by saying: "Jehovah will rescue us."*

Then Rabshaken continued: *"Have any of the gods of the nations rescued their land out of the hand of the king of Assyria? Where are the gods of that and this and that nation (*listing the nations that had been conquered*)? Who among all the gods of the lands has rescued their land out of my hand, so that Jehovah should rescue you out of my hand?"*

The Israelites remained silent, as they had been requested not to reply to the Assyrians, by their King. King Hezekiah's envoys went back to him with their garments ripped apart, a sign of despair and distress in the Jewish culture. King Hezekiah in turn ripped his garments apart and covered himself with sackcloth, then went into the house of Jehovah, the temple to pray. He then sent envoys to the prophet Isaiah, the son of Amoz, requesting him to pray for them and to enquire what Jehovah said, regarding the king of Assyria. The prophet Isaiah told the king's envoy that Jehovah Himself would take care of this matter, so these envoys returned with positive news for King Hezekiah.

In the meantime, the king of Assyria himself sent letters to King Hezekiah, boasting how none of the nations he conquered so far had been rescued by their gods; it concluded: **2 Kings 19:10**; ***"Do not let your god in whom you trust deceive you by saying: "Jerusalem will not be given into the hand of the king of Assyria."***

Hezekiah took these letters out of the hands of his messengers and read them, then he went into the temple with them and spread them before Jehovah and Hezekiah began to pray before Jehovah and say: *"O Jehovah the God of Israel, sitting enthroned above the cherubs, you alone are the true God of all the kingdoms of the earth. You made the heavens and the earth. Incline your ear, O Jehovah, and hear! Open your eyes, O Jehovah, and see! Hear the words that Sennacherib has sent to taunt the living God. It is a fact, O Jehovah, that the kings of Assyria have devastated the nations and their lands. And they have thrown their gods into the fire because they were not gods but the work of human hands: wood and stone. That is why they could destroy them. But now, O Jehovah our God, please save us out of his hand, so that all the kingdoms of the earth may know that you alone are God, O Jehovah."*

In the meantime, a message came from the prophet Isaiah, saying, (I have written only the beginning and the conclusion): Therefore, this is what Jehovah says about the king of Assyria,

2 King 19:6-7; "Tell your Master, this is what Jehovah says: *"Do not be afraid because of the words that you heard, the words with which the attendants of the king of Assyria blasphemed me. Here I am putting a thought in his mind, and he will hear a report and return to his own land;* **and I will make him fall by the sword in his own land."**

"He will not come into this city, or shoot an arrow there, or confront it with a shield, or cast up a siege rampart against it, by the way he came he will return; he will not come into this city," says Jehovah.

"I will defend this city and save it for my own sake and for the sake of my servant David."

In **2 Kings 19: 28,** this is what Jehovah says about King Sennacherib:

"Because you rage against me and because your insolence has reached my ears, I will put my hook in your nose and my bridle between your lips, and I will lead you back the way you came."

On that very night, an angel of Jehovah went out and struck down 185,000 men in the camp of the Assyrians. **When people rose early in the morning, they saw dead bodies.** See **2 Kings 19: 35.** King Sennacherib survived the slaughter; he had come to personally witness the surrender of Jerusalem. So, Sennacherib king of Assyria, broke camp and withdrew. He returned to Nineveh, his capital city and stayed there. And it came to pass, as he was worshipping in the house of Nisroch, his god, that Adrammelech andSharezer, his sons, smote him with the sword and they escaped into the land of Armenia; and Esarhaddon, his son, reigned in his place.

A historical record of the Assyrian conquests has been discovered, written in cuneiform, on clay prisms, or prism-shaped clay pillars; they record a siege of Jerusalem but do not mention its conquest. Jerusalem was surrounded by the Assyrian Empire but never became part of it.

From the above event, we see that if you trust in God, then nothing is impossible.

16

Three Israelites challenge the mighty king of Babylon

I will give another and my final account of God's interaction with the Israelite nation. This account is taken from Chapter 3 of the Book of Daniel, present in the Old Testament. Daniel is considered a prophet by Christians, Jews and Muslims. During this period, concerning the events written in **Daniel, Chapter 3,** Babylon was the dominant political power in the Middle East, after the fall of the Assyrian empire; and Nebuchadnezzar II was the then reigning king of Babylon.

King Nebuchadnezzar made a Golden statue, 27 metres or 90 feet high and 2.7 metres or 9 feet wide; this statue was set up in the plains of Dura, in the province of Babylon. The king then held a great inauguration ceremony, to which all the people who count were invited. During the inauguration ceremony, as all the people stood in front of the statue, the herald, that is, the court's master of ceremony, loudly proclaimed: *"You are commanded O peoples, nations and language groups, that when you hear the sound of the horn, pipe, zither, triangular harp, stringed instrument, bagpipe and all other musical instruments, you must fall down and worship the image of gold that king Nebuchadnezzar, has set up."*

"Whoever does not fall and worship will immediately be thrown into a burning fiery furnace." So, when all these people heard these musical instruments, they fell down and worshipped the king's golden statue.

It is obvious that King Nebuchadnezzar had no concept of what a god really is. His golden god was made from gold, a lifeless material, therefore this god was bound to be as lifeless as the gold itself and really would have been of no benefit to him at all. King Nebuchadnezzar must have looked down on all the gods of the nations that he himself had captured because if their gods were more powerful than him or his gods, they ought to have protected these nations from his capture. Sometime later, after the inauguration of Nebuchadnezzar's golden god, some Babylonians reported to the king that some high-ranking Jews: Shadrach, Meshach and Abednego who had been appointed to administer the provinces of Babylon, (**Daniel 2: 49**) were not following his orders. Then Nebuchadnezzar, in a furious rage, ordered Shadrach, Meshach, and Abednego to be brought in. So, these men were brought in before the king.

The king then enquired: *"Is it really true, that you, Shadrach, Meshach and Abednego, are not serving my gods and you refuse to worship the image that I have set up? Now when you hear the sound of the horn, the pipe, the zither, the triangular harp, the stringed instrument, the bagpipe, and all the other musical instruments if you are ready to fall down and worship the image that I have made, fine. But if you refuse, to fall down and worship my god, you will immediately be thrown into the burning fiery furnace. And who is the god that can rescue you out of my hand?"* See **Daniel 3:14-15.**

Shadrach, Meshach and Abednego replied to him, *"O Nebuchadnezzar, we have no need to answer you in this matter. If it must be, our God whom we serve is able to rescue us from the burning fiery furnace, O king, and to rescue us from your hand. But even if he does not, let it be known to you, O king, that we will not serve your gods or worship the image of gold that you have set up.* **Daniel 3: 16-18.**

The king became so furious with their reply that he ordered the furnace to be heated up to seven times the usual temperature. He ordered some of the mighty men from his army to bind up Shadrach, Meshach and Abednego and throw them into the burning fiery furnace. So, these men were tied up unceremoniously, with all their clothes still on and were thrown into the burning fiery furnace. Because the furnace was exceptionally hot, the men who threw Shadrach, Meshach and Abednego into the fiery flames were killed by the high temperature, while the three men fell, still bound and unharmed into the burning fiery furnace.

Now, one wonders; where did these three Israelites, Shadrach, Meshach and Abednego get such confidence in their God that they felt free to challenge this most powerful king, Nebuchadnezzar and his gods; risking their very lives? It is clear that they must have had particular experiences in their lives, that convinced them they could rely on their God, Jehovah, in all circumstances.

Let us see the background of these three men

These three Israelite men, together with their friend, Daniel, who was not with them at this particular event, had survived catastrophic events in their lives. They had been given away as hostages by their king Jehoiakim, to the Babylonians after Jerusalem, their home city, had surrendered to the Babylonian army. This was after the first encounter of Jerusalem with the Babylonian army.

The scripture says: **Daniel 1:1-2**; In the third year of the reign of Jehoiakim king of Judah, Nebuchadnezzar king of Babylon came to Jerusalem and besieged it. And Jehovah delivered Jehoiakim king of Judah into his hand, along with some of the utensils of the house of the true God. These he carried off to Babylon and put in the treasure house of his god in Shinar.

Siege definition: A military operation in which the enemy forces surround a city, town or building, cutting off essential supplies, to compel those inside to surrender. Lay siege is equivalent to, besiege, the act of making a siege.

**Let's see a brief history of Jerusalem
before its first destruction.**

Jerusalem has been destroyed twice in its history, first by the Babylonians in **586 BC** and the second destruction, in **70 AD**, by Rome. As regards Daniel and his friends, they lived in the period of Jerusalem's first destruction.   .

In **2 Kings chapter 21**, we read of a very evil king, Manasseh, the son of King Hezekiah; he made Israel sin in such a terrible manner, that Jehovah made a definite decision to punish this nation: **2 Kings 21: 12-15**. Manasseh's son, Amon, was also evil, but Menasseh's grandson, King Josiah, was a righteous king: **2 Kings 23: 25.** After King Josiah, all the other kings of Israel who ruled, up until the destruction of Jerusalem by the Babylonians, were evil men and did what was wrong in the eyes of Jehovah.

Jerusalem, the capital city of Judah, was an independent nation and the only large city in Judah that had not been conquered, (assisted through divine intervention), by the Assyrian empire.

During this period, before the first destruction of Jerusalem, there came to be a time of power struggle in the Middle East. The then-dominant Assyrian empire rapidly lost control to Babylon and other regional powers. This struggle concluded with the destruction of the Assyrian Empire and the emergence of a new regional power, Babylon. This rapid fall of the Neo-Assyrian Empire had always been attributed to internal conflicts, but of late, it is attributed to a mega-drought and consequently a decline in Assyria's agrarian productivity, contributing to its eventual political and economic collapse. (See: NCBI-2019 Nov. PMC-6853769).

During this period of a power struggle between the Assyrians and the Babylonian Empire, Josiah, the then-ruling king of Judah and the great-grandson of King Hezekiah, became entangled in this regional power struggle. The Judean king, Josiah, died from a wound inflicted in the battle at Megiddo, in **610 BC**, by the army of Egyptian Pharaoh Neccho II. King Josiah had tried, without success, to stop Neccho's army from passing through Judah on their way to support their Assyrian allies, who were fighting for survival against Babylon. Officers from the Israelite army transported their wounded king back to Jerusalem, where he died and was buried. See **2 Chronicles 35:20-27.**

Egypt was an ally of the Assyrian empire. In **612 BC,** Nineveh, the capital of the Assyrian empire, was conquered. It fell after a siege of three months to the combined forces of the Babylonians, the Medes, the Persians, the Scythians and the Cimmerians. The Assyrian king, Sinsharishkun, died in the battle but was succeeded by his brother, Ashuruballit II who fled to the city of Harran, about 44km North West of Nineveh.

Shortly after the fall of Nineveh, Harran fell to the combined forces of the Medes and Babylonians, in **609 BC**. This marked the end of the Assyrian Empire. The remnant of the Assyrian army fled to Carchemis, a city on the Euphrates River controlled by Egypt. In **609 BC**, the combined forces of Egypt and the remnant Assyrian army, crossed the Euphrates together, from Carchemish, a city under Egyptian rule on the Euphrates River, to Harran, in an attempt to take back the city of Haran. They **lay siege** for two months; Babylon had established a garrison there after conquering it, but they failed to retake it. It was on his way to Carchemish, bringing reinforcements for the battle of Harran, that Pharaoh Neccho II fought the battle of Megiddo with King Josiah of Judah.

2 Kings 23:29; While Josiah was king, Pharaoh Neccho II, King of Egypt, went up to the Euphrates River to help the king of Assyria. King Josiah marched out to meet him in battle, but Neccho faced him and killed him at Megiddo.

2 Chronicles 35:20: *"After all this, when Josiah had set the temple in order, Neccho king of Egypt went up to **fight at Carchemish on the Euphrates**, and Josiah marched out to meet him in battle."* **This is not exactly correct, Pharaoh Necco II went to Carchemish to collect reinforcement for his army,** this included the remnant of the Assyrian army, **who had fled to Carchemish after the fall of one of their last cities, Haran. He then moved his forces to Harran where his army lay siege for two months, see above.**

The battle of Carchemish was eventually fought in 605 BC, while the siege of Harran took place in 609 BC, the year that King Josiah was killed.

Note that, Pharaoh Neccho had to get first to Carchemish, then to Harran.

On his way back to Egypt from his failed Siege of Harran, Pharaoh Necho II passed through Judah. Jehoahaz, the then reigning king, who had succeeded his father, King Josiah, was deposed, (by pharaoh Neccho II), after just three months in power and exiled to Egypt, where he eventually died. Eliakim, Jehohaz's elder brother, was put on the throne instead by Pharaoh Neccho II and renamed Jehoiakim. This name could also be spelt as Jehoikim. Egypt imposed heavy taxes on Jehoiakim.

Jehoiakim ruled Jerusalem **for eleven years; 609-598 BC.** See **2 Kings 23:30- 37**.

Please note, that Eliakim, later renamed Jehoiakim by Pharaoh Neccho II, was Josiah's eldest son. It is said that he was passed over at his father's death as being unworthy to be his father's successor and the throne was given to his younger brother, Jehoahaz.

In **605 BC**, at the **Battle of Carchemish,** the Babylonian and Median army led by Nebuchadnezzar II destroyed the combined Egyptian and the remnant Assyrian forces. The Assyrian Empire ceased to exist as an independent power and Egypt retreated and lost all its influence in the ancient Middle East. Following the victory at the Battle of Carchemish, King Nebuchadnezzar II, then turned his attention to Judah.

Please note, Jerusalem was still existing as an independent state because it had not been destroyed or assimilated into the Assyrian Empire.

In the Tanakh and the Old Testament, **Daniel 1:1** says: "In the third year of the kingship of King Jehoiakim of Judah, King Nebuchadnezzar of Babylon came to Jerusalem and besieged it." This is when King Nebuchadnezzar II of Babylon **first** invaded the land of Judah. Nebuchadnezzar besieged Jerusalem, by surrounding it with military forces to intimidate the city to surrender, which it did immediately.

Daniel 1:2; And Jehovah delivered Jehoiakim king of Judah into his hand, along with some of the articles from the temple of God. These he carried off to the temple of his god in the land of Shinar and put in the treasure house of his god. Shinar is the name of the southern region of Mesopotamia and was part of the Babylonian Empire.

According to **Jeremiah 46:2**; **Nebuchadnezzar first invaded Judah in the fourth year of Jehoiakim's reign, not the third year as written by Daniel**. Nebuchadnezzar came after the battle of Carchemish, (605 BC), which he won; this was actually the fourth year of Jehoiakim's kingship. Jeremiah and Daniel both lived in Jerusalem during this period of the first siege of Jerusalem. I believe this difference regarding exactly in which year, the third or the fourth year of King Jehoiakim's reign, King Nebuchadnezzar first besieged Jerusalem might be explained if this event took place at the end of the third year and into the fourth year.

Quoting from Wikipedia's: "Jehoiakim King of Judah":

*"However, after the Egyptians were defeated by the Babylonians at the battle of Carchemish in 605 BC, Nebuchadnezzar II besieged Jerusalem, and Jehoiakim changed allegiances to avoid the destruction of Jerusalem. He paid tribute from the treasury in Jerusalem, some temple artefacts, and **handed over some of the royal family and nobility as hostages. In the Book of Daniel, Daniel is described as being one of these hostages.**"*

After the first siege of Jerusalem by the Babylonian army, Jehoiakim King of Judah, who had been paying tribute to Egypt, imposed by pharaoh Necho II, was forced to change allegiances and began paying tribute to Nebuchadnezzar II of Babylon.

After the battle of Carchemish, Egypt's eastern frontier was now next to the lands conquered by Babylon and made Egypt, extremely vulnerable to an invasion. In **601 BC**, Nebuchadnezzar tried to invade Egypt but was defeated with heavy losses, therefore some states rebelled and stopped paying tribute to Babylon. Judah was one of them and Jehoiakim, the then-reigning king in Jerusalem, switched his allegiance back to Egypt.

This is confirmed in **2 Kings 24:1**. *"During Jehoiakim's reign, King Nebuchadnezzar of Babylon invaded the land of Judah. Jehoiakim surrendered and paid him tribute for three years **but then rebelled**."*

Please Note, the scriptures of **1 Kings and 2 Kings** were written by the prophet Jeremiah, who lived in Jerusalem when Jehoiakim reigned.

In **late 598 BC,** Babylon invaded Judah and laid siege to Jerusalem for **three months**, from late **598 BC-597 BC, because** King Jehoiakim of Judah had rebelled against Nebuchadnezzar. Nebuchadnezzar arrived in Judah when the siege was going on. The then reigning king of Jerusalem, **Jehoiakim died during this siege** and his son **Jeconiah,** also known as **Jehoiachin,** became king; he was eighteen years and he ruled Jerusalem for just three months.

Jerusalem surrendered in **March 597 BC** and the then-ruling King Jeconiah came out to meet Nebuchadnezzar; he and all his household were exiled as captives to Babylon. King Nebuchadnezzar II then pillaged Jerusalem and took the following to Babylon as captives, most of the nobles and princes of Judah, skilled craftsmen and professionals, skilled soldiers, treasures from the king's house and treasures from Jehovah's temple. **A total of ten thousand Israelites were led away to Babylon, as captives.**

After taking away the captives, King Nebuchadnezzar installed in Jerusalem a king of his choice, Mattaniah, who was Jeconiah's uncle, his father's brother, King Josiah's son. King Mattaniah was renamed Zedekiah by King Nebuchadnezzar II. Zedekiah was 21 years old when he became king, and he reigned for 11 years in Jerusalem: **597BC-586 BC;** he did what was bad in Jehovah's eyes.

Jeremiah, the most prominent prophet in Jerusalem, had now been preaching for a long time, since the rule of King Josiah, of impending doom on the city of Jerusalem, if its inhabitants did not repent: **(Jeremiah 7: 1-7 and Jeremiah 26:1-6).**

After Nebuchadnezzar had installed Zedekiah as the king of his choice, there arose false prophets in Jerusalem, who were prophesying opposite to the prophet Jeremiah, saying that no harm would come to the city, there would be peace, Jerusalem would be freed from the Babylonians and all those who had been taken into exile would be brought back. See **Jeremiah chapter 28**. These false prophets were constantly persecuting, plotting to kill and killing Jehovah's real prophets. See; **Jeremiah chapter 26: 20-23.**

King Zedekiah, who had been installed by Nebuchadnezzar, after taking the then-ruling king of Judah, **Jeconiah or Jehoiachin** into exile, eventually rebelled against Babylon. **This was the second time that Jerusalem had rebelled against Babylon.** Why on earth would Zedekiah have done something so unwise, to challenge a super-power like Babylon, risking the destruction of Jerusalem and therefore the death of his own people? I believe, he must have been convinced to do so by the prophecies of the false prophets.

Nebuchadnezzar had had enough of disloyalty from the kings of Judah and decided to give an exemplary punishment to Jerusalem, to discourage other nations from rebelling against him. The Babylonian army lay siege to Jerusalem, which lasted eighteen months; from **589 to 587/586 BC.** The Israelites trapped in this city suffered horrendous deaths from diseases, famine, cannibalism, and slaughter when the Babylonian soldiers finally breached the city's wall.

When Jerusalem was under the final siege from the Babylonians, Jehovah, always merciful, informed the Israelites through his prophet Jeremiah, how to escape from the oncoming Babylonian slaughter, that is to go outside to the besieging Babylonian army and surrender; **Jeremiah 21:8-9**; but very few Israelites believed him. Jeremiah also gave the same message to King Zedekiah: see **Jeremiah 38; 17-18,** but he too refused to go outside and surrender. When the Babylonians breached the wall of Jerusalem, the king and his army fled by night, going through a secret gate, but were later captured and brought to Riblah in the land of Hamath, to the presence of Nebuchadnezzar king of Babylon. Nebuchadnezzar had all the nobles of Judah slaughtered; the sons of Zedekiah were slaughtered before his eyes; then he blinded Zedekiah's eyes, after which he bound him with copper fetters and took him to Babylon. (**Jeremiah 39:6-7**).

According to the prophet Jeremiah, Jehovah had selected all righteous people who were then living in Jerusalem to be deported to Babylon, after the second siege of Jerusalem, that is before the third and final siege, which concluded with the destruction of Jerusalem. According to the scriptures, those who remained in Jerusalem were evildoers and destined for destruction; see **Jeremiah chapter 24**. This shows that God will not let the righteous be destroyed together with the evildoers; He always manages to protect them from harm.

Once Jerusalem had fallen, Nebuchadnezzar sent one of his commanders, Nebuzaradan, with a mission to totally destroy Jerusalem. The entire city wall of Jerusalem was uprooted and **the entire city burnt down**, even Jehovah's temple. Jerusalem was razed to the ground. Jehovah had finally executed judgement on this city; **Jeremiah 7: 16-20.**

Let us now continue the story.

Again, I will quote Daniel 1:1-3; *"**in the third year** of the kingship of King Jehoiakim of Judah, King Nebuchadnezzar of Babylon came to Jerusalem **and besieged it**. In time, Jehovah gave King Jehoiakim of Judah into his hand, along with some of the utensils of the house of the true God, and he brought them to the land of Shinar to the house of his god. He placed the utensils in the treasury of his god.*"

According to Wikipedia's "Jehoiakim king of Judah", the king of Judah, paid tribute from the treasury in Jerusalem, some temple artefacts and handed over some of the royal family and nobility as hostages to Nebuchadnezzar. This was when Nebuchadnezzar first lay siege to Jerusalem. It is from this point onwards, that Daniel started to write of his life in Babylon, therefore, it is clear that he and his friends came to Babylon after the first presence of the Babylonian army in Judah, when the city of Jerusalem, was **first surrounded and besieged** by the Babylonian army after their victory in the battle of Carchemish in 605 BC.

Daniel, the narrator of this story and his three friends, were brought to Babylon from Jerusalem after Nebuchadnezzar's first contact with Jerusalem. They were given away by their own king, Jehoiakim, to Nebuchadnezzar as hostages to do with them as he willed. This must have been a very distressing moment for these youngsters; torn away from the comfort of their families, community and country and forced to emigrate to a distant, foreign land, with little hope of ever seeing their loved ones again. Some of these men, however, had nothing to fear; they trusted that their God Jehovah would take care of them, even in this foreign land of Babylon.

Once the Israelite exiles arrived in Babylon, King Nebuchadnezzar ordered his chief court official to select from the Jewish captives, young people of noble descent, with no defect and of good appearance, endowed with wisdom, knowledge and discernment, capable of serving in the king's palace. These young people were to be trained for three years, which included learning the language and writing of the Babylonians, and after that, they were to enter the king's service. Furthermore, all the young men selected for this training were to be fed on the same diet as that of king Nebuchadnezzar himself. King Nebuchadnezzar must have been a very generous man!

A young man called Daniel, who later became a prophet, and his three friends, Hananiah, Mishael and Azariah, were among those who had been selected for the training ordered by the king. The names of these Israelite youths chosen for the king's training were changed to Babylonian names; Daniel became Belteshazzar, Hananiah became Shadrach, Mishael became Meshach and Azariah became Abednego.

Unlike all the other Israelite trainees, these four friends refused to eat the king's diet which they considered to be "unclean food," instead, they requested a vegetarian diet, which was given to them. These four friends ended up looking a lot healthier than all the other Israelite trainees. They had considered the food from the king's table unclean, most probably because it included animals that Jehovah's Law forbids to the Israelites, **Leviticus chapter 11,** and/or the food might have contained blood from the slaughtered animals, which was also forbidden food to the Israelites: **Deuteronomy 12: 23-25.**

This decision regarding their feeding, pleased Jehovah, as they were upholding his law and He sustained them throughout their training period.

After three years of training, King Nebuchadnezzar requested that all the trainees be brought out to him. When the king spoke with them, no one in the entire group was found to be like Daniel, Hananiah, Mishael, and Azariah. In every matter requiring wisdom and understanding that the king would ask them about, he found them ten times better than all the magic-practising priests and the conjurers in his entire realm. They continued to serve before the king.

These three young men could clearly perceive that it was Jehovah who had led them to this privileged life of living and working in the king's court and then; (see Daniel 2:49), working in high-ranking jobs in the province of Babylon. Such positive experiences were bound to have made these three men acquire full confidence in their God, in that they could always rely on Him.

Let's continue the story from when three high-ranking Judean men, employed in the king's service, had been thrown into a fiery furnace by King Nebuchadnezzar because they had refused to worship his golden statue, images and his other gods. To verify that these culprits had been fully punished, King Nebuchadnezzar peered into the burning furnace. To his surprise, he saw **four** men walking among the flames, unbound. **He became frightened** and quickly rose up and said to his officials, "Did we not tie up three men and throw them into the fire?" They answered the king, "Yes, O king." He said, "Look, I see four men walking about free in the midst of the fire and they are unharmed, and the fourth one looks like a son of the gods!" **Daniel 3: 25.**

Nebuchadnezzar approached the door of the burning fiery furnace, and called out: "*Shadrach, Meshach, Abednego, you servants of The Most High God, step out and come here.*" The three men stepped out and became the object of inspection from the king's high-ranking officials, assembled there. They witnessed that the fire had had no effect on their clothing and bodies, not even one of their hairs had been singed and they did not even smell of fire.

The king then declared: "***Praise be to the God of*** *Shadrach, Meshach and Abednego, who sent his angel and rescued his servants. They trusted Him and went against the command of the king and were willing to die rather than serve any other god, except their own. I am therefore issuing an order,* **that any people, nation or language group, that says anything against the God of** *Shadrach, Meshach and Abednego, should be dismembered and their houses turned into public latrines, a garbage dump and a pile of ruins;* **for there is no other** *God, who is able to rescue like this one.*" Daniel 3: 28-29.

God's ID   *111*

The king then gave a promotion to all three of them; Shadrach, Meshach and Abednego.

Why was Nebuchadnezzar frightened when he saw the four men walking among the fiery flames? It is because he realized that there existed someone else more powerful than him and his gods; he felt vulnerable. Nebuchadnezzar was in the process of executing these three men in an incredibly brutal manner and their God snatched them out of his hand. It was obvious that this God would now have turned His attention on him; therefore, before this could happen, Nebuchadnezzar acted swiftly to remedy his very vulnerable position; first, by publicly acknowledging that this God is the real and true God, *"for there is no other God, who is able to rescue like this one."* Second, Nebuchadnezzar authorized the worship of this particular God, freely, without fear of persecution, because: "anyone challenging this fact would be "dismembered", that is killed and their homes destroyed. Third, he tried to compensate for his wrongdoing to appease this God; he gave a promotion to the followers of this God, whom he had just attempted to execute; King Nebuchadnezzar was a smart guy.

By resisting the king, these three men, Shadrach, Meshach and Abednego upheld Jehovah's name; furthermore, they acquired the right to free worship for their fellow citizens and anyone else who wanted to worship The True God.

This event, of challenging a most powerful king, shows that those who really trust in God can rely on him always, wherever they happen to be.

17

Jesus Christ

The other source of knowledge regarding God's identity is Jesus Christ.

Who was Jesus Christ and why should I consider him, when talking about God's identity?

Jesus Christ **(1-33AD),** was a first-century Jewish prophet and preacher, on whose teachings the Christian faith is based. Christians believe that Jesus Christ was the long-awaited Jewish Messiah as foretold in the Old Testament and the Jewish Bible, the Tanakh. Christians also believe that Jesus Christ was the incarnation of The Son of God, **Jesus himself claimed to have been in existence before his birth**; see **John 8: 57-58;** Then the Jews said to him: "You are not yet 50 years old, and still you have seen Abraham?" Jesus said to them: *"Most truly I say to you, before Abraham came into existence, I have been."* John the Baptist, a prophet also prophesied this fact; **John 1: 29-30**; The next day he saw Jesus coming toward him, and he said: "See, the Lamb of God who takes away the sin of the world! This is the one about whom I said: *"Behind me, there comes a man who has advanced in front of me, for he existed before me."* Actually, John the Baptist was born before Jesus Christ.

According to Jesus Christ, his main mission in life was to make God's name known to man, by preaching and by performing numerous miracles and to redeem mankind from their sins, by sacrificing his life. The death of Jesus Christ served to atone for man's sin. The full significance of "atonement" is explained later.

Christians believe that after his death, Jesus was resurrected to everlasting life and ascended into heaven. This explains why, although Christ lived in the past, over 2,000 years ago, Christians believe that he is alive today, and hence talk about him in the present tense, for instance, they say: "I do believe that Christ **is** the Son of God" instead of: "I do believe that Jesus **was** the Son of God." I will try and use the past tense only in my account here, regarding the life of Jesus Christ. I am a Christian and believe that Jesus Christ was the Son of God, died and was resurrected to eternal life.

Jesus is important in providing information on God's identity, due to his extremely close relationship with God, whom he addresses as: "My Father," or "My Father in Heaven" or as "Our Father in Heaven." Jesus claimed to be God's son, to have come from Heaven and to have been sent on earth as **God's representative** and also that his earthly mission was directed by God Himself.

Please note that: In all his life, Jesus never claimed to be God.

The name, Immanuel in Hebrew or when translated in Latin, Emmanuel, means God is with us. Christians believe that this term refers to Jesus Christ, due to his unique nature of being God's son and hence his presence on earth, represented God Himself, being near to mankind.

Judaism, the main religion of the Jewish people, (Jesus was a Jew), does not acknowledge Jesus as the son of God or even as a prophet; Islam regards Jesus only as a prophet but denies that he is God's son and denies that Jesus ever died. **Surah An- NiSa 4: 155-158**.

In the Hebrew scripture, the term Messiah means The Anointed One, that is: someone officially appointed into God's service, through an initiation act, such as anointing his head with oil. The word Christ originates from Greek, Christos, meaning The Anointed One; it is a title equivalent to the Hebrew Messiah. Christians refer to Jesus, as Christ, that is the Anointed One, the Messiah, because they believe this title, according to the Jewish scriptures, refers to Jesus. Judaism does not believe that the

Messiah mentioned in their holy scripture refers to Jesus Christ and to date, they are still awaiting the forthcoming Messiah.

According to the Jewish belief, the Messiah will be a political leader, (Jesus was apolitical), and a descendant of King David, who will rule and judge Israel. He will create a fair government in Israel, which will become a centre for all politics worldwide. The Messiah will also bring awareness of the true God to all people, unite all people, regardless of differences like religion or culture, bring about the end of war so that everyone can live in peace, signal the end of the world and he will also rebuild the Temple in Jerusalem.

According to Judaism, Jesus did not fulfil their messianic prophesies. However, Christians believe that the remaining unfulfilled prophesies will be fulfilled in the second coming of Jesus Christ, when a New Earth will be created. According to the Christian faith, at the End of Times, all mankind will be resurrected and there will be a Universal Judgement of Humanity; those deemed worthy will gain access to God's Kingdom, while the unworthy people will be destroyed by fire, through an everlasting fire and **they will cease to exist.** There will be a destruction of all evil and consequently, the establishment of an Everlasting Kingdom, **on earth**, with "The New Jerusalem" as its headquarters. See: **Daniel 2: 44 and Revelation 21:1-2.**

Judaism also claims that Jesus was not a descendant of King David, as he had no biological father. According to the scriptures, God made the following promise to King David: *"When your days are over and you are laid to rest with your fathers, I will raise up your offspring to succeed you, who will come from your own body, and I will establish his kingdom. He is the one who will build a house for my Name, and I will establish the throne of his kingdom forever."* See **2 Samuel 7: 12-13 and Chronicles 17:11-14**, now the temple was built by David's son, Solomon, and his reign did not last forever, therefore, Jehovah was not referring to Solomon in these prophesies. Now you can see why the term, "The son of David" refers also to the Messiah, a term that was constantly applied to Jesus by those who considered him to be the Messiah.

When out preaching, Jesus was frequently addressed as "Son of David" and he did not deny or object to it, but responded to it. Mathew, one of Christ's apostles, opens his scripture by tracing the genealogical line of Jesus Christ, through his father, Joseph, back to that of King David.

According to the scriptures: **Luke 1: 30-33**; the angel Gabriel was sent to a Virgin, Mary, Jesus' mother, to inform her of having been chosen to be the mother of Jesus Christ; And the angel said to her, "*Do not be afraid, Mary, for you have found favour with God. And behold, you will conceive in your womb and bear a son, and you shall call his name Jesus. He will be great and will be called the Son of the Most High.* **And the Jehovah God will give to him the throne of his father David,** *and he will reign over the house of Jacob forever and there will be no end to his kingdom.*"

In this particular message, also called, "The Annunciation", the angel Gabriel uses this phrase: "...*Jehovah God will give him the throne of his father David.*"

It could be that Mary was also a descendant of King David, or it could be that Jesus had the genetic composition of Joseph, who was a descendant of King David, or Jesus might even have had the genetic composition of David himself; with God, everything is possible.

Everyone, however, is entitled to their own opinions, in these religious matters.

Did Jesus actually say he was the Son of God?

Jesus repeatedly referred to himself as The Son of Man. It is clear that the Jewish public understood the significance of this title, as nobody ever asked Jesus to explain it. What does it mean in Judaism? It is used frequently to refer to man with the qualities of human weakness, that is "ben Adam" in Hebrew, and, "I am just human, therefore, not perfect."

Son of Man is also used in a very different way in **Daniel 7:13-14**; *"In my vision at night I looked, and there before me was one like a son of man, coming with the clouds of heaven. He approached the Ancient of Days (God) and was led into his presence. **He was given authority**, glory and sovereign power; all nations and peoples of every language worshipped him. His dominion is an everlasting dominion that will not pass away, and his kingdom is one that will never be destroyed."* Here, the term, Son of Man, refers to the Messiah, because: *"His dominion is an everlasting dominion that will not pass away, and his kingdom is one that will never be destroyed."*

From how Jesus used the term, Son of Man, it is clear he was referring to the manner it is used in the book of Daniel. Here are some examples: **Matthew 12:8**; "For the Son of Man is lord of the Sabbath."

John 3:13; No one has ever gone into heaven except the one who came from heaven—the Son of Man.

Matthew 9:6; "But that you may know that the Son of Man has authority on earth to forgive sins," he then said to the paralytic, "Rise, pick up your bed and go home." The paralysed man got up, cured, picked up his bed and walked away.

See what happened when Jesus was arrested and taken to the courtyard of the high priest to be interrogated; (**Matthew 26:63-64**): But Jesus kept silent. So, the high priest said to him: "I put you under oath by the living God to tell us whether you are the Christ, the Son of God!" Jesus said to him: "You yourself said it. But I say to you: From now on you will see the Son of man sitting at the right hand of power and coming on the clouds of heaven."

Matthew 16:13-17; Now when Jesus came into the district of Caesarea Philippi, he asked his disciples, "Who do people say that the Son of Man is?" They replied, "Some say John the Baptist; others say Elijah; and still others, Jeremiah or one of the prophets." "But what about you?" he asked. "Who do you say I am?" Simon Peter answered, "**You are the Messiah, the Son of the living**

God." Jesus replied, "Blessed are you, Simon, son of Jonah, for this was not revealed to you by flesh and blood but by my Father in Heaven."

Jesus being the Son of God must know God better than anyone else and this is why, I have written about Jesus Christ.

18

A Prologue of the
Life of Jesus Christ

Jesus Christ was an Israelite; he lived from about 1 AD to 33/34 AD. He led a quiet, uneventful life and not much is known about his early years before he started his earthly mission. **Luke chapter two** tells of a few events of Jesus, as an infant and child. As an adult, Jesus worked for his father, Joseph, as a carpenter, until he left home at about the age of thirty. His earthly mission started after he was baptized in the River Jordan, whereby he also got anointed by the Holy Spirit, God's active, living presence. His earthly mission was to make God's name known to mankind, through preaching extensively, performing numerous miracles and redeeming mankind from sin through his death.

Jesus Christ died by a public execution, ordered by the Roman authorities; the Jewish clergy had falsely accused him of subverting the rule of Rome. Present-day Israel and the surrounding countries were then all part of the Roman Empire and therefore under Roman jurisdiction.

The Birth of Jesus Christ

It was associated with some extraordinary events; it is important to note these events because they identify Jesus as the Messiah. To start with, his birth was very unusual, in that, he was born from a virgin.

The angel Gabriel was sent from God to a virgin called Mary, Christ's mother, and informed her that she would give birth to a child. **Luke 1: 31**; "*And look! you will become pregnant and give birth to a son, and **you are to name him Jesus.**"

Luke 1:34-35. But Mary said to the angel: *"How is this to be, since I am still a virgin?"* In answer, the angel said to her: *"Holy Spirit will come upon you, and power of the Most High will overshadow you. And for that reason, the one who is born will be called holy, God's Son."*

From the above account, Jesus did not have a biological father. Both Adam, the first man created and his wife Eve, did not have any biological parents; with God, all things are possible.

The name Jesus is derived from the Jewish name, Yeshua, which is Joshua in English. In Hebrew, the name Yeshua means God is salvation. (The definition of salvation is: preservation or deliverance from harm).

Note, during Christ's time on earth, the name Yeshua, was quite common among the Israelites. The Jewish prophet, who took over from the prophet Moses and delivered the Israelites to the Promised Land, was called Yeshua i.e.Joshua in English. Why then is Jesus not called Joshua? This is because, the books that compose the New Testament were first written in Greek, (note: the Canonical Gospels and the Epistles might have been written originally in languages used in Christ's time: Hebrew, Greek or Aramaic but **Greek was the dominant/official language at that time**).

In Greek, Yeshua is Ieosus. The Greek alphabet does not have the letter "y," which is transliterated (translation using the closest corresponding letters of a different alphabet or script) with "IO," which should sound as letter "u" in English. The Greek language does not have a "sh" sound, so it is substituted by an "S" sound and to make it a masculine name, they added another "s" to sound at the end. Note: Greek is gendered language; the gender of Greek nouns is assigned arbitrarily. Some nouns are Masculine, some are Feminine, and some are Neuter.

Therefore, I would say, Jesus is the anglicised Greek word, Ieosus., which in turn represents: Yeshua, a Hebrew/Jewish name, which is really the original name of Jesus.

I believe the name Ieosus, got into public domain, from the Greek scriptures and therefore remained circulation as such. The early Christians were mainly concerned with the teachings of Jesus and many had no access to the Old Testament; this would explain why the name Yeshua in the Old Testament, did not to Ieosus.

Here is another account of Christ's birth from the apostle Mathew; **Mathew 1: 18-21;** But this is how the birth of Jesus Christ took place. During the time his mother Mary was promised in marriage to Joseph, she was found to be pregnant before they were united. However, because her husband Joseph was righteous and did not want to make her a public spectacle, he intended to divorce her secretly. But after he had thought these things over, look! Jehovah's angel appeared to him in a dream, saying: *"Joseph, son of David, do not be afraid to take your wife Mary home, for what has been conceived in her is by Holy Spirit. She will give birth to a son, and you are to name him Jesus, for he will save his people from their sins."*

In **Deuteronomy 22: 20-21**, the fate of any Jewish woman who became pregnant and was not yet married, was death by stoning; this is why Joseph did not want to make his wife Mary, "a public spectacle."

See **Luke 2: 1**; Now in those days, a decree went out from Caesar Augustus for all the inhabited earth to be registered. That is Caesar, the Roman emperor, wanted a census of the population in his empire; all the territories of present-day Turkey, Syria, Jordan and Israel, were part of this empire when Jesus was born.

Now, Joseph, Mary's husband, went up from the city of Nazareth, in the province of Galilee into Judea, to David's city, which is called Bethlehem, because he was a member of the house and family of David. He went to get registered with Mary, who had been given him in marriage as promised and who was heavily pregnant. This is how Jesus came to be born in Bethlehem.

According to the gospel of **Luke 2: 8-20**, after Christ's birth, there was a heavenly apparition to shepherds grazing out in the fields, whereby an angel invited the shepherds to go and see: *"a new-born saviour, Christ the Lord."*

According to the gospel of **Matthew 2: 1-6**; After Jesus had been born in Bethlehem of Judea in the days of Herod the King, look! astrologers from the East came to Jerusalem, saying: *"Where is the one born king of the Jews? For we saw his star when we were in the East, and we have come to do obeisance to him."* At hearing this, King Herod was agitated and all of Jerusalem with him. On gathering together all the chief priests and scribes of the people, he inquired of them where the Messiah/Christ was to be born. They said to him, "In Bethlehem of Judea, for this is how it has been written through the prophet: And you, O Bethlehem of the land of Judah, are by no means the most insignificant city among the governors of Judah, for out of you will come a governing one, who will shepherd my people Israel."

Herod the King advised these three astrologers to go to Bethlehem because it had been identified by the priests as the place where the scriptures stated, the king of the Jews, the Messiah, was to be born. Herod then requested the astrologer to report back to him, when they found the child, so that he too would go and pay his respects, but the Astrologers were warned in a dream, not to go back to King Herod. When King Herod learned that these astrologers had departed without informing him of the whereabouts of "The new-born King of the Jews," he was furious and gave an order that all babies below two years of age in Bethlehem and its surrounding districts, should be massacred, in a bid to eliminate his new-born rival.

However, following divine inspiration, Joseph had moved his young family to Egypt, to safeguard Jesus from King Herod. See **Matthew 2:13;** After they (Astrologers) had departed, look! Jehovah's angel appeared to Joseph in a dream, saying: "Get up, take the young child and his mother and flee to Egypt, and stay there until I give you word, for Herod is about to search for the young child to kill him." So, Joseph got up and by night took along the young child and the child's mother and went into Egypt. He stayed there until the death of Herod.

This means that Jesus Christ was a refugee at a very tender age. When King Herod died, Joseph, the husband of Mary, was alerted through a dream by an angel and so the family of Jesus returned to Judea. However, Joseph did not feel comfortable living under Herod's son in Judea, so he moved his family to the town of Nazareth, in the district of Galilee. See **Matthew 2:19-23.**

At the age of about thirty, Jesus went to the River Jordan and got himself baptized by John the Baptist, a prophet. During his baptism, Jesus Christ was anointed, that is he was conferred divine office by God, through God's Holy Spirit.

John 1: 31-34; John the Baptist also bore witness, saying: *"Even I did not know him, but the reason why I came baptizing in water was so that he might be made manifest to Israel. I viewed the spirit coming down as a dove out of heaven, and it remained upon him. Even I did not know him, but the very One who sent me to baptize in water said to me: 'Whoever it is upon whom you see the spirit coming down and remaining, this is the one who baptizes in holy spirit.' And I have seen it, and I have given witness that this one is the Son of God."*

After being anointed, Jesus was then led by the Holy Spirit into the wilderness, the desert, where he fasted for forty days. During his fasting, Christ had a close encounter with the Devil, see; **Luke 4: 1-13**; who tried to derail him from his earthly mission, by tempting him, but failed. After fasting, Jesus started his mission on Earth, which lasted for about three years. The temptation of Jesus shows that Jesus has a free will to decide if to obey or to disobey God and therefore, he himself cannot be God.

After being baptized in the River Jordan and after fasting for forty days, Jesus set about selecting twelve men, his twelve apostles, who were to be his close companions, until his death. **The word apostle** originates from Greek, it means, emissary, or one who is sent off to convey a message. The purpose of these apostles was to learn God's word and also to be witnesses of the events in Christ's life so that they in turn would teach others what they had learned and witnessed.

Disciples: those who believe and followed the teachings, of their "master." Therefore, in this case, the term disciples defines anybody who had acquired faith in Jesus and was his follower. Therefore, the apostles of Jesus were also his disciples. After being anointed by God's Holy Spirit during his baptism, Jesus acquired special powers to support him in his earthly mission.

Here is a brief account of the transformation of Jesus after his baptism.

Before baptism, Jesus was just a normal person who did not stand out from the crowd, but after his baptism, all that changed. Jesus returned to Galilee, his home district, filled with power of the spirit, that is transformed by God's Holy Spirit.

When he had come to his own country, he taught them in their synagogue, so that they were astonished and said, "Where did this man get this wisdom and these mighty works? Is this not the carpenter's son? Is not his mother called Mary? And his brothers James, Joseph, Simon and Judas? And his sisters, are they not all with us? Where then did this man get all these things?" So, they were offended by him. **Matthew 13:53-57.**

Please note: Jesus was the firstborn, but he had other brothers and sisters. See more on Christ's brothers; **Matthew 12: 46-47** and **John 2:12**.

His fellow citizens had already heard of some miracles that Jesus had already performed, before arriving at his home town, Nazareth. They found it difficult to accept that from being one of them and from his humble upbringing, Jesus "the carpenter's son", had become, overnight, someone very important; a prophet.

But Jesus said to them, *"A prophet is not without honour, (that is he has honour) except in his own town and in his own home."* And he did not do any more miracles there, because of their lack of faith and their disbelief.

Luke 4: 31-32; He then went down to Capernaum, a city of Galilee. And he was teaching them on the Sabbath in the synagogue of Capernaum, they were astounded at his way of teaching because he spoke with authority.

Jesus had deep knowledge of the scriptures.

Now in the synagogue in Capernaum, there was a man with an unclean spirit. Jesus evicted it and it came out of the man, saying, "Did you come to destroy us? I know exactly who you are, the Holy One of God." Jesus ordered it to leave the man and it left him. At this, they were all astonished and began to say to one another, "What kind of speech is this? For with authority and power, he orders the unclean spirits, and out they come!" So, the news about him kept spreading into every corner of the surrounding country. (**Luke 4: 36-37**).

Luke 4: 38-44; After leaving the synagogue, he entered Simon's home, that is in one of his newly chosen apostles' home. At a later period, Jesus changed Simon's name, to that of Peter. Now, Simon's mother-in-law was suffering with a high fever, and they asked him to help her. So, he stood over her and rebuked the fever, and it left her instantly; she got up and began ministering to them.

Jesus most probably remained at Simon's home in Capernaum, as Luke writes: *"After leaving the synagogue, Jesus entered Simon's home."* At sunset, all those who had people sick with various diseases brought them to him; practically the whole city was gathered right at his door. By laying his hands on each one of them, he cured them. Demons also came out of many, crying out and saying: *"You are the Son of God."* But rebuking them, he would not permit them to speak, for they knew him to be the Christ.

According to **Matthew 4:23-25**; *Jesus went throughout Galilee, teaching in their synagogues, proclaiming the good news of the kingdom, and healing every disease and sickness among the people. News about him spread all over Syria, and people brought to him all who were ill with various diseases, those suffering severe pain, the demon-possessed, those having seizures, and the paralyzed; and he healed them. Consequently, large crowds from Galilee, the Decapolis, Jerusalem, Judea and the region across the Jordan followed him.*

Therefore, after Jesus was anointed, all these supernatural powers of healing and excellent preaching, became manifest.

19

Now let's get to the key question. What proof is there that Jesus Christ was the son of God?

I would say, mainly because of four things:

1. The events of Christ's life conformed to what had been prophesied in the Old Testament, that is in the Jewish Holy scriptures, identifying Jesus as the long-awaited Messiah.

2. The content of the message and preaching that Jesus delivered.

3. No normal human being could perform the numerous, diverse and extraordinary miracles that Jesus performed during his earthly mission.

4. The fact that Jesus came back to life after his death and resurrected, as he had predicted, appeared to and interacted with many people.

Some events of the life of Jesus Christ were foretold in the scriptures of the Old Testament.

When Jesus' apostles wrote their scriptures, they highlighted the different events in Christ's life, foretold in the Jewish scriptures. Just a few examples; the birth of Christ has been foretold in **Micah 5: 2** and his mission is foretold in the whole chapter of **Isaiah 53.** The prophecy in **Daniel 7: 13-14** is quoted by Jesus Christ when he talks about his second coming; **Matthew 24:30** and **Matthew 26:62-64**. Many Christians claim that the scripture of **Daniel 9: 24-27,** identifies when the Messiah would have started his mission on earth and which coincides with when Jesus began his mission, not when he was born. I do not know how to interpret or calculate the dates from this piece of scripture, of Daniel chapter nine.

Jesus and his apostles settled in Capernaum, a city in Galilee, quite distant from his home town, Nazareth. Today, this distance by road is about 48 km. Capernaum was a city by the sea, in the districts of Zebulun and Naphtali. This fulfilled what was spoken through **Isaiah the prophet 9: 1-2**, who said, *"However, there will be no more gloom for those who were in distress, as in former times when the land of Zebulun and the land of Naphtali were treated with contempt. But at a later time, He will cause it to be honoured—the way by the sea, in the region of the Jordan, Galilee of the nations.*

The people who were walking in darkness; Have seen a great light, and as for those dwelling in the land of deep shadow; light has shone upon them."

In **Luke 24: 44**; After the resurrection, Jesus says to his apostles: *"These are my words that I spoke to you while I was yet with you, that all the things written about me in the Law of Moses and in the Prophets and Psalms must be fulfilled."*

The teachings of Jesus Christ

Although Jesus resided in Capernaum, he spent most of his three-year mission away from home. Jesus went everywhere on foot, preaching mainly in all the territories occupied by the Israelites, starting with his home territory, Galilee; he preached the Good News to as many people as he could. The scriptures also record visits of Jesus, to non-Jewish territories: Samaria and Phoenicia.

Why did Jesus preach?

When the festival was half over, Jesus went up into the temple and began teaching. And the Jews were astonished, saying: *"How does this man have such a knowledge of the Scripture when he has not studied at the schools?"* Jesus, in turn, answered them and said:

"What I teach is not mine, but belongs to him who sent me." **John 7: 15-16**

The reason why Jesus preached is summarized as follows: **John 12: 49-50**; *"For I have not spoken of my own initiative, but the Father who sent me has himself given me a commandment about what to say and what to speak. And I know that his commandment means everlasting life. So, whatever I speak, I speak just as the Father has told me."*

The above scripture summarizes how Jesus perceived the purpose of his mission on earth: he was sent on earth by His Heavenly Father with a mission, to preach, to make God's name known to mankind, because, by acquiring this particular knowledge and by living according to this knowledge, it would lead you to into everlasting life, that is, into the Kingdom of God, because there is nowhere else that one can live forever.

What did Jesus preach about?

At the beginning of his mission, Jesus gave an extensive talk on the side of a mountain, known as the **Sermon on the Mountain**, as recorded in the scriptures of Matthew, Mark and Luke. Here, I have chosen to refer to the scripture of **Mathew, Chapters 5-7**. The preaching of Jesus regarded; how to gain access, to the Kingdom of Heaven; see explanation below.

The Beatitudes are the blessings listed by Jesus in the Sermon on the Mount; Jesus explained eight different states of mind or ways of behaving that are pleasing to God and therefore, have God's blessings and will lead into the Kingdom of Heaven. See **Matthew 5:3-12**. Jesus further explained some Laws of Moses: divorce, adultery, murder, the use of oaths, the right to revenge and the type of attitude to take towards your enemy, but he affirmed that he did not come to change the Law but to fulfil it.

Please note: In this particular sermon, Jesus preached against taking vengeance, and proposed non-violent behaviour which was quite revolutionary, in that it differed from the Law of Moses; see **Exodus 21:24-25, Leviticus 24:17-21**; see below.

Matthew 5:38-39; You heard that it was said: *'Eye for eye and tooth for tooth.' However, I say to you: Do not resist the one who is wicked, but whoever slaps you on your right cheek, turn the other also to him."*

I believe this new teaching of Jesus, of non-violence to aggression is one of the most revolutionary teaching and also one of the most difficult for any Christian to follow. You'll need to appeal for God's help, to follow this teaching, successfully.

See **Luke 6: 27-36**; "***Love your enemies and do good to those who hate you.***" No one had ever taught such a doctrine before. Jesus explains why we should do these things: *Be merciful, just as your Father is merciful;* because he is kind to the ungrateful and wicked.

If God does good to those who hate Him, why should you not do it too? Are you superior to God? I would say one is only human with human weakness, and following these teachings of Jesus is extremely difficult. However, one could always pray and appeal to God for support. Doing what God does must be the right way to behave because God is the source of all knowledge and all righteousness. It is God who sets the standards of what is right and wrong. God is positive and requires people to make that extra effort to be positive. If you retaliate against evil actions, you are no different from your enemies; they did it first and you do it after. Retaliation is bound to create and perpetuate a cycle of revenge, of evil. By imitating God, you will be children of the Most High and also your reward will be great. Be merciful, just as your Father is merciful.

If someone has wronged you, leave it in the capable hands of Jehovah. He is also the source of justice and He Himself will deal with that person. This attitude could be an extremely difficult thing to do and could also be a source of never-ending problems, during wartime. Men and women who object to war and its atrocities, in that one is obliged to kill another human being, fall into the category of **conscientious objectors, or Cos.**

People who are conscientious objectors claim the right to refuse military service on the grounds of freedom of thought, conscious or religion. Around 16,000 men refused to take up arms or fight during the First World War and 70,000 men in the Second World War; for any number of religious, moral, ethical or political reasons. These people were known as COS, Conscientious objectors. These men had to suffer a lot of hostility and persecution, for instance giving them unpleasant jobs like cleaning latrines, and imprisonment and were even executed in some countries. Prominent among the Christian groups persecuted for being conscientious objectors is the Christian denomination of Jehovah's Witnesses. This Christian denomination is zealous in preaching about the kingdom of God and also practises autonomy from politics, consequently, they do not get employed in organizations linked to the political system such as the military or police; where by Law, you are required to obey. During the Second World War, the German Jehovah's Witnesses paid heavily for following their religious principles; many were heavily persecuted, interned in concentration camps and some were even executed. They were also offered the option to opt out of their religion, but many refused to do so. The practice of this Christian denomination was banned by the Nazi Government from 1933 to 1945.

Note: conscientious objectors could also belong to other non-military professionals such as doctors who refuse to perform abortions or give certain contraceptives.

The Amish, another Christian Community in the USA, that practises non-violence, are targeted by thugs, who do things like slapping them in public because the Amish people will not slap them back or fight back. The thugs who do this find their response to violence "very funny!" See the film, Witness; starring Harrison Ford.

There are many other Christians who have refused to engage in violence against others and have had to pay for it or have succeeded, through legal challenge, in upholding this Christian principle of non-violence.

It is clear that this principle of non-violence continues to be ignored today by many Christians; most have heard it preached but have never given it much thought. Also, most of us Christians tend to identify ourselves on national or ethical grounds and forget God's Law: You should love your neighbour as yourself. It is very difficult to follow this principle of non-violence when others exercise violence towards you, your family, your friends or your country but God can assist you in upholding it.

In **Matthew 5:23-24** and in **Matthew 18: 15-17**, Jesus advised on how to behave when you have been wronged by others, that is to do everything possible to solve your problems with others in a peaceful way.

Leviticus 19: 18 says: *"Do not seek revenge or bear a grudge against anyone among your people, but love your neighbour as yourself. I am Jehovah."*

Jesus advised against hypocrisy regarding religious matters; **Matthew 6:1**; *"Take care not to practice your righteousness in front of others,"* for example giving charity in front of people or making it obvious to all that you are fasting, so as to be noticed by them. Jesus says that God will not consider your actions favourably because your actions were aimed at self-gratification, by getting praise from people, rather than pleasing God.

I will outline here what I believe is important from the teachings of the Sermon on the Mountain.

Jesus advised against being tied down by earthly material or wealth; it is not durable, but let your treasures be in heaven, where it doesn't get destroyed. **Matthew 6:21**; *"For where your treasure is, there your heart will be also."*

Jesus advised people not to worry. Why do people worry? They worry because they know that there is a possibility that things could go wrong and there is also the possibility that they will not be able to prevent or to solve whatever problem that might show up. People know that they do not have full control of future events.

If you are a believer, then acknowledge that it is God who really takes care of you. Therefore, seek first the Kingdom of God, live according to God's Law and your worries will be resolved because God will take care of your problems. See **Matthew 6:33**: *"But seek first his kingdom and his righteousness, and all these things will be given to you as well."*

People worry that things could go wrong and therefore some become so anxious, to the point of getting sick and requiring medication. It is true that things could actually go wrong, **that is very correct** but are you able to do anything about it? Worrying cannot help you resolve your problems; it is just a waste of time. Why then do you worry? **Adopt another strategy; acknowledge your limits, you are just human, you cannot foresee the future and cannot manage certain problems present in your life.** Get informed on various strategies for dealing with anxieties, but believers have the privilege of requesting assistance from someone who cannot fail them, God.

Why then are you worrying? Don't you have confidence and faith that God will take **good care** of you? Pray to Him and then wait and see that all will be fine.

Jesus concluded the Sermon on the Mountain by saying: *"Not everyone **saying to me**, 'Lord, Lord,' will enter into the Kingdom of the heavens, but only the one doing the will of my Father who is in the heavens will."* See **Matthew 7:21**. From this specific verse, Jesus identifies himself as the one who will do the judging, to decide who is worthy of entering and being part of God's Kingdom.

The main theme of Christ's preaching was the Good News, that is: The Good News of God, The Good News of the

Kingdom, The Good News of the Kingdom of God, The Good News of the Kingdom of Heaven, that is, how to gain access to this Kingdom.

The scripture of Mark says, (**Mark 1: 14-15**); Now after John was arrested, Jesus went into Galilee, preaching the Good News of God and saying: "*The appointed time has been fulfilled, the Kingdom of God has drawn near, repent, and have faith in the Good News.*"

Which I interpret as this: the decisive moment that was foretold is now happening; it is here! God's authority and presence are right here, among you, (because, I myself here, represent God), therefore repent, acknowledge your transgressions against God, to be forgiven and trust and therefore be a recipient of the Good News.

Luke 4: 42-44: However, at daybreak, he departed and went to an isolated place. But the crowds began searching for him and came to where he was, and they tried to keep him from going away from them. But he said to them: "*I must also declare the good news of the Kingdom of God to other cities **because for this I was sent.**"* So, he went on preaching in the synagogues of Judea.

In **Luke 17: 20-21:** when asked by the Pharisees when the Kingdom of God was coming, he answered them: "The Kingdom of God is not coming with striking observableness; nor will people say, 'See here!' or, 'There!" For look! t*he Kingdom of God is in your midst.*" I interpret this phrase to mean "*I myself, here with you, at present, is representing God's authority/presence and therefore, God's Kingdom.*"

In his teachings, Jesus used parables, simple short stories to illustrate what he was talking about, especially in his teaching regarding "The kingdom of God." Jesus also preached about the other purpose of his mission on earth, to redeem mankind from sin, see: **John 6:28-68** and the **whole of John chapter eight; his teachings were questioned and ridiculed**. It was quite difficult for those who knew the Law to understand and therefore to accept what Jesus was preaching about.

What exactly is "The Good News?"

This is the message preached by Jesus and later by his disciples and it regards: what was or is required for one to enter, or to be a part of God's Kingdom.

What is the definition of the word, "kingdom?"

It is defined as a state or country ruled by a king or queen, that is by someone with absolute **legal** authority.

In Christianity, God's Kingdom has the same meaning, that is a territory ruled by God and where God has absolute authority. However, God's kingdom includes both a physical and a spiritual reign. In these "territories" God's spirit or God's presence **and hence God's authority is present and in action.**

What is required for anyone to be part of a kingdom?

The requirements are:

- First, you should acknowledge the ruling political authority, the King or Queen and the ruling government.
- Second, one should be born a citizen, or one could acquire citizenship, after fulfilling the requirements established by the government of that kingdom; or one could be granted citizenship as an honour for something he or she did.
- Third, one should live according to the Law of that kingdom.

All the above requirements also apply, to God's Kingdom.

When preaching, Jesus described God's kingdom in **two ways; as a physical entity and as a spiritual entity.**

Jesus was God's son, therefore his physical presence anywhere represented God's authority and therefore, God's kingdom. God's spirit, that is, God's active power or presence was in action through

Jesus Christ. See **Isaiah 61:1-2/Luke 4:18-22:** *"The Spirit of the Sovereign Lord Jehovah is upon me, for He has anointed me."* This Spirit manifested itself through what Jesus did, his numerous miracles, his deep knowledge of the scriptures and his excellent preaching. This is precisely what Jesus meant by: *"The kingdom of God is at hand,"* or "The *kingdom of God is in your midst.*" That is I myself here am acting for and representing God's authority.

Monarchies will frequently send their partner or children to represent them in worldly events if they themselves cannot make it. These members of the royal family are accorded all the royal honours given to the monarchy they are representing. Likewise, God sent his own son, Jesus Christ to represent him here on earth, during his earthly mission, but people refused to give him his due honour.

The kingdom as a physical entity, to be established in the future: Luke 13: 28-29:

*"There is where your weeping and the gnashing of your teeth will be, when you see Abraham, Isaac, Jacob, and all the prophets **in the Kingdom of God**, but you yourselves thrown outside. Furthermore, people will come from east and west and from north and south, and will **recline at the table in the Kingdom of God."***

The kingdom as a spiritual entity

Jesus described the Kingdom of Heaven also as something alive, active and dynamic, growing exponentially. In **Luke 13: 18-19**, So he went on to say: "What is the Kingdom of God like, and with what can I compare it?" It resembles a **growing mustard seed** and Jesus goes on to describe this growth. **Luke 13: 20-22**, And again he said: "With what can I compare the Kingdom of God? It resembles **leaven or yeast**, mixed with three measures of floor and left to ferment; I believe these parables were referring to the rapid expansion of the early Christian Church, due to God's Holy Spirit sustaining the early Christian disciples, despite their being heavily persecuted.

As a spiritual entity: Matthew 13: 45-46; "*Again, the **kingdom of heaven** is like a merchant seeking beautiful pearls, who, when he had found one pearl of great price, went and sold all that he had and bought it.*" Meaning that when one understands the value of being part of God's kingdom, you will sacrifice everything you have, in order to be part of it.

As a spiritual entity: Matthew 10: 7-8; *As you go, preach, saying: 'The Kingdom of the heavens has drawn near.' Cure the sick, raise up the dead, make lepers clean, expel demons. You received free, give free.*" (God's Spirit will be made manifest through your miracles; the public will see for themselves, God's Spirit in action).

As a spiritual entity; John 14: 23; In answer, Jesus said to him: "If anyone loves me, he will observe my word and my Father will love him, and we will come to him and make our dwelling with him." This means God's presence will be with this individual.

As a spiritual entity; John 15: 5; "*I am the vine; you are the branches. Whoever remains in union with me and I in union with him, this one bears much fruit; for **apart from me, you can produce nothing at all**.*" Meaning that God's Spirit will guide and sustain you, if you remain in union with me; that is, by following my instructions. **John 15:6**: If you do not remain in me, you are like a branch that is thrown away because it does not produce any fruit and withers; such branches are picked up, thrown into the fire and burned.

As a spiritual entity: in the last supper, Christ prays for the unity of Christians: **John 17: 20-21**; "*I make request, not concerning these only, but also concerning those putting faith in me through their word, **so that they may all be one**, just as you, Father, are in union with me and I am in union with you, that **they too may be in union with us**, so that the world may believe that you sent me.*"

As a spiritual entity: In **Mathew 12: 22-27**; Jesus had just cured a blind and speechless and demon-possessed man and some people in the crowd were saying that he was surely, "The Son of David," that is, the Messiah, but some Pharisees outraged by this observation made the following comment: *"This fellow does not expel the demons except by means of Beelzebub, the ruler of the demons."* So, Jesus started reasoning with them: *Every kingdom divided against itself comes to ruin, and every city or house divided against itself will not stand. And in the same way, if Satan expels Satan, he has become divided against himself; how, then, will his kingdom stand? Moreover, if I expel the demons by means of Beelzebub, by whom do your sons expel them? This is why they will be your judges."*

Some Jews, mainly disciples of the Pharisees, could actually expel demons. These exorcists were all religious people and they expelled the demons by the power of prayer; see **Acts 19: 13-17**. Christ was pointing out to these Pharisees that if they believed he expels demons by the power of Satan or Beelzebub, it must be by the same evil power that their disciples used to expel demons, but if this fact was not true, the comments they had just made about Jesus, would be condemned and considered very offensive by their very own disciples. **Mathew 12: 28**; *"But if it is **by means of God's spirit** that I expel the demons, then the Kingdom of God has really overtaken you".* This means, that these "unbelievers" have been left behind; they have been excluded from being part of God's Kingdom because of their lack of faith; they do not acknowledge God's authority or power which Jesus manifested by expelling the demon and second, they blasphemed against the Holy Spirit, equating God's power to a demonic power; **a sin that is unforgivable, according** to Jesus Christ; see **Mathew 12:31- 32:** *"For this reason I say to you, every sort of sin and blasphemy will be forgiven men, but the blasphemy against The Spirit will not be forgiven. For example, whoever speaks a word against the Son of man, it will be forgiven him; but whoever speaks against the Holy Spirit, it will not be forgiven him, no, not in this system of things nor in that to come*."

No Trinity: Jesus makes a distinction between himself and The Holy Spirit.

A physical entity: **Matthew 7: 21**; "*Not everyone **saying to me,** 'Lord, Lord,' will enter into the Kingdom of the heavens, but only the one doing the will of my Father who is in the heavens, will.*" Is this a repetition, view preaching on Sermon.

As a physical entity: In **John 18: 36**, Jesus explained to Pontius Pilate, the Roman Governor interrogating him during his prosecution: "My Kingdom is no part of this world. If my Kingdom were part of this world, my attendants would have fought to prevent my arrest by the Jewish leaders. But as it is, my Kingdom is not of this source."

A physical or spiritual entity? The Church, the people who follow God's Laws and not necessarily the institutions of the church, are the living testimony of God's spirit in action and through this church. The Church, therefore, must be part of God's kingdom because, through it, God's will, that is, God's authority is executed. Those who live according to God's will, are part of God's kingdom.

A physical kingdom to be established in the future

God's kingdom also refers to a physical kingdom, an everlasting government to be set up in the future, which will be ruled by Jesus Christ; (**Luke 1:32-33**) "*Jehovah God will give him the throne of David his father and he will rule as King over the house of Jacob forever, and there will be no end to his Kingdom.*"

A physical entity: Luke 22:28-30; "However, you are the ones who have stuck with me in my trials; and I make a covenant with you, just as **my Father has made a covenant with me, for a kingdom,** so that you may eat and drink at my table in my Kingdom, and sit on thrones to judge the 12 tribes of Israel.

Matthew 25:31-32; When the Son of man comes in his glory, and all the angels with him, then he will sit down on his glorious throne, **of his kingdom.** All the nations will be gathered before him, and he will separate people one from another, just as a shepherd separates the sheep from the goats.

Please note: The term, "Everlasting life," is equivalent to "being part of God's kingdom" because, according to the scriptures, there is no other place in the universe where one can live eternally, except in God's Kingdom.

According to Jesus, one has to keep God's Law to have everlasting life and therefore be part of God's kingdom; **Luke 10: 25-28 and Mark 10: 17-22.**

From my understanding, obeying God's Law also means, acknowledging the sacrifice of his son, Jesus Christ, in that his death has a key role in the reconciliation of mankind with God, enabling man to gain access to the Kingdom of God. Without this acknowledgement, one cannot acquire everlasting life. **John 17:3** says; *"This means everlasting life, their coming to know you, the only true God, and the one whom you sent, Jesus Christ."*

As a spiritual entity

The terms Sheol in Hebrew and Hades in Greek, both refer to where people go after death; they are both used frequently in the Bible.

The Bible, in the Old Testament, describes the afterlife of man as "resting in Sheol." The New Testament, which was first written in Greek, uses the word Hades, instead of the Hebrew word of Sheol.

Jesus, God's representative, could also raise the dead, that is he could call the dead back to life from Sheol or Hades. This means that God's power and therefore God's authority and therefore God's Kingdom extends into the land of the dead.

See **John 11:39-44**; Jesus said, "Take the stone away." Martha, the sister of the deceased, said to him, "Lord, by now he must smell, for it has been dead now four days." Jesus said to her, "Did I not tell you that if you believed you would see the glory of God?" So, they took the stone away. **Then Jesus raised his eyes heavenward and said: "Father, I thank you that you have** heard me. True, I knew that you always hear me; but I spoke on account of the crowd standing around, so that they may believe that you sent me." When he had said these things, he cried out with a loud voice: "Lazarus, come out!" The man who had been dead came out with his feet and hands bound with wrappings, and his face was wrapped with a cloth. Jesus said to them: "Free him and let him go."

God's authority is far superior to that of the evil spirits. When Jesus exorcized evil spirits, these evil spirits would become unsettled just by his presence and many, if not all, would acknowledge him as the Son of God. When Jesus commanded the evil spirits to leave, they would obey and leave the demonized individual, **instantly.**

I know it comes naturally to us to fear death for various reasons, but as a Christian, one should try to overcome this fear and trust in God. As a Christian, one should be confident that God will take care of you, wherever you happen to be, even in Sheol or Hades, because God created all things, visible and invisible. God's dominion extends to include Sheol or Hades and all the invisible world. In conclusion, God's kingdom is where God exercises His authority; heaven, earth, the spiritual realm and also your heart if you submit to His authority.

From the Book of Revelation, the Kingdom of God **also regards a physical and political kingdom, a real government** to be established on earth, a newly created earth, in the future, accessible to mankind and governed by Jesus Christ.

20

The miracles performed by Jesus Christ

Why did Christ perform miracles?

- Jesus said that the purpose of his performing miracles was to testify the fact that he was sent by God, His Father and also to prove that he was who he claimed to be, The Son of God. See **John 3:1-2; John 10: 19-21**, **John 10: 24-25, John 10:31-39, Luke: 7: 18-23.** If you believe that someone is sent by God, that he is a prophet, surely you must also believe that he speaks the truth, because a real prophet cannot lie by claiming to be The Son of God. Also, God cannot empower someone who is blaspheming by making a false statement, saying that he is the Son of God, by giving them the power to perform miracles. T**ake note: Jesus did not claim to be God, but God's representative and also that he was the son of God.**

- Performing miracles, made people not dismiss Jesus, instead, they took note of what he was saying and he was, therefore, able to preach the word of God to them; see: **John 6: 1-2 and Mark 2: 1-2.**

- Many of the miracles done by Jesus, were also because he had pity on people. Jesus himself reached out to people, who did not even know him and resolved their misfortunes, miraculously; see **John 5:1-9:** a man sick for 38 years, **Luke 7: 11-17;** in Nain, death of an only son, of a widow and **Luke 13: 10-13;** a woman bent double**.**

Please note: When you read the New Testament, you will note that when Jesus performed miracles, the Jewish people glorified God **only and not Jesus**. It was obvious to them that the power in Jesus could only have come from one source, God **and Jesus never made any objection to it**.

What kind of miracles did Jesus perform?

All kinds of miracles; let's see some examples from the scriptures.

Jesus cured anyone who was ill, disabled, demon-possessed, epileptic, paralyzed etc. wherever these people happened to be, by the roadside, in the temple or the marketplace etc. While out preaching, Jesus would find sick people waiting for him everywhere he went. I**t is not recorded of any case where Jesus refused or failed to cure or remedy the problem. It is not reported of any case where Jesus used his miracles to hurt or kill someone or even to damage their property.**

All the miracles that Jesus performed were of great benefit to someone or to some people; Jesus never used his power to harm anyone and this testifies to God's positive power. Jesus travelled on foot, and it was while out preaching that he performed most of his miracles in the midst of the people. Once the word had spread about him, that he could cure miraculously, sick people were constantly brought to him wherever he happened to be, even when at home.

Please note: If sick people went to Jesus, they must have had the conviction that he could cure them, that is, they had full faith in him. It is reported in **Mark 9:17-29**, an occurrence where Jesus questioned a man who had brought his demon-possessed son to be cured, for saying: *"Help us if you can."* in **Mark 9:22**, clearly showing a lack of faith, however, Jesus did cure his son.

Jesus could forgive sins, on earth. See in **Mark 2: 5-12**, Jesus claimed that he had the authority to forgive sins on earth. Where did the authority come from? The scribes were questioning in their hearts why Jesus should make such a claim, which according to them, was the equivalent of blasphemy. Jesus perceiving what they were thinking, reasoned with them; if God could empower him to perform miracles, this was also a confirmation that what he said was the truth, that is he could actually forgive sins. God cannot give such power to someone who is blaspheming Him.

A usual scene of Jesus performing miracles: See Mark 6: 53-56. But as soon as Jesus and his apostles got out of the boat, people recognized him. They ran around all that region and started to bring on stretchers those who were ailing to where they heard he was. And wherever he would enter into villages or cities or the countryside, they would place the sick ones in the marketplaces, and they would plead with him that they might touch just the fringe of his outer garment. And all those who touched it were made well. Please note: Christ's miracles, especially those regarding people who touched his garments and got cured, were active events, **(Luke 8:43-48)** because power went forth from Jesus in order to cure them.

Often, Jesus would ask the people he cured not to tell anyone because when they did, it became practically impossible to enter the cities; so many people would show up, that practically he couldn't move. The crowds, however, would still come looking for him, even when he stayed outside their cities; see **Mark 1: 40-45**.

Here is a list of miracles, performed by Jesus Christ that I find extraordinary

All of Christ's miracles were amazing, but some really testify to the uniqueness of his power. These particular miracles are transferring Godly power to his disciples and apostles; curing at a distance; resurrecting the dead and command over nature and exorcism.

Empowering his disciples and apostles with godly power. When Jesus sent off **seventy-two of his disciples to preach** (not his apostles), he also gave basic instructions on what to do and say; see **Luke 10: 1-17**. Then the seventy-two returned with joy, saying: "Lord, even the demons submit to us *by the use of your name.*" At that, he, Jesus, said to them: "I see Satan already fallen like lightning from heaven. Look! I have given you the authority to trample underfoot serpents and scorpions, and over all the power of the enemy, and nothing at all will harm you."

Jesus also sent out his own apostles to preach; see **Matthew 10:1**; "*So he summoned his twelve disciples and* **gave them authority** *over unclean spirits, in order to expel these and to cure every sort of disease and every sort of infirmity.*" He also instructed them what to do, see below. To be more precise, these were actually the twelve apostles of Jesus as listed in **Matthew 10:2-4**.

In **Matthew 10: 5-6;** Jesus sent out his twelve apostles, giving them these instructions: "*Do not go off into the road of the nations, and do not enter any Samaritan city;* **but instead, go continually to the lost sheep of the house of Israel.**"

Mathew 10: 7-11; As you go, proclaim this message: 'The Kingdom of the heavens has drawn near.' Cure the sick, raise up the dead, make lepers clean, expel demons. You received free, give free. Do not acquire gold or silver or copper for your money belts or a food pouch for the trip, or two garments, or sandals, or a staff, for the worker deserves his food and wages."

"Into whatever city or village, you enter, search out who in it is deserving, and stay there until you leave."

By these instructions, we see Jesus is asking his apostles to entrust all their care, entirely to God.

Curing at a distance

Jesus could cure at a distance; without him being present.

Example: **Matthew 8: 5-13**. A **high-ranking** Roman army officer, a centurion, came looking for Jesus because his slave or servant was very ill. Jesus told him that he would cure his slave, later, when he got to the Centurion's home town. The Roman centurion then said to Jesus: *"Sir, I am not worthy to have you come under my roof, but just say the word and my servant will be healed."* Jesus praised his great faith and cured his slave there and then; without having to go to the Centurion's home.

Another example: **John 4: 46-53**; Then he came again to Cana of Galilee, where he had turned the water into wine. Now there was a royal official whose son was sick in Capernaum. When this man heard that Jesus had arrived in Galilee from Judea, he went to him and begged him to come and heal his son, who was close to death.

The royal official said to him: "Lord, come down before my young child dies." Jesus said to him: "Go your way; your son lives." The man believed the word that Jesus spoke to him, and he left. While he was on his way home, his slaves met him to say that his boy was alive. So he asked them at what hour he got better. They replied to him: "The fever left him yesterday at the seventh hour." The father then knew that it was at the very hour that Jesus had said to him: "Your son lives." So he and his whole household believed.

The Resurrection of the Dead

See, **Mark 5:21-24 and 35-43;** This miracle regards the daughter of Jairus, the Presiding officer of a synagogue. Then in **Luke 7:11-17,** Jesus comes across a funeral procession at the gate of the city of Nain; the dead man was an only son to a widow. Jesus is moved with pity for this widow and resurrects her son.

Command over nature

- Calming the storm; see: **Mark 4: 35-41**
- Walking on water in **Matthew 14: 23-34**
- Jesus communicating to fish: **Matthew 17: 24-27 and Luke 5:4-8**

Exorcism/casting out demons

Take note that Jesus could communicate with the demons and all demons recognised him as an authority over them and also that he was the Son of God because, when he ordered them to: "Get out!" they would all depart, immediately. See the following two examples: **Luke 4: 33-35** and **Mark 5: 1-20.**

According to the apostle John, the scriptures do not write all the miracles that Jesus performed.

See: (**John 20: 30-31**); To be sure, Jesus also performed many other signs before the disciples, which are not written down in this scroll. But these have been written down so that you may believe that Jesus is the Christ, the Son of God, and because of believing, you may have life by means of his name.

21

How big were the crowds, that followed Jesus?

The scriptures say in many places that Jesus was followed by a large crowd without giving a specific number. Let's just take a look at the first three chapters of the apostle Mark: **Mark 1:32-34:** That evening after sunset the people brought to Jesus all the sick and demon-possessed. The whole town gathered at the door, and Jesus healed many who had various diseases. He also drove out many demons, but he would not let the demons speak because they knew who he was.

Mark 2: 1-2: A few days later, when Jesus again entered Capernaum, the people heard that he had come home. They gathered in such large numbers outside his home that there was no room left, not even outside the door, and he preached the word to them.

Mark 3:7-12: Jesus withdrew with his disciples to the lake, and a large crowd from Galilee followed. When they heard about all he was doing, many people came to him from Judea, Jerusalem, Idumea, and the regions across the Jordan and around Tyre and Sidon. Because of the crowd, he told his disciples to have a small boat ready for him, to keep the people from crowding him. For he had healed many so that those with diseases were pushing forward to touch him. Whenever the impure spirits saw him, they fell down before him and cried out, "You are the Son of God." But he gave them strict orders not to tell others about him.

As you can see from the above three chapters, Jesus was constantly pursued by very large crowds.

I will pick two occasions in the New Testament scriptures, **that give the numerical size of the crowds following Jesus and both regard** when Jesus provided food, miraculously, to feed crowds that had followed him to a very isolated place, with no shops or market, to buy food.

The first episode is recorded in Matthew 14:14-22.

When he came ashore, he saw a large crowd, and he felt pity for them, and he cured their sick ones. But when evening fell, his disciples came to him and said: "The place is isolated and the hour is already late; send the crowds away, so that they may go into the villages and buy themselves food." Jesus instead, had already decided to feed this crowd. However, Jesus said to them: "They do not have to leave; you give them something to eat. They said to him: "We have nothing here except five barley loaves and two fish." According to **John 6: 9,** these barley loaves and two fish were supplied by a boy in the crowd. Jesus requested his apostles to bring these barley loaves and two fish to him; he then instructed the crowds to recline on the grass. Then he took the five loaves and two fish, and looking up to heaven, he said a blessing, and after breaking the loaves, he gave them to the disciples, and the disciples gave them to the crowds. Those eating were about **5,000 men,** as well as women and young children. then, after the meal, as it was very late, Jesus made his disciples board the boat and go ahead of him to the opposite shore, while he sent the crowds away.

Luke 9:10-17 talks of this same episode, it took place near the city of Bethsaida. **Luke 9:11** says: But the crowds, getting to know it, (that Jesus was in the area), **followed him. and he received them kindly and began to speak to them** about the Kingdom of God, and he healed those needing a cure.

The second occasion is reported in Matthew 15: 29 to 39.

Departing from there, Jesus next came near the Sea of Galilee, and after going up on the mountain, he was sitting there. Then large crowds approached him, bringing along people who were lame, maimed, blind, speechless, and many others, and they laid them at his feet, and he cured them. So the crowd felt amazement as they saw the speechless speaking and the maimed being made sound and the lame walking and the blind seeing, and they glorified the God of Israel.

But Jesus called his disciples to him and said: "*I feel pity for the crowd because they have already stayed with me for three days and they have had nothing to eat.*" The crowds had brought their sick to be cured, then remained. "*I do not want to send them away hungry, for they may give out on the road.*" Jesus ended up multiplying what had remained of their own food supplies; **seven loaves and a few small fish**, to feed a crowd of **4,000 men**, as well as women and young children. Jesus himself sent them away to their homes, after feeding them.

Why should this particular crowd have followed Jesus for three days? it is just crazy.

The crowds remained with Jesus, first because they needed to get healed (the sick were accompanied by the healthy people), others might have had psychological problems, others wanted to witness what they had heard; that Jesus could perform miracles, last but not least, Jesus welcomed them, that is, he received them kindly. See: **Luke 9:11**. These crowds were enchanted to witness God's power, manifested through Jesus by his superb preaching, by the many miracle cures and by the demons being exorcised; they had never witnessed anything of the sort. Once someone was healed, it would have come naturally to remain to see and hear what else Jesus had to say or do.

The people healed, glorified God and when they left, they would talk of their miraculous cures to other people they met. Not only had they been healed physically, but they had been reconciled to their Creator because they felt grateful to God; He had had pity on them and had removed their suffering.

22

Moses the prophet
mentioned Christ

Jesus affirmed two important things about himself that the prophet, Moses had written about him.

In **John 5: 45-47**; *"Do not think that I will accuse you to the Father;* ***there is one who accuses you, Moses, in whom you have put your hope. In fact, if you believed Moses, you would believe me, for he wrote about me.*** *But if you do not believe his writings, how will you believe what I say?"*

There are only two places in the scriptures written by Moses, which fit this description: **Deuteronomy 18:15 and Deuteronomy 18: 18-19.**

Deuteronomy 18: 15: *"Jehovah your God will raise up for you from among your brothers a prophet like me. You must listen to him. This is in response to what you asked of Jehovah your God in Horeb on the day of the assembly when you said, 'Do not let me hear the voice of Jehovah my God or see this great fire anymore so that I do not die.' Then Jehovah said to me, 'What they have said is good."*

Deuteronomy 18: 18-19; *"I will raise up for them from the midst of their brothers a prophet like you, and I will put my words in his mouth, and he will speak to them all that I command him. Indeed, I will require an account from the man who will not listen to my words that he will speak in my name."*

The apostles of Jesus recognized right from the start of Christ's earthly mission that, it was him whom Moses had referred to. See **John 1:45**: Philip found Nathanael and said to him: *"We have found* *the one of whom Moses, in the Law, and the Prophets wrote: Jesus, the son of Joseph, from Nazareth."*

Luke 24: 25-32 tells of an account where Jesus after his death, appeared incognito to two of his disciples, who are travelling to a village called Emmaus. A discussion among them came up, regarding how Jesus had been sentenced to death at the hand of chief priests and rulers; but then these disciples said that they had been hoping that this (Jesus Christ), was the man who would have delivered Israel from the rule of Rome.

So, after listening for a while to what these two disciples were saying about his death, Jesus said to them: *"O senseless ones and slow of heart to believe all the things that the prophets have spoken! Was it not necessary for the Christ to suffer these things and to enter into his glory?"* And **starting with Moses** and all the Prophets, he interpreted to them what was said in all the Scriptures concerning himself.

This verse here means that it is Jesus Christ that Moses had referred to, in Deuteronomy 18:18-19.

Jesus affirmed that: he was sent first to the nation of Israel.

It is important to note, that Jesus Christ affirmed that he was sent first to the nation of Israel.

In **Matthew 10: 5-6;** Jesus sent out, his twelve apostles, giving them these instructions: *"Do not go off into the road of the nations, and do not enter any Samaritan city;* **but instead, go continually to the lost sheep of the house of Israel."**

In another event; **Matthew 15: 21-28**; Jesus had gone to Sidon and Tyre, a non-Jewish territory, and was being followed by a Phoenician woman, who was pleading for mercy: *"Have mercy on me, Lord, Son of David. My daughter is cruelly demon-possessed."* Jesus continued moving on, deliberately ignoring her pleas, but she persisted, pleading and following him. He answered: **"I was not sent to anyone except to the lost sheep of the house of**

Israel. But the woman came and did obeisance to him, saying: "Lord, help me!" Jesus replied: *"It is not right to take the bread of the children (the Jews) and throw it to the little dogs (the Gentiles/non-Jews)."* Some people get quite angry at Jesus; I too, became angry on reading this phrase, but as it was very unlike Jesus, I decided to investigate its significance. This phrase could be misinterpreted, whereby Jesus might be perceived to be a racist, and it could be assumed that Jesus was insulting the woman because she was not an Israelite. This is not true, also because, Jesus had never asked anybody their nationality, before curing them, nor made any racist comments or speech, before this episode. If Jesus had gone to Sidon and Tyre, non-Jewish territory, surely this shows an interest in the Gentiles? That is the non-Jewish people.

With that phrase, Jesus was specifying the priorities of his mission and he was also testing the woman's faith. "The bread," was Jesus' earthly mission of preaching and doing miracles, which was directed first to the nation of Israel: "The children."

From the reply the Phoenician woman gave to Jesus, we understand that the term: "little dogs," is referring to the children's pets. To "take the bread of the children and throw it to the little dogs," means to deprive the little children the rightful recipients of their bread in favour of other secondary recipients: their pets. By doing so, Jesus would be failing in his duty of feeding "The Children" that is he would be contravening his mission.

The Phoenician woman replied, *"Yes, Lord, but really the little dogs do eat of the crumbs falling from the table of their masters."* What she was really saying was: "The gentiles are also bound to benefit from the breadcrumbs, falling down from "your table" That is, *"Lord, the crumbs of your mission, of your power, are sufficient for me."* Then Jesus replied to her: *"O woman, great is your faith; let it happen to you as you wish."* And her daughter who was not present, was healed instantly, from that hour on.

I will emphasize again that Jesus was not racist. **John chapter 4:7-42;** describes an encounter between Jesus and a Samaritan woman, near a well. It was Jesus who initiated talking to this woman and she remained very surprised and asked Jesus: *"How is it that you, despite being a Jew, ask me for a drink even though I am a Samaritan woman?"*

On the above occasion, Jesus breached the barrier of hatred between the Jews and the Samaritans; he ended up being invited to the Samaritan city of Sycar (this woman's city), where he stayed for two days. He preached to the Samaritans during his brief stay there and many put faith in him.

In the time of Jesus, Jews shunned Samaritans. This fact is clear from another passage of the scriptures, where there was a heated exchange of words between Jesus and some Pharisees in the temple: **John 8: 47-48;** Jesus says: *"The one who is from God listens to the sayings of God. This is why you do not listen because you are not from God."* In answer, the Jews (the Pharisees) said to him: *"Are we not right in saying, 'You are a Samaritan and have a demon?'"*

Please note: Jesus made the following statement while talking to the Samaritan woman near Jacob's well; **John 4:22;** *"You worship what you do not know; we worship what we know **because salvation begins with the Jews."***

God spoke to Abraham: **the whole world will be blessed through your offspring**... See **Genesis: 12:3; Genesis 18:18 and Genesis 22:15-18.**

After the death of Jesus, the News of the Kingdom was preached also to other non-Israelite nations, (the Gentiles), but starting from Jerusalem; by the disciple and apostles of Jesus, who were Jews, however, they soon recruited other non-Jewish disciples, who also participated in the spread of the Good News.

23

How does Jesus take away
the sins of the world?

The events regarding the death and resurrection of Jesus Christ are extremely important to us Christians. Very often you will hear Christians say, "Jesus died for our sins" or "Jesus died to save us from our sins." For a long time, I really did not understand what this phrase meant. I often wondered how the death of Jesus translates into "saving people from their sins?" Why did Jesus not do other things to save people from their sins? He could have prayed, he could have fasted, he could have run a 100 km marathon, etc. Why did he have to die?

One has to know the Jewish scripture, that is the Old Testament, to understand why Jesus Christ had to die to save man from sin, instead of doing something else. I believe we should start first by defining what sin is. According to the scriptures, to sin is to violate God's Law, voluntarily or involuntarily. When one sins, they break their relationship with God; they create a barrier between themselves and their Creator. Due to sin, one is no longer able to approach God freely in prayer, without first seeking forgiveness from God.

The second point is: the Kingdom of God will not be accessible to sinners; see: **Matthew 7:22-23**; "Not everyone who says to me 'Lord, Lord,' will enter the kingdom of heaven, but only the one who does the will of my Father in heaven.

The violation of God's Law also acts as a barrier between you and your fellow man, if they do believe in God's authority. If someone insults his father or mother, it would be inappropriate for his siblings to continue having a normal relationship with them;

they are bound to sympathise with their parents. In the same way, believers, will sympathise with their Heavenly Father and retreat from those violating God's Law.

According to the Christian faith, man was created to rely on God

Why did God do such a thing, is it an act of bossing, coercing or intimidating man? No, I believe it is an act of taking responsibility for his creation: man; an act of caring for man, an act of loving kindness. God knows that man has his limits, he knows also, that He, Himself is the source of everything and if man relies on Him, everything man needs will be taken care of. It is a great privilege for man, to have Jehovah taking care of him.

According to Genesis, the first book of the Bible, when man was created, he was placed in a paradise, called the Garden of Eden i.e. in the best possible environment one could desire; is this not loving kindness from God? Man relied on the fruits of this paradise for his food. (The first man created was called Adam and his wife, Eve). It would have come spontaneously for man to worship Jehovah (God) i.e. have a very high regard, for God, the source of all his benefits. Adam was free to do all he pleased in this paradise, except one thing; God ordered him, please note: he did not request him, but ordered him, i.e. commanded him, not to eat from The Tree of Knowledge of Good and Bad, which grew at the centre of this garden, **besides** The Tree of Life. Man was created to live forever if he did not disobey God, so the Tree of Life did not really interest him.

God informed the man he had just created that, if he ate from the Tree of Knowledge of Good and Bad, he would die; **Gen 2:16-17**: "But you must not eat from the tree of the Knowledge of Good and Evil; for in the day that you eat of it, you will surely die."

Man's life relied on obeying this single commandment.

This fact in itself means that man was not free to do all he wanted, right from his existence; God put a small restriction or limitation on him, as a sign of His authority over him. This command also establishes a relationship between man and God, meaning that man was to live under God's authority and his life depended on following this single commandment, of not eating from the Tree of Knowledge because if he broke this commandment, he would die; his life relied on doing God's will.

If man was created "perfect," he would never have had any need for a God, because he could do everything he liked to perfection and all by himself; a kind of God but independent of God, but according to the Bible, this was not God's intention when he created man. Man's perfection was connected with doing God's will.

This commandment was not difficult to obey; because Adam and Eve lacked nothing, all their needs were fully satisfied. By obeying this single commandment, Adam and Eve acknowledged God's authority over them. Only someone superior to you can give you a command i.e. orders. Both Adam and Eve had been informed of the consequence of breaking God's commandment: death.

Now, who would not like to live forever, when he or she lives in paradise?

Adam and Eve eventually broke this commandment and as a consequence, did not live forever; furthermore, they were both punished for disobeying God and were driven away from paradise. See **Genesis 3: 16-19**. All their offspring too, did not live forever. Why the offspring had to pay for their parent's faults, is another debate.

According to the Christian faith, Adam and Eve brought death, pain, suffering and sin into the world, as part of God's punishment for disobeying him. In **Genesis 3: 5**, Eve, Adam's wife, had a close encounter with the Devil, who convinced her to disobey God and she, in turn, convinced her husband, Adam. Apparently, Adam preferred pleasing Eve more than obeying God. The Devil's argument was: "*For God knows that when you eat from it, (The tree of Knowledge, of Good and Bad) your eyes will be opened, and you will be like God, knowing good and evil*" Besides the Devil lied to Eve, saying, they would not die if they disobeyed God. Both Adam and Eve; decided that the Devil had a point; they wanted to be, "just like God."

From the moment they disobeyed God, they came to know evil; their own perception changed, in that they now perceived negative things, for example, they perceived themselves to have a defect; they "realised" that they were naked. Before sinning, they did not realise that they were naked and they did not know of any bad or evil; they were innocent. Now they knew both good and evil, according to their own personal perception or let's say according to their own standards.

When God created them naked, He saw that it was good, but now, after eating from the Forbidden Tree, Adam and Eve, saw that this was not good; they were no longer in harmony with their Creator.

God permitted Adam and Eve, to live as they had chosen to; **free from His authority. By disobeying his commandment, they had actually challenged his authority, by refusing to submit to his command. Deciding means making a conscious choice, after consideration; therefore, Adam and Eve made a conscious, voluntary decision to disobey God.**

Any man who lives autonomously of God is bound to sin because he will have to decide what is right and wrong according to his own personal standards, which will not always conform to the same standards of God, also man without God's protection is easy prey for the Devil. Man's perfection is based on relying on God because God is perfect. This means that Adam and Eve and all their offspring were extremely vulnerable to sin, once they had been distanced from God, the source of righteousness; therefore man has to seek God constantly, in order to avoid sinning.

If your parents or your teacher or the Law of the Land prohibits you to do something, but you willingly choose to do what you have been requested not to; you have deliberately ignored the authority of your parents or the authority of your teacher or the authority of your country; you have **despised their authority** and there are always consequences to face; you have to be held accountable for your actions.

Note: According to the Law of Moses, the punishment for sinning intentionally is death. Why? If one sins intentionally, this is being defiant of God's authority, it is showing contempt for God's Law and therefore for God Himself; it is blasphemy.

Blasphemy definition: the act of insulting or showing contempt or lack of reverence to a deity.

God has instructed man on what to do and what not to do, in His commandments or Law, as given to Moses. When we sin, we disregard His law and instead do what we desire. Breaking God's commandments is equal to challenging God's authority, this is exactly what happens when we sin; we challenge God's authority; we deliberately refuse to submit to his commandments.

See the scriptures **Numbers 15: 30-31**; "But anyone who sins defiantly, that is, **deliberately/intentionally**, whether he is native-born or a foreign resident, is blaspheming Jehovah and must be cut off from among his people. Because they have despised Jehovah's word and broken his commandment, that person should be cut off without fail. His own error is upon him."

The Hebrew term, "cutting off," is "kareth". It could mean premature death, inflicted by man or Divine intervention or could be interpreted as the opposite of "being gathered to one's people," therefore, being deprived of the afterlife, hence leading to the extinction of the soul. All these interpretations, all lead to death.

In the Talmud, kareth means not necessarily physical "cutting off" of life, but the extinction of the soul and denial of a share in the world to come.

The Talmud is a record of the rabbinic debates/reasoning on the teachings of the Torah. This book is considered holy and is a central text of Jewish theology.

The punishment for sinning **is from God** because you have sinned against him. According to Jehovah's Law, intentional sin is equal to blasphemy and hence, it is punishable by death; see above, **Numbers 15: 30-31**. This means that officially and according to the Torah (Law of Moses), the punishment for sinning against God was/is death.

When God governed Israel, through his prophets and when the Israelites sinned, it would have been against God's nature to ignore their sins, just like a father should not ignore mistakes made by his children or a teacher should not ignore mistakes made by his or her pupils. Their sins had to be accounted for, one way or another.

Jehovah is a merciful God, so He came up with an alternative for preserving the Israelite nation from death. The Jewish people have different festivals, but the holiest of the Jewish festivals is The Day of Atonement; which in Judaism is referred to as **Yom Kippur**; see **Leviticus chapter 16**.

On this particular day, The Day of Atonement, Jehovah decided to accept the death of certain selected animals as "compensation or reparation" for the sins committed by the Israelites. I will not write the particulars involving this religious rite of The Day of Atonement, one can read it from **Leviticus chapter 16)**.

Please note that: The animals used for this sacrifice were innocent, in that they had committed no sin, at all, against Jehovah and therefore, did not merit to die. These animals, which had to be perfect i.e. without defect or blemish, were killed instead of the Israelites, who merited death, because, it is them who had deliberately, transgressed Jehovah's law. This is why it is said that; these animals were "sacrificed."

On this, "Day of Atonement" all the Israelites had to take note of the fact that they had actually transgressed Jehovah's law and they had to afflict their souls, that is, feel remorseful and deeply sorry for their sins, in order to be forgiven.

On this day, the sins of all Israel, intentional and non-intentional, were cleared away, by Jehovah. Also from this day on, all Israelites were now free to approach Jehovah in prayer, as their relationship had been restored by the forgiveness of their sins, through the sacrifices of some animals.

Leviticus 16: 30; On this day, atonement will be made for you, to declare you clean. You will be clean from all your sins before Jehovah.

Leviticus 16: 34; "This (The Day of Atonement) will serve, as a lasting statute for you, to make atonement for the Israelites concerning ALL their sins, once each year."

Please note: It was the blood from the slaughtered animals that was used to atone for sins. The corpses of the sacrificed animals were taken outside the camp and burned up. See **Leviticus 16: 26-28.**

The surplus blood from the slaughtered animals, that remained after the sprinkling was done, was **poured out** at the base of the altar, as part of the offering.

See an example: **Leviticus 4:7**:" *The rest of the bull's blood he shall pour out at the base of the altar of burnt offering at the entrance to the tent of meeting.*"

During the meal of Jesus with his apostles (the Last Super), Jesus says what his death means. See **Matthew 26:27-28;** And taking a cup, he offered thanks and gave it to them, saying: "Drink out of it, all of you, for this means **my blood of the Covenant, which is to be poured out on behalf of many for forgiveness of sins.**

See **Luke 22:20**; In the same way, after the supper he took the cup, saying, "This cup is the new covenant in my blood, which is **poured out** for you."

Sin offering was done privately, by individuals, to atone for non-intentional sin.

Leviticus chapter four explains the significance of Sin Offering.

Why should one be accountable to God, for non-intentional sin? Ignorance, especially regarding the Laws of God is inexcusable. Not being attentive to your actions is being negligent and could lead to sin, this also has to be accounted for.

When man sins, it is God who has been wronged and it is Him who decides what he requires to atone or make reparation for the sins, but the key to being forgiven is: one has to acknowledge their sins and feel remorseful for having committed them, also one must have faith and complete confidence and trust that God has the power to forgive all their sins.

God had destined Jesus Christ, right from his birth, to be the sacrifice that would atone for the sins of mankind; for all times, through his own death. The name Jesus is derived from the Jewish name Yeshua; in Hebrew it means "Yahweh is salvation" and salvation means: preservation or deliverance from, harm, ruin or loss. In short, the name Jesus is interpreted to mean: "to deliver" or "to rescue," it identifies the main purpose of Christ's life, that is, to deliver mankind from sin and death.

It is God's right to choose what He requires, to appease for the sins of mankind, because it is He, who has been wronged.

The ransom that was paid, so that mankind may be released from his sins and reconciled to God, was the precious life of God's own son, Jesus Christ. Let's see an example of "a ransom." In New York, a Mafia boss was kidnapped by bandits, who then demanded from his family a ransom of $50,000. The family of this Mafia boss refused to let this request go public; they were very humiliated because of the small sum of money requested as ransom; in their opinion, the Mafia boss was worth a lot more, than $50,000.

God chose something extremely precious to Him, to atone for man's sins, his own son; this means that God has a very high regard for human life if he required his own son's death as reparation for sins committed by mankind. This explains one of the most quoted verses of the scriptures;

John 3:16; For God so loved the world that he gave his one and only Son, that whoever believes in him shall not perish but have eternal life.

Believing in Jesus means believing and practising what he preached.

The death of Jesus Christ served as a sacrifice for the forgiveness of sins for all mankind, in a similar manner to the animals sacrificed in the Jewish festival of: "The Day of Atonement," this is why Jesus is sometimes referred to as, "The Lamb of God, who takes away the sins of the world."

See John 1:29; The next day he (John the Baptist), saw Jesus coming toward him, and he said: "*See, the Lamb of God who takes away the sin of the world.*"

This also explains the very popular quotation: **Romans 6:23**; "For the wages of sin is death, but the gift of God is eternal life in Christ Jesus Our Lord."

24

What led to the death
of Jesus Christ?

The mission of Jesus Christ on earth lasted for, let's say about three years. He was then arrested, prosecuted and executed. The Jewish clergy were responsible for arresting Jesus and then presenting him before a Roman tribunal with false allegations, which then led to his being executed, on the orders of the Roman Governor, Pontius Pilate.

Who made up the Jewish clergy in the days of Jesus?

Definition of clergy: the body of people ordained for religious duties.

At the time of Jesus Christ, it was made up of the priests, the Pharisees, the scribes and the Sadducees.

The priests were ordained to perform rituals in the temple and were well-trained in the Law, Jewish literature and traditions.

Scribes were elite professionals involved in copying documents, keeping records and administration. They transcribed God's Law and other official documents; some also taught the Law. Most of the Jewish population was illiterate in Christ's time and relied on the oral teachings of the Law. Also a large part of the Jewish population, perhaps even Jesus Christ, spoke Aramaic and not Hebrew. The Jews had acquired this language, during their seventy years of exile in Babylon. Hebrew language remained in use mainly in religion, in government and in the learned upper class of society.

The Pharisees were respected because they specialized in the interpretation of the law and in enforcing it, a kind of religious police. They also claimed to be strict observers of the traditional, man-made laws and the written law or God's Law. In the Bible's New Testament, they are portrayed as having a holier-than-thou attitude and of being hypocrites.

The Sadducees, on the other hand, were a sect of Jews of higher social economic rank, mainly of aristocratic background; they were also responsible for the maintenance of the temple. They believed only in the written Law of Moses; this means they must have been literate, and denied the obligation of oral tradition and other things outside this Law, for example, the resurrection, evil spirits etc. However, they must have collaborated with the priests if they had the competence of maintaining the Temple. The Sadducees formed an important part of the Sanhedrin.

The Jewish Elders were wise, God-fearing, elderly men with distinctive social grades, this was not a profession, and they represented their local community in presiding over certain social functions, for example confirming the act of Levirate, a man marrying his brother's widow etc. The Elders were also aligned with the priests and Pharisees.

The Sanhedrin was the supreme religious council or tribunal, which controlled civil and religious law. It was made up of priests, Sadducees, scribes and Pharisees. Its meetings were made either of twenty-three or seventy-one members.

The clergy had incredible power because they were the custodians of God's Law; they could also block someone from accessing the synagogue.

Let's now continue with,
"What led to the death of Jesus Christ?"

During Christ's third and final year of active mission on earth, the Jewish clergy felt that they were being progressively marginalised due to a new rising star, Jesus Christ, who was also openly hostile to them and whose popularity was increasing with every passing day. He had to be stopped. See **Matthew 5:20, Matthew 15:1-9, Mark 12:38-40, and Luke 18:11**.

With the resurrection of Lazarus, many people put their faith in Jesus, making him even more popular; this miracle was undeniable proof that he was a prophet. Jesus became so popular that the Pharisees dared not arrest him in public, for fear of the public's reaction. See **Mathew 21: 45-46;** When the chief priests and the Pharisees heard his illustrations; (The Parable of the Two Sons and The Parable of the Tenants), they knew that he (Jesus), was speaking about them. Although they wanted to seize him, they feared the crowds, because they regarded him as a prophet.

The Pharisees and scribes had the competence of teaching the public, God's Law, but they were the most crooked beings alive. According to Jesus, see; **Mathew 23:1-3**; *"The Scribes and the Pharisees have seated themselves in the seat of Moses,"* Jesus acknowledged that they were responsible for teaching the public, God's Law/The Law of Moses, but then he goes on to say: "So you must be careful to do everything they tell you. **But do not do what they do, for they do not practise what they preach."**

In almost all of **Mathew chapter 23,** Jesus denounces the scribes and Pharisees in public for what they really were, evil people, who were always trying to impress the public with their self-righteousness.

The popularity of Jesus was not the only grudge the Jewish clergy had against him. The clergy was envious of Jesus; he knew the scriptures better and preached better than them, although no one had taught him, hence none of the clergy or their institutions could take credit for it. When Jesus preached, people were enchanted by the word of God, See; **John 7: 14-15** & **John 7:45-48.** They also envied Jesus because he was able to perform miracles. **See Matthew 12:22-24.**

The Pharisees and the scribes often interrogated Jesus to test his knowledge of The Law, in a bid to humiliate him if he failed to give the correct answer. See: **Luke 11: 53-54; Matthew 22: 15-17 & 34-36,** but Jesus **always** got it right. On one of these occasions and tired of their constant interrogations, Jesus asked them a question, to which they could not reply. From that day on, they never asked Jesus any more questions. See **Matthew 22: 41-46**.

Jesus was repeatedly accused of breaking the Law by the Pharisees or some other person involved in religious matters. However, he **always** managed to give a sensible and legal explanation and always got it right. See the following example, when Jesus had just healed a crippled woman in **Luke 13: 10-17**; But in response, the presiding officer of the synagogue, indignant because Jesus did the cure on the Sabbath, said to the crowd: *"There are six days on which work ought to be done; so come and be cured on those days, and not on the Sabbath day."* However, Jesus answered him: *"Hypocrites, does not each one of you on the Sabbath untie his bull or his donkey from the stall and lead it away to give it something to drink? Should not this woman, who is a daughter of Abraham and whom Satan held bound for 18 years, be released from this bondage on the Sabbath day?"* Well, when he said these things, all his opposers began to feel shame, but the entire crowd began to rejoice at all the glorious things he did.

Jesus explained to the crowd, including the Pharisees, why he was doing miracles on the Sabbath; see **John 5: 17-18:** But Jesus answered them, *"To this very day My Father is at His work, and I too am working."* This is why the Jews (the clergy), began seeking all the more to kill him, because not only was he breaking the Sabbath, but he was also calling God, his own Father, making himself equal to God. Judaism does not believe that God has a Son, therefore, making such a claim would have been considered as blasphemy.

John 5: 1-19; "Very truly I tell you, the Son can do nothing by himself; he can do only what he sees his Father doing because whatever the Father does, the Son also does."

Jesus testified that God is at work on the Sabbath, that is the Sabbath applies only to man, because God is always at work whenever He likes, He is above the Sabbath. In another incident where the disciples of Jesus were accused by the Pharisees of working on the Sabbath because they had picked a few heads of grains in the fields and eaten them, Jesus gave the following reply to the Pharisees: **Matthew 12:8;** *"For the Son of Man is Lord even of the Sabbath."*

The priests in the Jewish communities were permitted to work on the Sabbath by Law, because they were administering sacred services to God. By doing miracles on a Sabbath, Jesus was doing acts that glorified God; the crowds who witnessed his miracles and the people healed glorified God; he was rendering sacred service to God, just like the priests.

To conclude, the main reason for getting rid of Jesus was that the clergy was in fear of losing public support in favour of Jesus, whose popularity was increasing each day.

25

Conspiracy to kill Jesus Christ

The decision to put Jesus to death was taken after he performed a miracle of resurrecting a man called Lazarus, who had been dead and buried for four days; see **John 11: 38-44.** When some Pharisees were informed about this miracle of Lazarus, they called for a Sanhedrin, a tribunal of rabbis. A rabbi is a Jewish teacher of the Law and religion.

See; **John 11: 47-50**; So, the chief priests and the Pharisees gathered the Sanhedrin together and said: *"What are we to do, for this man performs many signs? If we let him go on this way, they will all put faith in him, and the Romans will come and take away both our place and our nation."* But one of them, Caiaphas, who was high priest that year, said to them: *"You do not know anything at all, and you have not reasoned that it is to your benefit for one man to die on behalf of the people rather than for the whole nation to be destroyed."*

The meeting of the Sanhedrin, as officially reported, see above, had just one aim, to find a legal basis for the arrest and murder of an innocent man: Jesus Christ. This Sanhedrin was equating the miracles performed by Jesus as a means of acquiring converts, with the final purpose of gaining political consent and power; to resist the rule of Rome. **This was a deliberate misinterpretation of Christ's miracles, but it served their purpose, that of getting rid of Jesus.** The Sanhedrin condemned Jesus to death, in his absence, without any hearing at all, breaking its own rules. **See John 7:50-51**.

The deliberate distortion of the miracles performed by Jesus is obvious: first, Jesus did not do miracles to get political consent from people; he did not harbour any political ambition, he shunned politics. Jesus had never shown any hostility towards the foreign Rulers of Judea, that is, the Romans. See; **John 6: 14-17** and **Luke 20:20-26** he was not engaged in any kind of resistance to the Roman rule.

Note, however, that at the time of Jesus, there existed in Judea some groups of armed resistance against the rule of Rome, but some high-ranking Israelites, such as Caiaphas the High Priest, did not approve of their activity. They feared that if the resistance to Roman rule increased, it might have led Rome to retaliate and destroy the nation of Israel.

According to the Jewish scriptures, the Messiah was supposed to deliver the Jews from oppression, but the Jewish clergy in Christ's time had never acknowledged Jesus as the Messiah or even as a prophet. In **John 9: 18-23 and John 12:42** it says that; it had been made known that anyone acknowledging Jesus as Messiah, would be expelled from the synagogue; obviously by the Jewish Clergy.

Matthew 26: 4; writes regarding this meeting of the Sanhedrin: *"They conspired together to seize Jesus by cunning and to kill him,"* and he is correct; this meeting's aim was to plot how to get rid of Jesus. In fact, Mathew goes on to say, **Matthew 26: 5**; however, they were saying: *"Not at the festival, (i.e. they did not want to arrest Jesus, at the Passover Festival, which, was soon approaching), so that there may not be a riot among the people."*

The clergy feared that people might riot because many people had put faith in Jesus and regarded him as a prophet.

The scriptures say in **John 12: 10-11**; "The chief priests now conspired to kill Lazarus also, since it was because of him that many of the Jews were going there and putting faith in Jesus." People went to see Lazarus because they wanted to verify for themselves what they had heard; that a miracle had brought him back to life, four days after his death. This particular miracle created a surge of converts in favour of Jesus, but for the Jewish clergy, it created fear.

Matthew 21: 10-11; And when he entered Jerusalem, a few days before his crucifixion, the whole city was in an uproar, saying: "Who is this?" The crowds kept saying, "This is the prophet Jesus, from Nazareth of Galilee!"

A large crowd that had come to the festival of the Passover, heard that Jesus was coming to Jerusalem. Many people had believed in Jesus after he had raised Lazarus from the dead and it was these new believers, who went out to meet Jesus, hailing and cheering him, while entering the city of Jerusalem.

People took branches of palm trees and went out to meet Jesus, while he was entering the city of Jerusalem and they began to shout:

"Hosanna (save we pray) to the Son of David!"

"Blessed is he who comes in Jehovah's name!"

"Hosanna in the highest heaven!"

John 12: 19; So, the Pharisees said among themselves: "See, this is getting us nowhere. Look how the whole world has gone after him!"

Hosanna means save, rescue, Saviour. In the Hebrew Bible it is used as: "help," or "save, I pray," **Psalms 118:25**. Hosanna as used in the Gospels, means, special honour to the one who saves, literal interpretation is "save now."

Jesus arrived in the temple of Jerusalem, accompanied by a large crowd of followers. In **Matthew 21:12-13**: On arriving, Jesus entered the temple; he threw out all those involved in commercial activities, inside the temple, saying: "It is written, *My house will be called a house of prayer," but you are making it a cave of robbers.*" This act of kicking out merchants from the Temple of Jerusalem was a direct challenge to the temple's authority because it is this same authority that had, in the first place, authorized this commercial activity. Later, the chief priests and the elders challenged Jesus regarding this issue, that is, they wanted to find out, who had given him the authority to kick traders from the temple, but Jesus snubbed them, see **Mathew 21: 23-27.**

Once inside the temple, the presence of Jesus overshadowed every other activity there, to the dismay of the chief priests. **Matthew 21:12-16**; Also, blind and lame people came to him in the temple and he cured them. When the chief priests and the scribes saw the marvellous things he did and the boys who were shouting in the temple, "Save, we pray, the Son of David!" they became indignant and said to him, "Do you hear what these are saying?" Jesus said to them, "Yes. Did you never read this, 'Out of the mouth of children and infants, you have brought forth praise'?"

Therefore, the main reason for conspiring and eventually killing Jesus Christ was that he was perceived as a menace to the clergy's authority. Jesus was highly critical of the Jewish clergy of his time and towards the end of his life, many people were acknowledging him as a prophet; his popularity was skyrocketing, and this is why his removal had become even more urgent.

26

The Last Supper

The parting counsel of Jesus to his apostles during his last meal.

The last meal Jesus had with his apostles was a special meal; it also happened to be the Passover Meal. In Judaism, the Passover Meal is eaten in remembrance of the liberation of the Jewish people from their slavery in the land of Egypt. It was during this Passover Meal, that Jesus instituted a ritual to be performed in the remembrance of his death, the Eucharist, the Holy Communion or the Memorial, by requesting his apostles to always perform this ritual, in **remembrance of the sacrifice of his life, for the redemption of mankind.**

Luke 22: 19, says: Also, he took a loaf, gave thanks, broke it, and gave it to them, saying: "*This means my body, which is to be given in your behalf. Keep doing this in remembrance of me.*"

Please take note that this meal took place during the Jewish Passover Meal and therefore as part of that particular meal. The Passover meal occurs once a year and as written earlier on, it serves to commemorate the day the Jewish people were liberated from slavery in the land of Egypt. God had requested the Israelites to commemorate their delivery from slavery in Egypt, by eating the Passover Meal **once a year**. Most likely Jesus meant that we Christians should commemorate his death only once a year, because, on this particular day, his death would have freed man from sin, forever.

In Judaism, the Passover Meal starts in the evening, usually at sunset. Also, in Judaism, a day starts at sunset and ends at the next sunset. Jesus was dead before the next day's sunset; therefore, the Last Meal took place on the same day on which Jesus died.

The apostle John in his scripture does not give details of the ritual regarding the Last Meal, whereby Jesus instituted the sacrament of the Holy Communion. Instead, he writes of all the other things that took place that evening and especially the discussion that went on between Jesus and his apostles. It is clear that the apostle John regarded this last evening with Jesus, (just the evening, excluding the rest of the day), as extremely important, because **he has dedicated to it five whole chapters: chapters 13 to 17, of his twenty-one chapters of scripture**.

I will write a brief summary of the Last Supper, according to the apostle John, only.

During the last supper with his apostles, Jesus emphasized several important points: Jesus started that evening by washing the feet of his apostles; see **John13: 1-17**; a task usually reserved for slaves or servants, to underline an important point; that they should take care of each other, and no task should be considered too low for any of them when it comes to providing support and care for each other. **If Jesus who was their master could wash their feet, why should any of them consider such a task too low for them?** In other words, they should adopt an attitude of humble service and support towards each other at all levels, because of the love they have and should have, for each other. Among Christ's apostles, only John wrote of this particular episode in which Jesus washed the feet of his apostles.

After washing the feet of his apostles, Jesus reclined at the table and the evening meal proceeded. Jesus had previously warned his disciples against toxic competition for power among themselves; see **Mark 9: 33-35** and **Mark 10: 35-45.** This washing of feet was also meant to address this particular issue. The apostle John says that, shortly after Jesus had handed a piece of bread to Judas, telling him: "What you are doing, do it more quickly," Satan entered Judas, who went out in order to betray Jesus. It seems, according to the apostle John, that Judas left in the early phase of the evening meal.

As the evening meal proceeded, Jesus gave them a new commandment: **John 13: 34-35**; *"I am giving you a new commandment, that you love one another; just as I have loved you, you also love one another. By this, all will know that you are my disciples—if you have love among yourselves."* Jesus repeated this point several times throughout that evening. See **John 15:12, 17.**

In **John, chapter 14,** Jesus informed his apostles that he would be leaving them definitely. Jesus then reassured them and informed them of the steps he had taken to support them after his departure. **He was comforting his apostles** because they were very sad to hear that he would be leaving them.

Jesus started his discussion by underlining one fact, the necessity for his apostles to exercise faith and complete confidence in him and his Father, therefore, not to worry about the fact that he would be leaving them, because;

John 14:3-4; *"Also, if I go my way and prepare a place for you, I will come again and will receive you home to myself, so that where I am you also may be. And where I am going, you know the way."*

His apostles now started acknowledging for the first time, that Jesus would actually be leaving them because Jesus starts to talk of what will happen when he leaves them; see **John 14:2** *"My Father's house has many rooms; if that were not so, would I have told you that I am going there to prepare a place for you?"*

Jesus had previously spoken to his apostles several times about his forthcoming departure, but they had been in denial and had refused to believe it. However, now it was quite clear that Jesus was leaving them, definitely. The apostles felt bewildered and were in a bit of panic; how would they cope without Jesus? He had been at the centre of their lives for the last three years.

Previously, Jesus had spoken of "His Father" constantly but none of his apostles had ever requested him to show them this person, because they knew that Jesus was referring to God and were just content to have Jesus with them. Now in a state of distress and panic, because Jesus had just informed them that he was going to The Father definitely and they did not know how they could get into contact with Jesus once he had departed, Phillip, one of his apostles, asked Jesus to **show them**, "The Father" and Thomas, another apostle, pointed out to Jesus that **they really did not know "the way**," to where he would be going, that is they wanted Jesus to leave them his contact address.

Jesus replied to Phillip by telling him that actually, he already knew "The Father," because he, Phillip, had lived with Jesus now for quite a while and had seen Jesus active in his mission, preaching and doing miracles, all of which were directed by The Father; "who remains in union with me and is doing his works."

"I will not leave you bereaved. I am coming to you." In a little while the world will see me no more, but you will see me, ..." In **John 14:18-19,** Jesus informed his apostles that he would be coming back specifically for them after his resurrection, but they did not understand him. Jesus informed his apostles that, in support of his absence, He and His Father would still be with them, spiritually; **John 14: 20**, besides, Jesus would request the Father to send a Helper/The Spirit of the Truth/The Holy Spirit, to them. Regarding the Holy Spirit, Jesus says; I quote: **John 14: 16-17**: *"You know **it,** because **it** remains in you and is in you."* In some Bibles, this verse is written as: "But you know **him**, for **he** lives with you and will be in you."

Please note: The Holy Spirit has different names in different bibles: The Helper, The advocate, The Comforter and The Spirit of the Truth; all these names represent the Holy Spirit. As I have written above, the Holy Spirit is God's active presence, God's active force.

The Helper would illuminate their minds, concerning what he had taught them. Jesus repeated this fact several times that night: **John 14: 16-17 and 26, John 15:26 John 16:12-15.**

Then Jesus informed his apostles that they would be granted whatever they requested His Father, through his name and Jesus repeated this fact, several times that night: **John, 14: 13-14; John 15:16; John 16:23.**

John 14: 15, 21, 23: if **they obeyed his commandments**, all the above would take place, because they would remain in his love and therefore in the love of his Father.

In **John chapter 14:20**; *"In that day you will know that I am in union with my Father and you are in union with me and I am in union with you."*

Through the above statement, Jesus makes it very clear, the spiritual nature of God, because it is the only way that this verse makes sense. Lastly, in order to overcome this world's fears and troubles, Jesus, gave a special gift of peace, (not as the world gives it), to his disciples, **(John 14: 27)**.

In Chapter 15, Jesus primed his disciples about their forthcoming mission. Jesus informed his apostles that he had chosen them from the world, and therefore they are not part of it. He forewarns them that they would become objects of hatred and persecution and their mission would not be an easy ride, however: *"if they have persecuted me, they will also persecute you; if they have observed my word, they will also observe yours,"* in other words, his apostles would also have success in their mission. See **John 15:20.**

Jesus informed his apostles, why he chose them: *"I appointed you to go and keep bearing fruit and that your fruit should remain. You are to bear witness about me and therefore about the Father, (Jesus represents the Father), because you have been with me from the beginning."*

Chapter 15 starts with the parable of The True Grapevine and Jesus then explains its significance to his apostles. Jesus started by informing his apostles, that "They must bear fruit" that is teach others of the kingdom and make converts of them. This would be possible only if they kept his word and relied on his teachings, because "no branch can bear fruit by itself; it must remain in the vine, that is, in line with his teachings." Take note, that the teachings of Jesus came from His Father, so if they followed his teachings, they would be following the teachings of God, Himself.

John 15:1-2; "I am the true vine, and my Father is the cultivator and gardener. He takes away every branch in me not bearing fruit, and he prunes every one bearing fruit, so that it may bear more fruit."

- In **James 2:14**; What does it profit, my brethren, if someone says he has faith but does not have works? Can faith save him?

- **James 2: 19-20**; You believe that there is one God. You do well. Even the demons believe—and tremble! But do you want to know, O foolish man, that faith without works is dead?

- **Matthew 5:16**; Likewise, let your light shine before men, so that they may see your fine works and give glory to your Father who is in the heavens.

John 15:8; "My Father is glorified in this, that you keep bearing much fruit and prove yourselves my disciples."

Jesus informed his apostles that, if they needed anything at all, for this their mission, it would have been granted to them by The Father, because their success in "bearing fruit" was ultimately to his glory, therefore, God would sustain them in their mission. On the other hand, if they did not bear fruit, they would be destroyed; *"Anyone who does not remain in union with me, is like a branch, that is thrown away and withers, such branches are picked up and thrown into the fire and burned."* **John 15:6.**

The teachings of Jesus are truth and life, in that they lead to eternal life; on the other hand, living independently of these teachings will surely lead you astray into the hands of Satan and death, **to being excluded from eternal life and finally to**

destruction. See **John 8: 31-32**; Jesus was preaching in the temple courts, and he made this statement: *"If you hold on to my teaching, if you remain faithful to my teaching, then, you are really my disciples. Then you will know the truth and the truth will set you free."* Free from what? **John 8:34**: Jesus replied, "Very truly I tell you, everyone who sins is a slave to sin." That is, one is a slave because he is bound by sin and cannot free himself from sin, that is why he keeps sinning.

The teachings of Jesus are the word of God because Jesus was directed by his Father and his teachings would free you from ignorance, they would illuminate your mind and free you from uncertainty about what is right or wrong, they would free you from sin and therefore, free you in order to worship God.

See **John 17:7**; "Sanctify them by means of the truth; your word is truth."

In **John 15:12 & 17**; **Jesus points out to his apostles that he is commanding them, not requesting them, to love one another,** just as he himself has loved them, He then quotes **John 15:13**; *"Greater love has no one than this: to lay down one's life for one's friends*. Consequently, he told his apostles that he considered them to be his friends because he had revealed to them all the things he heard from His Father; **John 15: 15**. Generally, you will reveal intimate things, for example, what your father tells you, only to your friends and not to your slaves or servants.

Jesus also condemned the unbelievers: **John 15: 22-24**; If I had not come and spoken to them, they would not be guilty of sin; but now they have no excuse for their sin. Whoever hates me, hates my Father as well. If I had not done among them the works no one else did, they would not be guilty of sin. As it is, they have seen, and yet they have hated both me and my Father. **John 15:25**; "But this is to fulfil what is written in their Law. They hated me without reason."

In chapter 16; Jesus forewarned his apostles of the fact that they would be seriously persecuted and even killed on account of his name so that they would be aware of what to expect in the future.

See **John 14: 28:** *"You heard that I said to you, "I am going away and I am coming back to you. If you loved me, you would be glad that I am going to the Father, for the Father is greater than I."* See also: **John 16: 16**: *"In a little while you will see me no longer, and again, in a little while you will see me."* Jesus was telling his apostles that he would die in a short while, but then, he would resurrect to life and they would all see him alive, again, but they did not understand him. See **John 16:22**: *"So with you: Now is your time of grief, but I will see you again and you will rejoice, and no one will take away your joy."*

Jesus again, made it clear to his apostles, that his earthly mission as a representative of his Father was now over and he would be going back to his Father, definitely; **John 16: 28**; *"I came from the Father and entered the world; now I am leaving the world and going back to the Father."*

The apostles in turn, informed Jesus, that it was now clear to them, that he had come from God, but Jesus told them, that in a short while, **they would all abandon him**, that is they would soon be in doubt if he really came from God, but Jesus lets them know that he would not be alone, despite them abandoning him, because his Father would be with him.

Jesus concluded by saying, **John 16: 33**; *"In this world you will have tribulation* (great suffering/great trouble), *But take heart! /Be of good cheer! /Have confidence! I have conquered the world."*

In chapter 17, the apostle John writes of the last prayers Jesus made, in the presence of his apostles.

First, Jesus requested God to sustain him, to accomplish his mission in this last phase of his life. "Father, the hour has come. Glorify your Son, that your Son may glorify you. For you granted him authority over all people that he might give eternal life to all those you have given him. This means everlasting life, their coming to know you, **the only true God, and the one whom you sent, Jesus Christ**."

Jesus then prayed for his apostles requesting his Father to protect them from the Evil One and to sanctify them: **John 17:17**; "*Sanctify them by your truth, your word is truth*."

Jesus also prayed for the unity of his apostles and also for the unity of the future Christian Church; **John 17: 20-21**; "*I make a request, not concerning these only, but also concerning those putting faith in me through their word, so that they may all be one, just as you, Father, are in union with me and I am in union with you, that they also may be in union with us, so that the world may believe that you sent me.*"

Lastly, Jesus requested his Father; **John 17:24;** "Father, I want those whom you have given me to be with me where I am, so that they may look upon my glory, that you have given me."

To conclude, Jesus spent the last moments with his apostles, **comforting them, instructing them and praying for them.** Then Jesus went out with them to the Garden of Gethsemane, where he was eventually arrested.

Jesus had known for a long time when and how he was going to die.

In the last period of his life, Jesus had informed his apostles several times of his impending death, but they did not accept it; it seemed impossible to them, that anybody could kill "The Son of God."

For example, when Jesus informed his disciples that shortly he would be going to Jerusalem, where he would die, one of his apostles, Peter, thought he was just feeling a bit depressed and sought to comfort him; see below.

Matthew 16: 21-23. From that time on, Jesus began to explain to his disciples that he must go to Jerusalem and suffer many things at the hands of the elders, the chief priests and the teachers of Law and that he must be killed and on the third day be raised to life. But Peter, one of Christ's most outspoken apostles, reacted in this manner: Peter took him (Jesus) aside and began to rebuke him; *"Never Lord!"* he said, *"This shall never happen to you!"*

Jesus turned and said to Peter, *"Get away from me, Satan! You are a dangerous trap to me/a stumbling block to me. You are seeing things merely from a human point of view, not from God's."*

Here are some instances where Jesus foretells his forthcoming death.

Matthew 16: 21-22; Matthew 17: 22-23; Matthew 20: 17-19; Matthew 26:2

Mark 8: 31; Mark 9: 31 and Mark 10: 33-34Luke 9: 22; Luke 17:25; Luke18: 31-33

27

The death of Jesus Christ

Two days before the Passover Feast, one of Jesus' apostles, Judas Iscariot went to the chief priests and stipulated a deal, whereby he offered to bring them to Jesus when opportune; when he was isolated and free from the presence of the public, and he was paid 30 pieces of silver for this deal.

This opportunity presented itself on the evening of the Passover Feast. According to the Jewish tradition, every Israelite was bound to be at home, eating their Passover meal, to celebrate a most special day when Israel was freed from slavery, in Egypt. This meant, there would be no crowd at all, in any place, on that particular evening and night.

While Jesus was having his Passover meal with his twelve apostles, Judas Iscariot, one of his apostles, went out to the chief priests to betray Jesus, by bringing them to where he was. After the Passover meal, Jesus and his apostles went to the garden in Gethsemane, where they often met, but on this particular night, Jesus had gone there to pray, because he already knew what was about to happen to him; he was about to be betrayed and arrested and by the end of this particular day, he would be dead. In Judaism, the day starts at sunset and ends the next sunset, therefore, a new day had just started when Jesus and his disciples were having their last meal together.

Jesus said to the disciples, "Sit down here while I go over there and pray." And taking along Peter and the two sons of Zebedee, James and John, he began to feel grieved and to be greatly troubled.

Jesus had known for a long time that he was going to die and how he was going to die; he had predicted his death many times;

but now when the moment arrived, he needed support from his father and that is why, he was now praying. I do not believe Jesus was afraid of the ordeal that awaited him, most probably; he was praying to be able to restrain his Godly powers and to allow this final phase of his life to happen as programmed by his Father.

There was a real possibility of Jesus derailing from his main mission on earth; of failing to fulfil his mission; that of dying to redeem man from sin. Therefore, Jesus is now praying for support from his Father, to submit to what His Father had requested and required him to do.

Jesus had a choice, a free will, he could have refused to be crucified, but instead, he chose to restrain his Godly powers and to do what His Father had requested him; he chose to obey His Father; to submit to His Father's will. **Matthew 26: 42; Jesus prayed**, *"My Father if it is not possible for this cup to be taken away unless I drink it, may your will be done."*

After spending some time in prayer, Jesus was strengthened to face his tribulation. The three apostles who had accompanied Jesus to pray were unable to keep vigil on this very special night and had fallen fast asleep, after having had their evening Passover meal.

Jesus was ready when Judas, one of his apostles, who was also his betrayer, showed up and with him, a large crowd with swords and clubs, sent from the chief priests and the elders of the people. Judas went up to Jesus and gave him a kiss on the cheek, saying, "Greetings Rabbi." That evening, it had been agreed between Judas and the chief priests' crowd, that the person he kissed, should be the one taken into custody.

The apostle John does not mention the kiss of betrayal from Judas, but he says: "Now Judas, his betrayer, also knew the place, because Jesus had often met there with his disciples. So, Judas brought the detachment of soldiers and officers of the chief priests and the Pharisees and they came there with torches and lamps and weapons." Therefore, the apostle John also identifies Judas as a traitor.

Peter, one of Christ's apostles, noting the hostility from this crowd, drew his sword and cut off the ear of a slave to the High Priest. Christ ordered Peter to put away his sword, saying: *"Those who take up the sword will perish by the sword. Or do you think that I cannot **appeal to my Father** to supply me at this moment more than 12 legions of angels? In that case, how would the Scriptures be fulfilled that say it must take place this way?"* Jesus touched the slave's injured ear and it healed instantly; therefore, Jesus still had his Godly powers, but he chose not to use them in self-defence.

Christ did not resist his arrest, but he made a request that his apostles should be left free to go; none of Christ's apostles was arrested. All of Jesus' apostles fled, except Peter, but he too left later and abandoned Jesus.

In **John 16: 32** Jesus foretold their betrayal: *"Look! The hour is coming, indeed, it has come, when each one of you will be scattered to his own house and you will leave me alone. But I am not alone, because the Father is with me."*

When Jesus was arrested, **he had a choice, a free will, that is he could have** refused to get crucified, and he could easily have overcome and subdued his enemies, but he chose to restrain his Godly powers and submit to His Father's will, in order to accomplish his mission on earth.

Jesus' apostles could not understand why Jesus had not used his "super-powers" to stop his arrest; they knew the capabilities of Jesus because they themselves had witnessed Jesus do numerous glorious miracles. If Jesus was the Son of God, why did he allow these people to arrest him? The apostles were in shock after the arrest of their master; what future did they have now that Jesus had been arrested? If they were able to arrest their Master, they too were in danger of being arrested.

Jesus was arrested while in Jerusalem, to celebrate the Feast of the Passover. He was first taken to Ananias a chief priest then transferred to the courtyard of the High Priest, Caiaphas.

Now the chief priests and the entire Sanhedrin were looking for a testimony against Jesus **to put him to death** but did not find any. Jesus was **arrested with no evidence of wrongdoing**. A few testimonies showed up, but whatever evidence they gave, it was not sufficient to condemn Jesus to death. Finally, (**Matthew 26:63-68**) the High Priest exasperated, due to lack of evidence and because Jesus was silent in front of all his accusers said: "I put you under oath by the living God to tell us whether you are the Christ, the Son of God! Jesus replied to him: "*You yourself said it. But I say to you: From now on you will see the Son of man sitting at the right hand of power and coming on the clouds of heaven.*" The term "*You yourself said it,*" is an affirmation, equivalent to, "*That's correct.*" Then the high priest, Caiaphas, ripped his outer garments, saying: "*He has blasphemed! What further need do we have of witnesses? See! Now you have heard the blasphemy. What is your opinion?*" They answered: "*He deserves to die.*" Then they spat in his face and hit him with their fists. Others slapped him on the face, saying: "*Prophesy to us, you Messiah. Who struck you?*"

Jesus provided the evidence required to put him to death, by admitting that he was the Son of God. God identifies Himself as, "the truth," Christ represents God, and therefore, he too represents, "the truth." Jesus could not deny the fact that he was the Son of God, he was honoured to be a "Representative of his Father" right to the end of his life.

Please note: In all his lifetime, Jesus Christ never claimed to be God; the only claim Jesus made was that he was the Son of God.

When Jesus was born and during his lifetime, Judea, Samaria, Galilee, Decapolis and Syria were all part of the Roman Empire. When Jesus was arrested while in Jerusalem and consequently prosecuted, the province of Judea was governed by a Roman governor, Pontius Pilate, who also had the competence to preside over important trials.

When morning came, (after Jesus had been arrested the night before), all the chief priests and the elders of the people, after binding him, led him off and handed him over to Pilate, the governor.

The Jewish clergy realised that Pilate would never have sentenced anyone to death for "making himself like God," that is, blasphemy, which was their main accusation against Jesus, therefore, they modified their charge against Jesus to one which would definitely lead to death; they accused Jesus of undermining the rule of Rome, sedition, which was a very serious crime punishable by death. What the clergy really wanted was Jesus dead and extinct, no longer a menace to their authority.

See; **Luke 23: 1-5**; So, the multitude got up, one and all, and led him to Pilate. Pontius Pilate came outside, to the courtyard, of his office. The chief priests then started accusing Jesus of many things; *"We found this man subverting our nation, forbidding the paying of taxes to Caesar, and saying he himself is the Messiah, a king."* Now Pilate asked Jesus the question: "Are you the King of the Jews?" In answer, he said, "You yourself are saying it," meaning: "**It is as you say it**." Then Pilate said to the chief priests and the crowds: **"I find no crime in this man."** But they insisted, saying: *"He stirs up the people by teaching throughout all Judea, starting from Galilee even to here."*

Note: Although Jesus admitted to being a king, Pilate did not find him guilty of what he had been accused of, stirring up people to rebel against Rome.

Pilate observed the man brought in front of him; calm and collected, dressed in a simple manner not adorned like "earthly kings" then he observed the clergy vehemently accusing him of all sorts of things; instinctively, he realised that this man had been framed. Contrary to the allegations brought against him, Jesus did not present any hostility towards him, he being a first-class representative of the Roman authority in Judea. If Jesus had been fighting Rome, his attitude towards Pilate would have been very different.

See **John 18: 31**; *"So Pilate said to them: "Take him yourselves and judge him according to your law." The Jews said to him: "It is not lawful for us to execute anyone."* The clergy had already decided that Jesus had to be executed, by accusing him of sabotaging the rule of Rome, but only the Roman governor was authorized by law, to give capital punishment; this is why they refused to judge Jesus, themselves.

The **scriptures say in Mathew 27:18 and Mark 15: 10**: "Pilate was well aware that out of envy the chief priests had handed Jesus over," and this is why he kept trying to find a way to release him.

Just then, as Pilate was sitting on the judgment seat, his wife sent him this message: **See Matthew 27:19** *"Leave that innocent man alone. I suffered through a terrible nightmare about him last night."* However, Pilate had already understood, all by himself, even without his wife's message, that Jesus was innocent.

So, in **John 18: 33-35,** Pilate entered the governor's residence again and called Jesus and said to him: "Are you the King of the Jews?" Jesus answered: "Are you asking this of your own originality, or did others tell you about me?" Pilate replied: *"I am not a Jew, am I? Your own nation and the chief priests handed you over to me. What did you do?"*

And Jesus answered; **John 18:36;** *"My Kingdom is no part of this world. If my Kingdom were part of this world, my attendants would have fought that I should not be handed over to the Jewish leader. But as it is, my Kingdom is not from this source."*

John 18: 37-38; So, Pilate said to him: "Well, then, are you a king?" Jesus answered: "You yourself are saying that I am a king." This is an affirmation, equivalent to: **"It is as you say it. For this,**

I have been born, and for this, I have come into the world, that I should bear witness to the truth. Everyone who is on the side of the truth listens to my voice." Pilate said to him: "What is truth?" With this, he went out again to the Jews gathered there and said, "I find no basis for a charge against him."

According to the apostle Mark, once Jesus had accepted that he was a king, he did not reply to any more questions from Pilate; **Mark 15:4-5**: Now Pilate began questioning him again, saying: "Have you no reply to make? See how many charges they are bringing against you." But Jesus made no further answer so Pilate was amazed. Pilate then went outside into the courtyard, after interrogating Jesus and gave his own opinion to the Jews: **"I find no fault in him." (John 18: 38**).

Pilate then tried mediating the release of Jesus, by offering an alternative solution to the problem: (**John 18: 39-40**); "*Moreover, you have a custom that I should release a man to you at the Passover. So do you want me to release to you, the King of the Jews*?" Again, they shouted: "*Not this man, but Barabbas!*" Now Barabbas had taken part in an uprising.

According to the apostle Mark, I quote **Mark 15: 7**; "*At the time the man named Barabbas was in prison with the seditionists, who had committed murder in the uprising.*"

Sedition is: conduct or speech inciting people to rebel against the authority of a state or monarch.

During this period of the trial of Jesus Christ, there was actually an element of insurgence against Roman rule among some Jews. And this is why a charge of sedition was plausible against Jesus. Barnabas, the guy who was released from prison in preference to Jesus, was one of these rebels, as one of the charges for his imprisonment, was sedition.

Luke 23: 13-14; Pilate then called together the chief priests, the rulers, and the people and said to them: "You brought this man to me as one inciting the people to revolt. Now look! I examined him in front of you but found in this man no grounds for the charges you are bringing against him."

In **John 19: 12-16;** Pilate kept seeking a way to release Jesus, but the Jews shouted: *"If you release this man, you are not a friend of Caesar. Everyone who makes himself a king speaks against Caesar."* Then Pilate, after hearing these words, brought Jesus outside, and he sat down on a judgment seat in a place called the Stone Pavement, but in Hebrew, *Gabbatha.*

Now it was the Preparation Day of the Passover, and about the sixth hour. And he said to the Jews, *"Behold your King!"* But they shouted, *"Take him away! Take him away! Crucify him!"* Pilate said to them, *"Shall I execute your king?"* The chief priests answered, *"We have no king but Caesar!"* Then, he delivered Jesus to them to be crucified. They then took Jesus and led him away.

Now, no man could be a king in the Roman Empire, without the consent of Caesar. In **John 18:36;** "My kingdom is not part of this world," Jesus admits that he is a king. Pontius Pilate acknowledged that Jesus was innocent and that "The kingdom of Jesus," which is not part of this world, could not have been a serious threat to Rome, because, after interrogating Jesus, who admitted that his kingdom is not part of this world, Pilate went out to the crowds and said, "*I find no fault in him,*" **John 18: 38.**

Pontius Pilate found himself alone in defending Jesus, against a huge, wild, hostile crowd, incited by the Jewish clergy. It was Pilate's responsibility to uphold justice in the territories under the command of Rome; anyone in his jurisdiction, who challenged the authority of Rome, had to be dealt with very seriously. According to Roman Law, the correct, or let's say the legal punishment by law, for subverting the rule of Rome, was crucifixion, a most agonizing and humiliating type of capital punishment where one would have a slow and painful death, in full view of all the public; so that all could see and learn, what happens to those who dare to challenge Rome. This is why the priests and public were already shouting even before Pilate could pronounce his sentence: "Crucify him! Crucify him!" because they knew that the legal punishment for sedition was crucifixion.

When Pontius Pilate examined Jesus, he himself admitted that he did not find any fault in him, even when Jesus admitted that he was a king; see **Luke 23: 4, 14 and 22** and **John 18: 38** and consequently, Jesus did not merit to be executed. The only proof of the fact that Jesus had committed acts of sedition, came from the false testimony of the Jewish clergy and it was sufficient to condemn Jesus to death, though Jesus was innocent.

Pilate knew that it was his competence to uphold justice in his jurisdiction but if he had let Jesus go free, he would have lost the support of the High Priest, the Chief Priests, scribes and elders, who were "the cream" of the Jewish society. The clergy had a great influence over the Jewish public and the Jewish politicians, therefore, if he had ignored their requests, they might have ceased to collaborate with him and such a situation might have destabilized, his political position as governor. For example, without the intervention of the clergy, there might have been riots or civil disobedience, which might have led to Pilate being demoted or suffering other unpleasant consequences. Pontius Pilate decided to protect his own interests, by safeguarding his political career, instead of upholding justice and preventing the death of an innocent man.

According to **Matthew: 27: 24-25;** Seeing that it did no good, Pilate was trying to free Jesus, but rather an uproar was arising, Pilate took a bowl of water and washed his hands before the crowd, saying: "*I am innocent of the blood of this man. You yourselves must see to it!*" At that, all the people said in answer: "*Let his blood come upon us and upon our children.*" Then he released Barabbas to them, but he had Jesus whipped and handed him over to be executed on the stake, that is to be crucified.

When Pilate had Jesus whipped and then crucified, he was just following the normal praxis, the official procedure on how to punish those subverting Rome. Pilate then wrote a sign to be hung above Jesus on the cross; it was in Latin, Hebrew and Greek, showing the crime Jesus had been charged with: "Jesus the Nazarene, King of the Jews." **Therefore, the final charge of Jesus Christ, according to the Roman law, was death by crucifixion, for sedition.** It is worth noting that, although **Jesus had done only good works** while in Jerusalem, and elsewhere, there was a complete absence of any public support during his trial; **no one at all spoke up in his defence**. I believe this was due to the fact that people feared the clergy, and no one had the guts to come out publicly and oppose them, even during this particular trial.

See **John 12: 42-43**; All the same, many **even of the rulers** actually put faith in him, but they would not openly acknowledge him because of the Pharisees, so that they would not be expelled from the synagogue, for they loved the glory of men even more than the glory of God.

Now that Jesus had become famous for his miracles, it might be that many of the people attending his trial, had hoped to witness something spectacular, for example, a miraculous escape of Jesus from his execution, but this did not happen. **Matthew 27: 39-44;** describes how some people in the crowd were insulting and jeering at Jesus, inciting him to free himself, while he lay dying on the cross.

Before and after his crucifixion, Jesus underwent all kinds of humiliation; he was slapped, mocked, spat on etc. but did not defend himself from this mistreatment.

There were two other people, thieves, crucified alongside Jesus.

The last words of Jesus as recorded by the apostle Luke are in Luke 23:46; Jesus called out with a loud voice, "**Father, into**

your hands I commit my spirit" or "Father, into your hands I entrust my spirit." When he had said this, he breathed his last.

Dying by crucifixion in the Roman Empire was the ultimate of humiliation, a punishment reserved for the scum of society: despised enemies of the state, violent offenders, deserters, slaves, petty criminals, pirates and those committing high treason. The death of Jesus Christ was by public execution and although his apostles were absent, except the apostle who Jesus loved, **it was witnessed** by his mother and his mother's sister, disciples and acquaintances, for example, women from Galilee who had administered to him. **Matthew 27: 55-56; Luke 23: 49; Mark 15: 40-41** and **John 19: 25.**

The scripture of Luke talks of an eclipse of the sun, on the day Jesus died. **Luke 23:44;** Well, by now it was about the sixth hour, that is: midday according to Judaism and yet a darkness fell over all the land until the ninth hour.

After his crucifixion, Jesus died a few hours later, a soldier then pierced his chest to make double sure he was dead. It was not specified which side, but I would say the left side because that's where the heart is. The two thieves crucified with Jesus had their legs broken by the Roman soldiers to quicken their death. With legs broken, one cannot use the thigh muscles to support his weight on the cross, therefore all the weight will be supported by the outstretched arms. This position will make it impossible to expand the thoracic cage, to breathe. Also, the internal bleeding from the fractured legs and vasodilation from heat exposure, from the sun, would lead to hypovolemic shock and death.

Later that day, a man, Joseph of Arimathea, came and took down the corpse of Jesus from the cross, after being granted permission by Pontius Pilate, and transferred it into a new tomb**.**

Please note: **all four gospels testify that there was a corpse of Jesus Christ which was buried in a tomb, carved out of a rock**; see: **Matthew 27:57-61, Mark 15:42-47, Luke 23:50-54,**

John 19:38-42. Three of the Gospels, Matthew, Mark and Luke also write that some women from Galilee; two are named Mary Magdalene and Mary mother of the sons of Zebedee, those who administered to Jesus when he was alive, followed Joseph of Arimathea who buried Jesus and verified the burial site of Jesus. These women wanted to see where Jesus was buried because they planned to come later and embalm his body.

After the death of Jesus, the very next day was a Sabbath; the chief priests and Pharisees went to Pilate and requested permission to seal his tomb. See **Matthew 27: 62-66;** The next day, which was after the Preparation, i.e. the Sabbath, the chief priests and the Pharisees gathered together before Pilate, saying: "Sir, we recall what that impostor said while he was still alive, 'After three days I am to be raised up.' Therefore, command that the grave be made secure until the third day, so that his disciples may not come and steal him (his corpse) and say to the people, 'He was raised up from the dead!' Then this last deception will be worse than the first." Pilate said to them: "You may have a guard. Go make it as secure as you know how." So they went and made the grave secure by sealing the stone and posting a guard.

The clergy and Pharisees must have been well satisfied, that it would not have been possible to steal the corpse of Jesus after these measures; they could not tolerate the idea of Jesus being declared alive, after they themselves put him to death; it would have been too embarrassing.

The Pharisees had realized that should Jesus resurrect, their efforts to put him into extinction would have been nullified, because, he would now have acquired even more fame than when he was alive. The Pharisees and clergy had always believed that Jesus was pretending to be The Messiah, an imposter, they had never acknowledged that he was the real Messiah, but were not willing to take any risk; Jesus might have been the real Messiah.

In Israel, it was forbidden by Law to leave a dead body hanging up on a stake, throughout the night, after execution. See **Deut.**

21:22-23: "If someone has committed a crime worthy of death and is executed and their body is hung on a tree (or a pole), be sure to bury it that same day, because anyone who is hung on a pole or tree is under God's curse.

In the Israelite community, for anyone to be punished by hanging, one must have committed a very serious offence against the Law of God and therefore, the one hung up had to be, "something accursed of God."

The phrase: "because the one hung up is something accursed of God or under God's curse," could be interpreted by some to mean that the fact Jesus was crucified, means he himself was a curse to God.

The crime for which Jesus was hung up, was derived from false testimony, that of subverting the rule of Rome, and not for blasphemy or for breaching any of God's Law, therefore, he could never have been something accursed of God. Furthermore, the hanging of Jesus or his crucifixion was done by a foreign government, that did not know or follow the Law of Moses, but its own Law.

A human corpse left hanging would quickly rot and would have been a health hazard for any community and the sight was bound to been very distressing for any sensitive being. The man who committed the crime had already been punished and was already dead. Therefore, God orders the Israelites not to leave their dead hanging after an execution; it makes a lot of sense.

Jesus describes his death as "being lifted up" not as "being hung up." See **John 3:14**: And just as Moses lifted up the serpent in the wilderness, so the Son of man must be lifted up, so that]everyone believing in him may have everlasting life.

John 12:32; "And I, when I am lifted up from the earth, will draw all people unto myself."

See **Numbers 21:8-9**, where Moses lifted up a bronze serpent and saved the lives of those who looked upon it with faith.

See **Galatians 3:13**; Christ redeemed us from the curse of the law by becoming a curse for us, because it is written, cursed is everyone who is hung on a tree. This verse is referring to the fact that**: Jesus was crucified, for "the sins of the world," which are in effect, an offence and a curse to God."**

Well, each person is free to make their own interpretation regarding the significance of the act of crucifixion of Jesus; however, for us Christians, it is the actual death of Jesus Christ that is more important.

See **Deuteronomy 17: 1**: "You must not sacrifice to Jehovah your God a bull or a sheep that has a defect or anything wrong with it, for it would be detestable to Jehovah your God."

Apart from being God's son, Jesus was pure, innocent and without sin, therefore, a righteous, honourable and worthy sacrifice to God. See **John 8:46** *"Who among you can convict me of sin? If I am telling the truth, why don't you believe me?"*

Please note: it does not make sense to say: "I do believe Jesus Christ was a prophet but do not believe he was the Son of God." Jesus himself repeatedly said he was God's Son; he was executed for blasphemy, by affirming that he was God's son. Therefore, **if you believe that God has no son**, then Jesus blasphemed and this fact should make you reconsider your views on Jesus Christ.

28

The resurrection of Jesus Christ

It is written in the scriptures, **Matthew 28: 11-15,** that on the third day after the death of Jesus Christ, the guards went to report to the chief priests that the grave of Jesus Christ was empty. After a consultation with the elders, it was decided to bribe these guards, telling them to let it be known to the public that the disciples of Jesus had stolen his corpse, while the guards were sleeping; the chief priests also pledged to protect these soldiers from punishment, should they be accused of failure of duty, in protecting of the grave of Jesus. Sleeping while on duty is always a very serious matter in the army and for a Roman soldier, it might have led to a death sentence. The Jews have up until today, believed this version of the story, that the disciples of Jesus Christ stole his body and then spread the story that he had resurrected.

The act of stealing the corpse of Jesus would have surely woken up any guards, because it would have involved first, breaking the seal on the grave, second, rolling away a very heavy stone that blocked the grave, the rock cavity where the body of Jesus lay and would surely have made much noise and third, carrying away the corpse of Jesus would have been no easy task, more so if they had to denude the corpse because the linen clothing that had wrapped the corpse of Jesus was found to be in his tomb after his resurrection. See **John 20: 6-7**: Then Simon Peter also came, following him, and he went into the tomb. And he saw the linen cloths lying there. The cloth that had been on his head was not lying with the other cloth bands but was rolled up in a place by itself.

The Christians' belief in the resurrection of Jesus, is based on the fact that; after his death, Jesus Christ himself appeared alive, in his real body i.e. bone and flesh, to his disciples and interacted with them and not on the fact that his grave was found empty, on the third day after his death.

The day after Christ's death was a Sabbath; all work is forbidden in the Jewish communities, so no one went to the tomb of Jesus to embalm his corpse, however, the clergy had gone to Pontius Pilate, the Roman Governor to make a request for permission to seal the tomb of Jesus, which had been granted and done, on the same day.

All four gospels write of some women, Mary mother of James, Mary Magdalene, and Joanna, Salome, named in **Mark 16:1** and **others**; see **Luke 24:10**, who had gone early in the morning, after the Sabbath, to embalm the corpse of Jesus, but had found that the huge stone that had blocked the entrance to the grave of Jesus had been rolled away and his grave was empty. These women also had a close encounter with a heavenly being/s; who informed them that, Jesus was risen and requested them to take this news to the apostles, but the apostles did not believe them.

These women from Galilee were also present at the crucifixion of Jesus; see **Matthew 27:55-56** and **Mark 15: 40-41**; they used to administer to Jesus and his apostles. See **Luke 8: 1-2**: Shortly afterwards he travelled from city to city and from village to village, preaching and declaring the good news of the Kingdom of God. And the Twelve were with him, as were certain women who had been cured of wicked spirits and sicknesses: Mary who was called Magdalene, from whom seven demons had come out; Joanna the wife of Chuza, Herod's man in charge; Susanna and many other women, who were ministering to them from their belongings.

Most probably, the Galilean Women must have been horrified and mystified when they found the entrance stone rolled away and the tomb of Jesus empty. They were just recovering from the shock and sorrow after the brutal execution of their master. Then they witnessed the presence of a heavenly being or beings, near or inside the tomb of Jesus.

I must say that any shocking experience is bound to create some discrepancy, between what really happened and the perceived experience. This probably explains the variation of versions reported by these Galilean Women, regarding what happened when they went to the tomb of Jesus to embalm his corpse. However, **all of them confirmed that they found the tomb open; the stone that had covered the entrance had been rolled away and the corpse of Jesus had disappeared.**

In **Mark 16: 8,** "So when they came out, they fled from the tomb, trembling and overwhelmed with emotion **and they said nothing to anyone, for they were in fear." This last verse of the gospel of Mark, contradicts all the other gospels**, of **Matthew 28:8-10**, of **Luke 24:9-11** and of **John 20:14-18**, which confirm that the "Galilean Women" reported to the apostles what they had seen.

It could be that these women were at first frightened, then later decided to go to the disciples and tell them what they had actually seen, also because the angels had made this specific request to them, it would be very unlikely, that they had ignored it.

Mark 16:8 is the last verse, from the scripture of Mark. The last chapter of the apostle Mark is very short, it has only eight verses; surely, a piece of this gospel is missing because it ends abruptly with no real conclusion. **I am forced to conclude that, the Gospel of Mark does not write of any encounter with the risen Christ, because the concluding paragraphs are missing.**

Accounts of the Risen Christ

The scriptures give slightly different versions of the appearance of Jesus Christ, after his resurrection. The scriptures record that Jesus appeared first to "The Galilean Women" before anyone else.

Apart from Jesus' apparition to the Galilean women, **the gospel of Matthew reports only one other and final encounter with the risen Jesus to his apostles;** see **Matthew 28:16**;

"However, the 11 disciples went to Galilee, to the mountain where Jesus had arranged for them to meet."

In this encounter, Jesus commissioned his disciple to go out and preach to all nations and this particular encounter as recorded in **Matthew 28:16-20**, is called: **The Great Commission**.

The Gospel of Luke

The apostle Luke records three encounters with the risen Jesus. Luke 24:13-35. On the first day of the week after the Sabbath, some disciples who were **travelling to Emmaus had an encounter with Jesus**, after which, they returned immediately to Jerusalem, to give the good news of the risen Christ to the apostles and the other disciples who happened to be with them there.

Luke 24:33-34: They (the disciples who had been travelling to Emmaus), got up and returned at once to Jerusalem. There they found the Eleven and those with them, assembled together; the apostles were now saying, "*It is true! The Lord has risen and **has appeared to Simon**.*" That is the apostle Peter claimed to have had an encounter with Jesus earlier on during that day and earlier on in the morning, some Galilean women, disciples of Jesus, had informed the apostles that they too had had an encounter with the risen Christ. By now, the disciples of Jesus had become very unsettled about these claims of "a risen Christ." **Luke 24:35**; Then the two disciples told them what had happened on the way to Emmaus and how they had recognized Jesus when he had broken the bread.

Luke: 24:36-43, describes an event, on the evening of the first day of the week after the Sabbath, where the disciples who had been travelling to Emmaus had already returned from Emmaus to the house of the apostles in Jerusalem and were busy talking to the disciples about their encounter with Jesus, when J**esus himself materialized** among them and ate a piece of broiled fish, to prove to them that, he was real. **Luke 24:39**; "*See my hands and my feet,* *that it is I myself. Touch me, and see. For a spirit does not have flesh and bones as you see that I have."*

Luke 24:44-49; He said to them, "This is what I told you while I was still with you: Everything must be fulfilled that is written about me in the Law of Moses, the Prophets and the Psalms." **Then he opened their minds so they could understand the scriptures.** He continued: "This is what is written: The Messiah will suffer and rise from the dead on the third day, and repentance for the forgiveness of sins will be preached in his name to all nations, beginning from Jerusalem. You are witnesses of these things. I am going to send you what my Father has promised, but stay in the city until you have been clothed with power from on high."

The Gospel of John reports three encounters with the risen Christ.

The first apparition: **John 20:19-20**, on the evening of the first day of the week after the Sabbath, while still in Jerusalem, with the doors locked for fear of the Jewish leaders, Jesus materialises among them. The apostle Thomas was absent in this apparition and did not believe what the apostles told him: that Jesus had appeared to them.

The second apparition: **John 20: 26-29;** was a week after the first appearance **and Thomas was present**.

The third apparition: **John 21:1-23**, was by the Sea of Tiberius/Sea of Galilee/ Lake of Gennesaret, where some apostles and some disciples of Jesus had gone fishing, but had caught nothing, for the whole night.

Acts, one of the books of the New Testament, was written by the apostle Luke. **Acts 1: 3** says: After he (Jesus) had suffered, **he showed himself alive to them by many convincing proofs. He was seen by them throughout 40 days, after his resurrection** and he was speaking about the Kingdom of God.

God's ID

Therefore, up to forty days after his resurrection, Jesus appeared on several occasions, to his disciples; he talked and interacted with them, to prove that it was him and that he was actually alive and also to confirm what had been written about him, in the scriptures; that he would rise from the dead.

The New Testament scriptures have recorded twelve occasions, when Jesus appeared to his disciples, after his resurrection: **John 20: 16; John 20: 19, John 20: 26-29**; **John 21:9-14, Matthew 28: 9-10; Matthew 28: 16-20; Luke 24: 34, mentioned again in 1Corinthians 15:5; Luke 24: 13-31; Luke 24: 36; Acts: 9: 3-6 and 1 Corinthians 15: 6 & 7**.

Who raised Jesus from the dead?

Some Christians say Jesus raised himself from the dead, while others say that God, his Heavenly Father, raised him.

Please note: Jesus was dead, hence could not perform any task. This leaves only one person who qualifies to have raised Jesus because only he has such capabilities, his own Father. See also, **Luke 23:46**: Jesus called out with a loud voice, "*Father, into your hands I commit my spirit.*" When he had said this, he breathed his last. This means that, while physically dead, Jesus had entrusted his own spirit to his Father, who put the spirit back into his body, in order to resurrect him.

In the scriptures, Jesus says, regarding his forthcoming death, "On the third day, **I will be raised** from the dead." See **Matthew 16: 21-23; 20: 17-19**_and **Luke 9: 22**, raised by whom? While on other occasions, he says, "**I will rise** on the third day."

There is no information in the Bible, where Jesus says: **"I will raise myself up,"** besides the apostle Peter in his first preaching post-resurrection of Jesus and after being anointed by the Holy Spirit, makes this statement; **Acts 2:32**; "*God resurrected this Jesus, and of this, we are all witnesses.*"

Queries on John 20:22 and John 20:23

The gospel of John explains the nature of the Holy Spirit. See **John 14: 15-17 and 26, John 15:26 John 16:13-15**.

The Risen Christ then promised to send to his apostles, what he had already promised them some time back; The Holy Spirit. See **Luke 24: 49;** *"And look! I am sending upon you what my Father promised. You, though, stay in the city until you are clothed with power from on high."*

However, according to a verse: John 20:22; Jesus blows The Holy Spirit on his apostles, when he first appears to them after the resurrection. *"After saying this he blew on them and said to them: "Receive Holy Spirit."* This scripture that says Jesus himself blew The Holy Spirit on his apostles, **contradicts the same gospel of John**, which writes that, previously, before his crucifixion, Jesus had informed his apostles that The Holy Spirit would be coming from the Father because Jesus would request it from his Father; see **John 14:26, John 15:26 John**.

Also, in this particular occasion, of **John 20:22**, where Jesus blows the Holy Spirit onto the apostles, it is not recorded of any unusual or visible manifestation of The Holy Spirit in action, on any of the apostles or disciples present, that is, there was no transformation at all in any of them. Also, Thomas, one of Christ's apostles, was absent.

According to the gospel of **Acts 2: 1-4**; the Holy Spirit anointed the apostles and disciples fifty days after the death of Jesus.

A query on the verse of this scripture of John 20:22 remains.

I also noted the following scripture of **John 20:23**; *"if you forgive the sins of anyone, they are forgiven; if you retain those of anyone, they are retained."*

There is also a query, regarding this scripture of John 20:23.

In the scriptures, Jesus forgives sins publicly, in **Luke 7:48** and **Mark 2:10**. In the scripture of Mark he says: *"But I want you to know that the Son of Man (a name Jesus uses for himself), has authority on earth to forgive sins*." So, he said to the man, *"I tell you, pick up your mat and go home."* This public declaration of: *"*Your sins are forgiven*"* was challenged and questioned in people's minds, by some in the crowd, as it was common knowledge that only God could forgive sins.

As you can see, Jesus says he has authority, "on earth" to forgive sins and this authority must have been given to him by someone; his Father.

In the New Testament, when Jesus sent his disciples and apostles away to preach, he also gave them basic instructions on what to do and say and he bestowed on them Godly powers that allowed them to perform miracles. See the scriptures; **Luke 10: 1-16** and **Mathew 10:1-15**. <u>**But Jesus did not authorize them to forgive sins, and none of them reported having done so.**</u> It is not reported anywhere in the Bible that a prophet or a disciple of Jesus forgave sins.

Now, if it is true, that Jesus himself had authorized his apostles to forgive sins on earth, how come no such event in the lives of all the apostles and disciples has ever been reported anywhere?

If people commit sins against God, why should somebody else forgive them their sins on behalf of God? The query on John 20:23 remains.

29

The reception of The Holy Spirit

The Helper, The Advocate, and The Comforter are some terms used in some Bibles instead of: The Holy Spirit.

Before his death, Jesus had promised his apostles, to send them the Holy Spirit. See **John 14: 25-26**; "*I have spoken these things to you while I am still with you. But The Helper/The Advocate/The Comforter, The Holy Spirit, **whom the Father will send in my name, that one will teach you all things** and bring back to your minds all the things I told you.*"

See what Jesus says when he appears to his apostles after the resurrection: **Luke 24: 46- 48**; and said to them, "*This is what is written: that the Christ would suffer and rise from among the dead on the third day, and on the basis of his name, repentance for forgiveness of sins would be preached in all the nations—starting out from Jerusalem. You are to be witnesses of these things. And look! I am sending upon you what my Father promised. You, though, stay in the city **until you are clothed with power from on high.**"

The final departure and ascension of Jesus after the resurrection

After his resurrection, Jesus requested his apostles to stay in Jerusalem and await the Holy Spirit. It is written in **Acts 1: 3** that, **the final ascension of Jesus to heaven took place forty days after his resurrection**. See **Acts 1:3**; After his suffering, he presented himself to them and gave many convincing proofs that he was alive. He appeared to them over a period of forty days and spoke about the kingdom of God.

Jesus wanted his disciples helped and sustained by God His Father, through the Holy Spirit, because he gave them a very challenging mission; to spread the Good News to the rest of the world. This would be no an easy task.

See **Acts 1:4-11**; While he was meeting and eating with them, **he ordered them:** "*Do not leave Jerusalem, but keep waiting for what the Father has promised, about which you heard from me; for John, indeed, baptized with water, but you will be baptized with Holy Spirit, not many days after this.*"

Then they gathered around him and asked him, "*Lord, are you at this time going to restore the kingdom to Israel?*"

He said to them: "*It is not for you to know the times or dates the Father has set by his own authority.* **but you will receive power** *when the Holy Spirit comes on you, and* **you will be my witnesses** *in Jerusalem, and in all Judea and Samaria, and to the ends of the earth.*"

After he had said these things, while they were looking on, he was lifted up and **a cloud caught him up from their sight**.

They were looking intently up into the sky as he was going when suddenly two men dressed in white stood beside them. "*Men of Galilee,*" *they said,* "*why do you stand here looking into the sky? This same Jesus, who has been taken from you into heaven, will come back in the same way you have seen him go into heaven.*" This was the final earthly encounter recorded, of Jesus with all his apostles and it took place after his resurrection.

The Pentecost

The Pentecost is a Christian festival, celebrating the descent of the Holy Spirit on the disciples of Jesus. It is held on the seventh Sunday after Easter, which is **fifty days after Easter**. Pentecost comes from Greek, meaning fiftieth.

In some countries, namely Britain, Northern Ireland and throughout the world among Catholics, Anglicans and Methodists; the Whitsun, also Whitsunday or Whit Sunday, is the name used to represent The Day of Pentecost.

The disciples of Jesus receive The Holy Spirit

At the time of Jesus, the Jewish people celebrated a festival called; the **Feast of Weeks or the Wheat Harvest Festival**, which took place fifty days after the second day of the Passover, to give thanks to God for the first fruits of the harvest; see **Exodus 34: 22**. In Judaism, this feast is called **Shavuot.** Today, however, Judaism celebrates Shavuot as the day the Torah/the Law was given to the nation of Israel, through God's prophet, Moses.

Before his crucifixion and after his resurrection, Jesus had promised his apostles that he would make a request to his Father, to send them the Holy Spirit. Why? What did it serve?

Just to remind you, according to the Bible, the Holy Spirit is described as God's active or living power or God's living presence in a person. In the Old Testament, when someone was anointed, i.e. was officially selected by God for a specific and important role, God also sent his Holy Spirit to them to support them in their mission. For example, see **1 Samuel 16:12-13**, when David was anointed by the prophet Samuel, see when Jesus was baptized by **John the Baptist** in the River Jordan**: 1:32-33**, at the beginning of his Messianic mission on earth.

Jesus explained to his apostles what would happen when his disciples received the Holy Spirit; see: **Acts 1:8**; "But *you will receive power when the Holy Spirit comes upon you, and you will be witnesses of me in Jerusalem, in all Judea and Samaria, and to the most distant parts of the earth.*"

The first disciples of Jesus were all Jews and therefore followed Judaism. They were all in Jerusalem, seated in a room and were in the process of celebrating the first Feast of Weeks, after the resurrection of Jesus when they received the Holy Spirit. See **Acts 2: 1-4**; "*Suddenly there was a noise from heaven, just like that of a rushing, stiff breeze, and it filled the whole house where they were sitting. And tongues as if of fire became visible to them and were distributed, and one came to rest on each one of them, and they all* *became filled with Holy Spirit and started to speak in different languages, just as The Spirit enabled them to speak."*

On this occasion, the Apostles and Disciples of Jesus were "baptized by the Spirit" and this endowed them with special gifts, such as speaking in different languages, and deep knowledge of the scriptures so that their preaching became excellent and the Apostles were also able to perform extraordinary miracles, through the power of the Holy Spirit; see all of **Acts chapter two**. On this particular day, after having received the Holy Spirit, the apostle Peter in the company of the apostles started preaching to the public, many people, three thousand, converted and became believers of Jesus.

From this day onwards, the number of believers in Jesus from all nations, continued to grow, due to the excellent preaching and the miracles performed by the disciples of Jesus. This is why Pentecost is also considered to be the Birthday of Christianity.

Please note: The spread of Christianity started from Jerusalem, through the Jewish disciples of Jesus Christ and from there, spread to the rest of the world. The Jews were chosen by God for this important task, to initiate the spread of the Good News. The converts from the Gentiles, that is, the non-Jewish converts also participated actively in the spread of Christianity; many areas of the Mediterranean and beyond, gradually converted to Christianity. The disciples of Jesus Christ were empowered by the Holy Spirit and despite all the difficulties they encountered, they succeeded in this very difficult task of spreading the Good News of the Kingdom of God. By reading all the scripture of Acts, one sees clearly how the Holy Spirit was key to the spread of Christianity, through the disciples of Jesus Christ.

Please note: Not everything went smoothly, regarding the spread of Christianity. The first official Christian Church establishment, that is the Roman Catholic Church eventually, became involved in politics, became very rich and corrupt and false doctrines entered into the teachings of the Church. This led to the breakup of the Catholic Church, followed by two savage inter-religious wars, giving rise to the formation of new independent Christian Churches. The first big official division of the Christian (Catholic) Church was on 16 July 1054, with the formation of schisms between the Church of Rome and the Eastern Orthodox Church of Constantinople.

Unfortunately, divisions in Christendom continue to this day; but more important the Good News is still being preached all over the world and has been in continuous expansion over the years. However, it has been noted that from the twentieth century, specifically after the 1950s, Christianity is in decline in the Western world.

30

What did Jesus accomplish through his mission on earth?

Were the numerous prophecies about Jesus Christ fulfilled?

In this chapter, I will review two prophecies regarding Jesus, which were made to both his parents before his birth. They regard the most important and unique accomplishment of Jesus Christ. These same prophesies were also made way back by some Jewish prophets.

The prediction made to his mother Mary was: See **Luke 1: 30-33**; "And look! You will become pregnant and give birth to a son, and you are to name him Jesus. This one will be great and will be called Son of the Most High, and Jehovah God will give him the throne of David his father and **he will rule as King over** the house of Jacob forever, and there will be no end to his kingdom."

The prophecy made to his father Joseph was: **Matthew 1: 20-21**: But after he had thought these things over, look! Jehovah's angel appeared to him in a dream, saying: "Joseph, son of David, do not be afraid to take your wife Mary home, for what has been conceived in her is by Holy Spirit. She will give birth to a son, and you are to name him Jesus, **for he will save his people from their sins."**

Let's first look at the prophecy made to his father Joseph; **did Jesus save his people from their sins?**

According to the scriptures, not only did he save his people, the Jews, from their sins, but he actually saved the whole of mankind from sin. When Jesus was executed, his death served as a sacrifice similar to that of the animals sacrificed on the Day of

Atonement. The death of Jesus Christ atoned for the sins of all mankind; see the explanation here, in **Chapter 23 of this book.**

Was Jesus given the throne of his father David, as prophesied to his mother Mary and as prophesied by some prophets of the Old Testament?

In the Last Supper, Jesus mentioned his political kingdom. See **Luke 22:28-30**; "However, you are the ones who have stuck with me in my trials; and I make a covenant with you, **just as my Father has made a covenant with me, for a kingdom**, so that you may eat and drink at my table in **my kingdom**, and sit on thrones to judge the 12 tribes of Israel."

There was a covenant, an agreement, between Jesus Christ and his Father, for a kingdom.

When Jesus was arrested and taken to court, he was accused of sedition; that is inciting people to rebel against Rome and one of the charges was that he was calling himself a king.

In **John chapter 18:33;** when Jesus was being interrogated by the Roman governor, Pontius Pilate, he was asked: "Are you the King of the Jews?" Jesus answered: **John 18:36-37**; "My Kingdom is no part of this world. If my Kingdom were part of this world, my attendants would have fought that I should not be handed over to the Jewish leaders. But as it is, my Kingdom is not from this source."

Jesus **did not deny having a kingdom, instead, he confirmed it**: "My Kingdom is not from this source."

Where then is the kingdom that Jesus rules or will rule as a king?

God has made it known to man, his future plans for mankind, through his prophets and through his Son Jesus Christ; that those who live according to his Law, although they die, they will not perish. In God's own time, He will resurrect them to eternal life and will come to be part of God's Kingdom, which will never pass away.

That is, in addition to assisting you here on earth, if you live according to His Law, God will take care of you even after death and reward you for keeping His Law. If you keep God's Law, it shows that you fear God, that is, you acknowledge his authority, in that He is the source of righteousness **and therefore, His Law is righteous.**

God is pure, therefore, all the people who will make up God's Kingdom will also have to be pure. How can man attain this purity? Man has constantly sinned against God, damaging his relationship with his Creator and jeopardising his access to eternal life in God's kingdom. God decided that a sacrifice was necessary, to purify man from his sins and consequently give him access to eternal life in God's kingdom. Out of his great love for man, God made it such that, deliverance from sin, that is **Salvation**, should be brought about through the sacrifice and death of His Own Son, Jesus Christ.

God would like all people to acknowledge this sacrifice made by His Son, permitting the remission of sins for all mankind, so that all mankind can now be reconciled to God and can have access to eternal life in God's kingdom. **This acknowledgement of the sacrifice of Jesus Christ is a prerequisite to gaining access to eternal life.**

See **Chapter 23** for further explanation of the significance of the death of Jesus.

Now, let's get back to the subject of: Where is Christ's Everlasting Kingdom, The kingdom of Heaven or God's Kingdom as Jesus called it?

According to the Bible, God's Kingdom will be installed in the future. This information regarding the coming of God's Kingdom can be found in **the Book of Revelation,** which is the last book of the Bible. This book of Revelation discloses that, in the coming future, no one knows exactly when God's kingdom will be a reality;

it also reveals who will make up this kingdom and that God's kingdom will be installed after a Universal Judgement of mankind has taken place.

The Book of Revelation

The book of Revelation is based on visions given to the apostle John, by an angel sent by Jesus Christ. Jesus in turn received this information from his father, Jehovah. The visions were presented as signs that need to be interpreted. John was requested to write down the visions he saw in a scroll and to send a copy to each of the seven Christian congregations of Asia, part of the present-day Republic of Turkey because these visions were addressed to them. See **Rev. 1: 11.**

When the apostle John received these visions, he happened to be in Patmos, a Greek island, where he had gone to preach the word of God.

I am not an expert on the interpretation of this last book of the Bible, that is the Revelation, however, one can understand the basics. The book deals mainly with what will happen to the earth and to mankind at the End of Times, but the vision present in Chapters two and three of the book of Revelation, are letters from Jesus, addressed specifically to The Seven Christian Congregations of Asia. These letters regard the successes and failures that were present in these seven congregations; they identified the root causes of their failures and suggested ways to deal with them. The letters concluded by encouraging the congregations to hold onto their faith, despite heavy persecution and other difficulties.

I believe those martyred for their faith are what Jesus refers to as: **"those who have conquered."** Jesus says that in their afterlife, he will grant special privileges, to "those who have conquered," See **Rev 2: 7, 11, 17, 26 and Rev 3: 5, 12, 21**. Those who upheld their faith despite severe persecution and even death would have had to conquer fear, hatred, suffering and even death.

Here is a brief summary of Revelation's Chapters 4 to 22.

From **Chapters 4 to 11**, John had a vision of God's throne in heaven at the End of Times. In his visions, John witnessed the orders being executed by God's angels, which culminated in the destruction of the earth. In this vision, the destruction of the earth takes place in a series of events signalled by the **breaking of the Seven Seals** of a scroll by the Lamb/Jesus; there follows **the blowing of seven trumpets (Rev. 8:6)** and last of all, **the pouring out of God's anger onto the earth, from seven golden bowls**; see **Rev. Chapter 16**.

The above events led to a gradual destruction of the earth; sea, rivers, moon, sun, mountains, and cities and of the people living in the areas of destruction.

In **Chapter 5**, Jesus Christ was honoured in heaven, because, through his death, he had made the Kingdom of God accessible to man. He was the only person found worthy to break the seven seals **on a scroll** which was kept on the right hand of his Father, Jehovah. The breaking of seals on this scroll initiated the destruction of the earth and ushered in God's kingdom.

Chapters 12 to 19 showed the events that were taking place in Heaven and on Earth, just before the Day of Judgement. The earth had become dominated by an evil moral organization, **Babylon the Great,** and an evil political, social and economic system, of universal magnitude, **the Wild Beast and its Prophets;** the world, in general, had become extremely corrupted by these two systems and man had become extremely evil. The destruction of these two evil systems had become a necessity, to restore God's righteousness on earth.

In **Revelation 14:1-5,** the apostle John had a vision of 144,000 men sealed on the forehead with the name of God and of the Lamb (Jesus Christ); this group of men appeared on Mount Zion, accompanied by The Lamb.

Some other important events to note from Revelation

In **Revelation**: **11: 3- 13;** In a vision, John saw two final prophets sent to prophesy, for 1260 days; these two prophets were endowed with super powers which served to testify that God had sent them. They did not succeed in their task of drawing man to God because of the prevalence of evil on earth and man's aversion to God. Actually, these two prophets ended up being murdered and their corpses were left for public display; they were refused a burial. After three and a half days, their corpses were resurrected to the shock of everyone and these two prophets were taken up to heaven.

In **Rev. 11:15** There followed the blowing of the **seventh** trumpet; this signalled the inauguration of God's political kingdom on earth, which was proceeded by the Universal Judgement of Mankind.

Here is a brief summary of some of the final chapters of Revelation:

Rev. 17: Fall of Babylon the Great, (an evil moral organization)

Rev. 18: Earth mourns the destruction of Babylon the Great.

Rev.19: 1-3; Heaven celebrates the destruction of Babylon the Great.

Rev. 19: 19- 21; The fall of the Wild Beast and its followers.

Rev. 20: 4-6; John had a vision of **a first resurrection** of a special class of Christians; those who had been martyred for their faith. These martyrs are also mentioned in **Rev. 6: 9-11 and Rev. 7: 13-14,** they will have a millennial rule with Jesus Christ and during this period, of one thousand years, Satan will be locked up in an Abyss, that is, in a deep space/fissure present in the earth's crust. These first resurrected Christians **will not be subjected to a second death.**

Rev.20: 7-10: After the Millennial Rule of Jesus, Satan will be released from the Abyss and he will go out to mislead those nations in the four corners of the earth, Gog and Magog, to gather them together for the war. In number, they are like the sand on the seashore. They marched across the breadth of the earth and surrounded the camp of God's people, the city he loves. But fire came down from heaven and devoured them. And the Devil who was misleading them was hurled into the lake of fire and sulphur, where both the wild beast and the false prophet already were; and they will be tormented day and night forever and ever. Therefore, according to John's vision, the Devil will thus be defeated and permanently neutralized in a lake of fire.

In the vision of universal judgement: **Rev. 20: 12-15**, all human beings have been resurrected for judgement; anyone not found written in The Lamb's Scroll/book of Life, had **a second death**; they were **destroyed** in a lake of fire.

Please note: Those not found written in The Lamb's Scroll/book of Life, had **a second death," destruction by fire and were not subjected to "burn in eternal fire."**

Chapters 21 to 22 of Revelation

The visions John had from the two last chapters of Revelation, dealt with the installation of God's Kingdom after the Universal Judgement. God will create a new Heaven and a new earth and a New Jerusalem. Death is vanquished and God Himself in person will make everyone on the New Earth feel welcome and comfortable in his New Kingdom. See **Revelation 21: 3-7.**

The book of Revelation answers some important queries.

When will the kingdom of God start?

It is not yet known when the kingdom of God will come into existence; Jesus said that only his father knows it, and no one else; **even he himself did not know it.** See **Matthew 24:36**

The apostle John had a vision of the events that will herald God's Kingdom, but it was not revealed to him **when** this would happen.

See **Revelation 11:15-16; the seventh angel sounded his trumpet** and there were loud voices in heaven, which said: "The kingdom of the world has become the kingdom of our Lord **and** of his Messiah, and he will reign for ever and ever."

The blowing of this trumpet heralds the coming of God's kingdom because it is followed by the final execution of God's judgement on the earth and on his enemies. God is now reigning; he has taken charge of the earth and starts by using his almighty power to restore his righteousness, by destroying all the evil forces present on earth. God then proceeds to judge the Nations, through his son Jesus Christ.

Rev. 20: 11-15: Then I saw a great white throne and him who was seated on it. **From his presence earth and sky fled away, and no place was found for them**. And I saw the dead, great and small, standing before the throne, and scrolls/books were opened. Another scroll/book was opened, which is the scroll/book of life. The dead were judged according to their deeds as recorded in the books/scrolls. The sea gave up the dead that were in it, and death and **Hades** gave up the dead that were in them, and **they were judged (the dead who have been resurrected) individually according to their deeds. Then Death and Hades were thrown into the Lake of Fire. The Lake of Fire is the second death.** Furthermore, whoever was not found recorded in the scroll/book of life was thrown into the lake of fire.

Note: The scroll/book of life is described as: "the Lamb's."

See **Rev. 21:27;** But anything defiled and anyone who does what is disgusting and deceitful will in no way enter into it; (The New Jerusalem), only those written in the Lamb's scroll of life will enter.

Where will the Kingdom of God be?

It will be on earth; God will replace the present earth and heavens with a new creation. **Rev. 21: 1-3;** Then I saw a new heaven and a new earth, for the old heaven and the old earth had passed away, and the sea was no more. I also saw the holy city, New Jerusalem, coming down out of heaven from God and prepared as a bride adorned for her husband. With that I heard a loud voice from the throne say: "Look! The tent of God is with mankind, and he will reside with them, and they will be his people. And he will wipe out every tear from their eyes, and death will be no more, neither will mourning nor outcry nor pain be anymore. The former things have passed away."

Note: There is no mention of angels being part of the Kingdom of God. I believe God will still be ruling Heaven and there is a possibility that God has other kingdoms, (different or similar to the earth), somewhere else in the universe. See **Rev. 5:11**; And I saw, and I heard a voice of many angels around the throne and the living creatures and the elders, and the number of them was myriads of myriads and thousands of thousand.

Note: This "new earth," will also include, a holy city, "a New Jerusalem," which will descend on earth from heaven, all prepared and adorned and ready for use. See **Rev. 21: 10;** So, he carried me away in the power of the spirit to a great and lofty mountain, and he showed me the holy city Jerusalem **coming down out of** heaven from God; see: **Rev. 21: 9-27 and Rev 22: 1-5.**

Rev. 21: 16; And the city is laid out as a square, and its length is as great as its width. And he measured the city with the reed, 12,000 stadia; its length and width and height are equal.

Please note: **one stadium equals 185 metres or 606.9 feet**. The New Jerusalem is described as a cube of **12,000 stadia**; this is equivalent to **2,220 km or 1380 miles**. This means that, being a cube, the New Jerusalem will also measure **2,220 km upwards**, this is why the apostle John says: **Rev. 21:10**; "he showed me the holy city Jerusalem coming down out of heaven from God," **because it will be towering into the heavens.**

The largest city in the world is Tokyo and it occupies **an area** of about 2, 194 km squared. The New Jerusalem will occupy on the surface of the earth 2,220 km x 2,220 km, that is 4,928,400 km squared and will project upwards into the skies for 2,220 km.

The highest clouds on earth are about 60,000ft up which is about 18,288metres and about 18.228 km. This means that the New Jerusalem, will actually tower way up above the clouds.

This New Jerusalem **will be the new political headquarters** of the Kingdom of God because **the throne of God and of the lamb** will be in the city. **See Rev. 22: 3;** And there will no longer be any curse. But the throne of God and of the Lamb will be in the city, and his slaves will offer him sacred service, and they will see his face, and **his name will be on their forehead.**

Who will make up the Kingdom of God?

The following will make up the kingdom of God:

- God the Father, i.e. Jehovah
- Jesus Christ
- Those from the first resurrection including the 144,000 sealed/anointed
- Those from the second and final resurrection

In other words, all humankind will be part of God's kingdom, **except those not found written in the Book of Life. See Rev. 21: 27.**

God's authority and that of Jesus Christ will be perpetually present in this kingdom. "But the throne of God and of the Lamb will be in the city, that is, in the New Jerusalem. **Rev. 22:3**

See Rev. 7:17 "Because the Lamb, who is in the midst of the throne, will shepherd them and will guide them to springs of waters of life. And God will wipe out every tear from their eyes."

God's Kingdom will include a specific group of people; See **Rev. 14: 1-5**; Then I saw, and look! The Lamb **standing on Mount Zion**, and with him **144,000 men** who have his name and the name of his Father written **on their foreheads**. This group of people have the **seal/emblem** of the Living God and of his Christ on their forehead sand are standing on Mount Zion, an area of Jerusalem where the first and second temples had been built; an area associated with God's presence.

I believe that standing on Mount Zion, the seat of God's authority in ancient Israel, and having a seal of God and of Jesus on their forehead identifies this group of 144,000 men as having been anointed to be part of the ruling government of God's Kingdom. See: "... and his slaves will offer him sacred service, and they will see his face, and his name will be on their foreheads." **Rev. 22: 3-4.**

See further definition of Mount Zion at the end of this chapter.

Who will rule the Kingdom of Heaven?

Rev. 11: 15; The seventh angel blew his trumpet. And there were loud voices in heaven, saying: "The kingdom of the world has become the Kingdom of our Lord AND of his Christ, and he will rule as king forever and ever.

Rev. 11: 16-17; And the 24 elders who were seated before God on their thrones fell upon their faces and worshipped God, saying: "We thank you, Jehovah God, the Almighty, the one who is and who was because you have taken your great power and **begun ruling as king**.

Rev. 19: 6, praise Jehovah, because Jehovah our God the Almighty has begun to rule as king!

God will rule this Kingdom of Heaven; it is his kingdom, He created it; **Rev. 21:5**, he also created the New Jerusalem; **Rev.21: 10**, He created **all things.** However, **God will rule His kingdom, through His son, Jesus Christ.** We can deduce this to be true from the following facts.

The fact that "The Scroll of Life," is described as: "The Lamb's Scroll of Life," means that it is Jesus who will be deciding who should be part of God's Kingdom.

See **Rev. 21:27**, But anything defiled and anyone who does what is disgusting and deceitful will in no way enter into it; (referring to the New Jerusalem), only those written in the Lamb's scroll of life will enter.

See **Mathew 7:21**; "Not everyone **saying to me**, 'Lord, Lord,' will enter the kingdom of heaven, but only he who does the will of My Father in heaven."

The fact that New Jerusalem is described as: "The Lamb's wife," see: **Rev. 21: 9-10**; One of the seven angels who had the seven bowls that were full of the seven last plagues came and said to me: "Come, and I will show you the bride, the Lamb's wife." So he carried me away in the power of the spirit to a great and lofty mountain, and he showed me the holy city Jerusalem coming down out of heaven from God." **This means that Jesus, the groom, will look after his bride/wife, i.e. this holy city of "New Jerusalem" and he will be in charge of it, permanently.**

When a groom takes on a bride, he becomes permanently responsible for the welfare of his bride.

There is another place in Revelation that mentions "The marriage of the Lamb." See **Rev. 19: 7-8**: "Let us rejoice and be overjoyed and give him glory because the marriage of the lamb has arrived and his wife has prepared herself. Yes, it has been granted to her to be **clothed with bright, clean, fine linen,** for the fine linen stands for the righteous acts of the **Holy Ones**."

I believe the term "Holy Ones," refers to martyrs because clothing is mentioned only regarding them. They are first mentioned in **Rev. 6: 9-11**, as being stationed under the altar (of God), and then each of them was given a white robe. Then **Rev. 7: 9-17** mentions a great multitude, standing before the throne of God **wearing white robes** and holding palm branches in their hands.

Note: These two groups of people are in God's presence, therefore, they must be holy because nothing defiled or unholy can go near God. I believe these two groups of people mentioned in these two verses, represent just one group; that of the martyrs.

The father and son are in harmony, not in conflict and Jesus is part of God's authority:

- **Rev. 5: 6**; And I **saw standing in the midst of the throne** and of the four living creatures and in the midst of the elders **a lamb** that seemed to have been slaughtered.

- **See Rev. 7: 16-17**; They will hunger no more nor thirst anymore, neither will the sun beat down on them nor any scorching heat, **because the lamb, who is in the midst of the throne,** will shepherd them and will guide them to **springs of waters of life.** And God will wipe out every tear from their eyes."

- **John 16: 15;** Everything that belongs to the Father is Mine. That is why I said that the Spirit (which comes from the Father), will take from what is Mine and disclose it to you.

- **Rev. 22: 1-2**; And he showed me **a river of water of life**, clear as crystal, flowing out from the **throne of God and of the Lamb** down the middle of its main street. On both sides of the river were trees of life producing 12 crops of fruit, yielding their fruit each month.

Note: in the New Jerusalem, there will be two thrones, one of God and one of the lamb.

Rev. 3:12; The one who conquers, I will make him a pillar in the temple of **my** God, and he will by no means go out from it anymore, and I will write upon him the name of **my** God and the name of **the city of my God**, the New Jerusalem that descends out of heaven from **my God, and my own new name.**

From the statement above, Jesus himself confirms that the New Jerusalem belongs to his Father, who is also **his God**, but God has given Jesus the authority to reign in his Kingdom "on earth."

Rev. 3:21; To the one who conquers I will grant to sit down with me **on my throne.**

Rev. 1: 4-5; John to the seven congregations that are in the province of Asia: May you have undeserved kindness and peace from "the One who is and who was and who is coming," and from the seven spirits that are before his throne, and from Jesus Christ, "the Faithful Witness," "the firstborn from the dead," and "**the ruler of the kings of the earth.**"

Please note: Throughout this book of Revelation, a clear distinction is made between Jesus Christ and his Father Jehovah, the only true God and the Sovereign Lord of the Universe.

Please note: In the book of Revelation, in which John receives a vision of Heaven, there is no mention at all of the Holy Trinity.

Please note: Daniel Chapter seven, some visions of The End of Times are revealed to the Daniel.

The last book of the Bible, Revelation, concludes with; the accomplishment of The Kingdom of God/The Kingdom of Heaven, desired and prayed for by Jesus Christ and all Christians: "May Thy Kingdom come, Thy will be done on earth as it is in Heaven."

Zion: explained further

The term "Mount Zion" or "Mt Tzion," originally referred to a specific hill located south of Mount Moriah and which had served as a fortress for the Jebusites, the people who lived in Jerusalem before the arrival of the Israelites. This fortress was then captured by King David of Israel and became part of Israel's territory.

God requested Abraham to go to Mount Moriah to sacrifice his son Isaac. **See Genesis 22:1-2.**

Mount Moriah is where the first Temple was built by King Solomon and which is the highest point in Jerusalem, therefore, it became known as The Temple Mount and also came to be referred to as Mount Zion.

When King Solomon built and finished Jehovah's temple, the first temple, God appeared to him at night in a vision and said: "*I have heard your prayer and have chosen this place for myself as a temple for sacrifice.*" ... "*Now my eyes will be open and my ears attentive to the prayers offered in this place. I have chosen and consecrated this temple so that my Name will be there forever. My eyes and my heart will always be there.*"**2 Chronicle 7:11-12, 15-16.**

This is why, to this day, Jews who practise Judaism pray facing this Temple Mount. In Judaism, in Christianity and Islam, God's presence is identified with this area, where the first Temple was built and where Abraham took his son Isaac, in order to sacrifice him.

When the Babylonians destroyed the First Temple, a second Temple was rebuilt on the same site as that of the first temple; this temple was later destroyed by the Romans.

Today, the Temple Mount refers to the elevated plaza, an open space, surrounded by a retaining wall. Retaining walls are structures designed to restrain soil to a slope, to keep it from sliding out of the slope, **and this includes the Western Wall.** Today, this compound of the Temple Mount is found within the Old City of Jerusalem. Today, three major monumental structures of the Islam religion dominate the Temple Mount.

Jerusalem was conquered by Islamic forces (**Caliph Umar) in 638 AD** and has had a large Muslim presence since then. This explains the presence of Islamic monuments in the Temple Mount. These monuments are:

- Dome of the Rock/ Qubbat al-Shakhra
- the Al-As-quad Mosque
- the Western Wall, part of the Retaining Wall

You have to the North, **Dome of the Rock** /Qubbat al-Shakhra a beautiful building with a gold-topped dome and is located on the Temple Mount, which is **on the site of the previous first and second Judaic Temples.** Dome of the Rock was built **not as a place for public worship (mosque), but as a shrine for pilgrimage**. It was built **between AD 685 and 691** by the caliph 'Abd al-Malik ibn Marwan,

To the South of this open space, we have the al-Aqsa Mosque; the compound of this mosque **is the third holiest site in Islam**.

Muslims believe that it is from the Dome of the Rock that Muhammad, the founder of Islam, departed, on his trip to heaven; this trip is called Mi'raj, where he received instructions from God, saying: Muslims should pray five times a day/The Salah. As the Dome of the Rock was constructed much later after Prophet Muhammad's death, this means that the Mi'raj took off from that area, but without The Dome.

To the Southwest stands the Western Wall, a relatively small segment of a far longer ancient retaining wall, which originally was also known in its entirety as the "Western Wall." **This remnant of the ancient retaining wall is the holiest site in Judaism, today.**

The al-Aqsa Mosque draws tens of thousands of pilgrims from across Palestine and the wider Muslim world each year.

Today, the term Zion is applied to different things: to represent the entire city of Jerusalem, the entire biblical Land of Israel, and "the World to Come", from the Jewish understanding of the afterlife. The word "Zion" also has had special significance for the

Israelite diaspora, for them the word Zion is used to represent a land of future promise, that is, Israel. To conclude, Mount Zion is used to represent different things, earthly sites, a political identity and a spiritual identity; but one thing is constantly associated with this term: God's presence.

31

God is there to benefit man

My investigation of God's identity shows that one needs to know what the word "God" really means; something many people presume to know, but really do not. **Why do you need to understand what the word "God" means?**

A statement from the first commandment of God says: You shall love Jehovah your God with all your heart with all your soul and with all your mind. If you do not know God, how can you follow this commandment? How can you love something you don't really know?

According to the Bible, God Himself would like man to know that He does exist and who He really is, and has taken great measures to let Himself be known to man. He has done this through his prophets sent to the Jewish people but above all, through His Son, Jesus Christ. Over the centuries to the present day, through his worldwide Church and His Word in the Bible, God continues to make Himself known to mankind. When I say the Church, I do not necessarily mean the institutions of Christianity, but those individuals who live according to God's Law.

I would like to say that God has also sent non-Jewish prophets to non-Jewish people, all over the world.

God has also created man with the innate capacity to perceive Him. This fact is obvious because all peoples have always had a God or gods, whether an idol or idols or a real God; it seems like man has always known that God exists.

God is the best resource man has in life. He is there to benefit man; he takes care of us if we choose to live according to His Law; He is Our Heavenly Father.

God would like man to rely on Him above everyone and everything else, when in need. Why? The reason is **God cares for man;** He feels responsible for man's well-being and above all, He knows man, including his needs and problems, better than anybody else. He knows that He is capable of resolving your problems better than anybody else because he is God.

God is real and alive and present within reach of every man who seeks Him, wherever you happen to be. Despite all this writing on God's identity, it is only your personal experience with God that will confirm to you that He really exists and of His capabilities. One's personal experience is the most important route for one to acquire faith and confidence in The Almighty.

No worries, no stress, and take all your problems to God in prayer! Have full confidence and trust that God can resolve your problems in the best possible manner; because He is God.

32

Miscellaneous

In this chapter, I will be looking into various controversial topics.

The doctrine of the Holy Trinity

This is a concept, taught by some Christian Churches where **God is perceived as being unique but made of three coeternal, consubstantial (of the same substance) and distinct persons who are also gods**: The Father, The Son (Jesus Christ) and The Holy Spirit.

I am coming back again to this topic of the Holy Trinity because it is vital that man has a correct concept of God. It is also vital that we define God as defined in the Bible; a one and unique God.

The Bible writes about God the Father, the creator of the universe; it writes about Jesus Christ, the Son of God and it writes about the Holy Spirit, that is. God's Holy presence, **but there is no mention of "the Holy Trinity" or of "the Trinity."**

God defines Himself repeatedly in the scriptures in The Old Testament as a unique being. Let's see a few examples from just a single book of the Bible, that of the prophet Isaiah:

Isaiah 44:6; This is what Jehovah says, The King of Israel and his Repurchaser, Jehovah of armies: *"I am the first and I am the last. There is no God but me."*

Isaiah 45:22; "*Turn to me and be saved, all the ends of the earth, For I am God, and there is no one else."*

Isaiah 46: 9; "Remember the former things of long ago, That I am God, and there is no other. I am God, and there is no one like me."

In the first and second commandments, see below, God demands exclusive devotion to anyone who acknowledges him as God.

Note: These are commandments and not requests.

First Commandment: Exodus 20:2-3; "I am Jehovah your God, who brought you out of the land of Egypt, out of the house of slavery. **You must not have any other gods besides me."**

Second Commandment: Exodus 20:4-5; ... "You must not make for yourself a carved image or a form like anything that is in the heavens above or on the earth below or in the waters under the earth. You must not bow down to them nor be enticed to serve them **for I, Jehovah your God, am a God who requires exclusive devotion.**

This is the original Second Commandment which has been deleted and substituted with the Third Commandment by the Roman Catholic church and the Lutheran church, to accommodate illegal, according to the Bible, practices of praying to or through statues. To verify what the real original Ten Commandments are, one needs to read them from the Hebrew Bible, that is the Tanakh or from the Torah, (part of the scriptures written only by the prophet Moses), which have been handed down over the centuries.

Certain events and statements made by Jesus Christ confirmed the uniqueness of God, that is there is no other being in the universe like Him. Also, that Jesus is subordinate to his Father; see a few examples below.

The Temptation of Jesus is narrated in the Gospels of Matthew, Mark and Luke.

Query: If Jesus was God, would the Devil have tempted him to sin against himself?

Luke 4:6-8: Then the Devil said to him: *"I will give you all this authority and their splendour i.e. (All the kingdoms of the world) because it has been handed over to me, (obviously, not by Jesus Christ) and I give it to whoever I wish. If you, therefore, do an act of worship before me, it will all be yours."* It is obvious that such a request would not have made sense if Jesus Christ was God.

In reply, Jesus said to him: *"It is written, it is Jehovah your God you must worship, and **it is to Him alone** you must render sacred service."*

During the last meal with his apostles, Jesus makes the following statement when praying; **John 17:3**: *"This means everlasting life, their coming to know you, **the only true God, and** the one whom you sent, Jesus Christ."* Note that Jesus makes a distinction between himself and "The Only True God.

See; **Matthew 24:36**: *"Concerning that day and hour nobody knows, neither the angels of the heavens nor the Son, **but only** the Father."* In this scripture, Jesus affirms that **only God knows** when the end of the world will be but **not him** or anyone else. This means that he and God are two different individuals.

Mark 10:18; Jesus said to him: *"Why do you call me good? Nobody is good except **one**, God."*

Mark 12:28-30: One of the scribes who had come up and heard them disputing, knowing that he had answered them in a fine way, asked him: *"Which commandment is first of all?"* Jesus answered: *"The first is, 'Hear, O Israel, **Jehovah our God is one Jehovah**, and you must love Jehovah your God with your whole heart and with your whole soul and with your whole mind and with your whole strength."* This is another affirmation of Jesus, that God is "One."

Matthew 26:39; *"My Father, if it is possible, **let** this cup be taken from me, yet **not as I will, but as you will**."* If Jesus was God, why was he praying to His Father, for support?

John 12:49; "For I did not speak on my own initiative, but the Father Himself **who sent me has given me a commandment** as to what to say and what to speak." You command someone only if he is **under your authority, which means, he is inferior to you in authority.**

Jesus is subordinate to his Father, therefore, is not his equal and therefore, is distinct from Him. Second, if someone is a God, you would not need to rely on anybody else telling you what to speak, you would be self-sufficient; Jesus instead, relies on his Father, he does not speak of his own initiative, but what he has been **commanded** to speak.

John 6:38; *"For I have come down from heaven not to do my will but to do the will of him who sent me."*

John 13:16: *"Most truly I say to you, a slave is not greater than his master, nor is one who is sent greater than the one who sent him."*

A phrase in **John 1:1**; *"**In the beginning** was the Word, and the Word was with God, and the Word was a god,"* is frequently quoted to justify the notion that Jesus is God; this is because it is misunderstood. This phrase affirms that Jesus is not God because he had a starting point, that is: **In the beginning,** when he came into existence, God instead has/had no beginning.

The **Christian creed** says that Jesus was generated from the same substance as the Father. Generated by whom?

Christ has his own distinct identity; though **in communion** with his Father: **John 14: 10-11**; *"Do you not believe that I am in union with the Father and the Father is in union with me? The things I say to you I do not speak of my own originality, but the Father who remains in union with me is doing his works. Believe me that I am in union with the Father and the Father is in union with me; otherwise, believe* *because of the works themselves."* Jesus is **in communion with the Father and also has godly powers, conceded to him by his Father**. The works, that is, the miracles, testify that God is with him because no earthly man could do the miracles that Christ did autonomously, that is independently of God.

Jesus never claimed to be God, instead, he claimed to be a messenger, the Messiah and he also claimed to be the Son of God.

See **Matthew 16:13-17**; When Jesus came to the region of Caesarea Philippi, he asked his disciples, "Who do people say the Son of Man is?" They replied, "Some say John the Baptist; others say Elijah; and still others, Jeremiah or one of the prophets." "But what about you?" he asked. "Who do you say I am?" Simon Peter answered, "**You are the Messiah, the Son of the living God**." Jesus replied, "Blessed are you, Simon son of Jonah, for this was not revealed to you by flesh and blood but by my Father in heaven."

God himself affirms repeatedly in the Bible that he requires **exclusive, entire and undivided devotion. God would like you to pray directly to Him** and not through Mary the mother of Jesus Christ or the saints.

Is the Holy Spirit God?

According to the scriptures, the Holy Spirit **originates** from God the Father. The Holy Spirit is described as a kind of **living power**, a living presence of God sent from God the Father to someone, to guide and support them in accomplishing a specific mission. When one receives the Holy Spirit, we say that, he has been anointed.

If the Holy Spirit originates from the Father, it cannot be considered to be a God because it is not autonomous, its life or its existence depends on the Father.

Matthew 3:13-17: As soon as Jesus was baptised, he came up out of the water. Heaven was opened and he saw the spirit (power) of God descending like a dove and alighting on him. Then a voice said from heaven, *"This is my own dear son with whom I am pleased."* Jesus got anointed through his baptism.

When Jesus started his earthly mission, on the Sabbath, as was his custom, he went to the synagogue of his home town, Nazareth. He stood up to read, and the scroll of the prophet Isaiah was handed to him. Unrolling it, he found the place where it is written: The Spirit of Jehovah is upon me **because He has anointed me** to preach the gospel/the Good News to the poor; he has sent me forth to heal the broken-hearted, to preach deliverance to the captives, and recovering of sight to the blind, to set at liberty them that are oppressed. **Luke 4:18.**

In **Matthew 12:31-32**: *"For this reason I say to you, every sort of sin and blasphemy will be forgiven men, **but the blasphemy against the Spirit will not be forgiven**. For example, whoever speaks a word against the Son of man, it will be forgiven him; but whoever speaks against the Holy Spirit, it will not be forgiven him, no, not in this system of things nor in that to come."*

As you can see from the above scripture, Jesus makes a clear distinction between himself and the Holy Spirit.

The Bible overflows with other proofs which deny the existence of The Trinity/The Holy Trinity. This doctrine of the Holy Trinity is illogical; you cannot say a person is **unique**, but made of three **distinct** persons or God is unique but made of three distinct Gods. Many Christians who have questioned its logic, have been advised by the Christian clergy: "To have faith."

The early Christian Church did not have this concept of Trinity /Holy Trinity, it was introduced officially into the Christian Church after the First Nicean Council, of **325 AD** in the fourth century.

This doctrine of the Holy Trinity has been contested right from the moment it was introduced into the Christian Church and is still contested today by many Christian Churches, Christian scholars and various individuals. It has been a source of division among

Christians, right from its introduction. In the early Christian Church those who opposed it were expelled from the Church and excommunicated, that is officially banned from associating with other members of the congregation and denied from receiving any sacrament.

At that time, the only Christian Church was, the Catholic Church; which had become very powerful and hence difficult to challenge without incurring terrible consequences. Also, in those early days of the Christian Church, the Holy Bible was not accessible to the public; there were only a few handwritten and very expensive copies, under the absolute monopoly of the only Christian Church in existence; the Roman Catholic Church. This fact explains partially why this doctrine survived unchallenged for many years; the Bible was not accessible to the public, for many centuries.

In the year 1440, a goldsmith in Germany named Johannes Gutenberg invented the printing press, which started the Printing Revolution. This Printing Revolution now made the Bible accessible to any literate person, mainly the Christian clergy, scholars and nobles. With the newly-acquired knowledge of the Bible, some people now felt confident, in fact, they felt obliged, to challenge questionable doctrines present in the Catholic Church. They could now testify from the bible, that the Holy Trinity was a false doctrine, as it was not present in the Bible and could also testify, from the Bible, that God was one; a unique being.

This newly-acquired knowledge led to permanent divisions in the Christian Church, which remain to this day. The spread of accurate Bible knowledge in Europe led to Revolts against the Catholic Church and to terrible Religious Wars in Europe, which lasted from the 16th to the 18th century.

The Blasphemy Act of **1697** was an Act of the Parliament of England, which made it an offence to deny that, the Trinity was God.

In **1697**, **Thomas Aikenhead**, a twenty-year-old Scottish student from Edinburgh, **was the last person** in Great Britain to be executed (hanged) for blasphemy; he was charged with denying the Trinity. Thanks to people like Thomas Aikenhead, who stood up for the truth, they have made it possible today for Christians to be able to discuss religious matters without fear of persecution and for this we are eternally grateful to them.

Today there are **three verses** in the New Testament that seem to openly support the doctrine of the Trinity, but they have been declared fraudulent.

The first verse: Matthew 28: 19; *"Go, therefore, and make disciples of all nations, baptizing them in the name of the Father and of the Son and of the Holy Spirit, ...* this particular verse contains a phrase used by many Christian Churches to baptize: *"I baptize you, in the name of the Father and of the Son and of the Holy Spirit,"* this is why it is named: The Baptism Formula or The Trinitarian Baptismal Formula. This verse is also called; **the Great Commission**, because Jesus is commanding his disciples to go out, preach and baptize, that is to make new disciples from all nations.

It is claimed that the original script was: *"With one word and voice he said to his disciples: "Go, and make disciples of all nations IN My Name, teaching them to observe all things whatsoever I have commanded you."*

If you write on the Web, this particular query: **"Is Matthew 28:19 a forgery?"** or **"Is Matthew 28:19 a fraud?"** you will find some credible research done by renowned Christian scholars, who claim and provide evidence, to prove that the Baptism Formula, which uses the phrase: *"baptizing them in the name of the Father and of the Son and of the Holy Spirit"* is a forgery.

Please, check out sources of proof for yourselves, if you can.

The second verse which seems to validate the Trinity is 1 John 5:7-8: *"For there are three that bear record / that testify/ that* *are witnesses in heaven,_the Father, the Word, (Jesus) and the Holy Ghost: **and these three are one." And there are three that** bear witness on earth, the Spirit, the Water and the Blood, and these three agree in one, i.e. in* one testimony.

It has been demonstrated, that the phrase of 1 John 5:7: "... **in heaven, the Father, the Word, and the Holy Ghost: and these three are one,**" which support the Trinity doctrine, does not appear in **the original Greek scriptures**. It is said that this particular phrase was a marginal note that became interpolated/added into the main text and this is why this part of the false addition is called: **The Johannine Comma.**

Comma: to alter or corrupt something, such as a text by inserting new or foreign matter.

One of the main arguments against 1 John 5:7, is The first Greek manuscripts of the New Testament that contains the comma dates from the 15th century, that is, **all previous Greek scripts do not have it.**

The third biblical verse which seems to validate the Trinity doctrine is: **1 Timothy 3:16:** And without controversy great is the mystery of godliness: **God was manifest in the flesh**, justified in the Spirit, seen of angels, preached unto the Gentiles, believed on in the world, received up into glory.

This phrase: "***God** was manifest in the flesh,*" is meant to prove **the deity** of Jesus Christ and hence to confirm the doctrine of the Trinity.

One of the earliest contesters of this particular verse was none other than **Sir Isaac Newton**, (**1642-1727**) the English scholar, physicist, philosopher, theologian and mathematician, famous for having formulated the theory of Universal Gravitation; apparently, he also invented Calculus in maths. In his Thesis/Dissertation: "**A Historical Account of Two Notable Corruptions of Scripture,**" he provided evidence to prove that two scriptures of the Bible, 1

John 5:7 and **1 Timothy 3: 16**, were fraudulent. These findings of Newton were not published during his lifetime; he feared printing them due to the cruel persecution, present in his time, of those who denied the Trinity Doctrine.

I believe that this verse has now been proved fraudulent, because the majority of Bible translations today, read **1 Timothy 3:16** as: And without controversy great is the mystery of godliness: "***He*** *was manifest in flesh, justified in the Spirit, seen of angels, preached unto the Gentiles, believed on in the world, received up into glory*" and some other Bibles; "And without controversy great is the mystery of godliness: ***which*** *was manifest in the flesh, justified in the Spirit, seen of angels, preached unto the Gentiles, believed on in the world, received up into glory.*"

1 Timothy 3:16; New International Version; Beyond all question, the mystery from which true godliness springs is great: **He** appeared in the flesh, was vindicated/authenticated by the Spirit, was seen by angels, was preached among the nations, was believed on in the world, was taken up in glory.

When one finds controversies in the Bible, it is up to each individual to do their own private and personal research; do not try to shift this responsibility of researching for the truth, onto the clergy; they too might not have the correct answer or could have their hands tied by vows of obedience or other issues present in their church. Listen to what they say, but it is you yourself, that has to decide what to believe.

This controversy, regarding the existence or not of the Trinity, is still very present today among different Christian churches.

The Christian Church has inherited many doctrines and rites from paganism, it is important for us Christians, to review all this "stuff" and to select attentively what conforms to the Bible's teachings; the rest could be declared obsolete. For example, see The History of Christmas at: "SimpleToRemember.com"

Failure to do this will lead to people deserting the Church, once they find out that the doctrines taught are false or that certain rituals and ceremonies, very present in the Christian churches, have little to do with Bible teachings or with Christianity **and some have very dark pagan origins.**

Nowadays, information of all kinds is accessible to the public, through the internet. People can now find out things which were previously reserved only for certain groups of society. This is especially true regarding religion; for example, I was shocked to learn about the role played by the Catholic Church, during the Inquisition period of European history, 12th -19th century; this made me realize that the institutions of the Church are run by human beings and not by saints.

Note what Jesus had to say on some issues, some quite controversial subjects today.

Jesus and prayer

Please note; the fact that Jesus prayed to His Father, shows that he and is Father are two different entities.

Prayer was a very important part of Jesus' life; he was always praying to God, His Father. Before the start of his mission, Jesus was led into the wilderness by God's Holy Spirit for forty days and nights. I believe this period of isolation and prayer was meant to prepare Jesus for his earthly mission. **Luke 5: 16** says Jesus often went into desolate areas, free from the crowds, to pray. Prayer is a dialogue between man and God; this means that Jesus was always in contact with His Father. Before choosing his disciples, Jesus spent the whole night in prayer; see **Luke 6: 12-13**. While Jesus waited for the ordeal of his crucifixion to begin, he prayed intensively to His Father; **Luke 22:41-44**.

Jesus Christ's dying words on the cross were addressed to his Father; Luke 23:46 *"Father, into your hands I entrust my spirit."*

In **Matthew 6: 6-8**, Jesus advised his apostles how to pray: "Take care not to practice your righteousness in front of men, to be noticed by them. But when you pray, go into your private room and, after shutting your door, pray to your Father who is in secret. Then your Father who looks on in secret will repay you. Do not say the same things over and over again, for your Father knows what you need even before you ask Him.

From the advice that Jesus gives to his apostles, it is quite clear that prayer should be a private and personal dialogue between us and our Creator. The apostles have written down only episodes where Jesus prays with his apostles; the Last Supper and in the Garden of Gethsemane, before his arrest.

Following Christ's example, as he prayed frequently, prayer should also play a vital role in every Christian's life; prayer connects man to his creator, for support and guidance in life.

Hell, does it exist?

God's Law is positive for any society and it is made for the benefit of man. It doesn't serve God, it is an act of loving kindness for God to provide man with his instructions.

If God has given a Law, then there must be consequences for breaking this Law; **there must be accountability for breaking this Law.**

Many religions, including some Christian Churches, teach that those who reject God's Laws perpetually will be punished by God, by being thrown into Hell.

Definition of Hell: a spiritual realm in the afterlife; of evil and of suffering generally **depicted as a place of everlasting fire**, where the wicked are thrown as punished after death. It is perceived to be located underneath the earth.

I have always found this kind of punishment extremely distressing and contradictory to what is taught about God: "God is Love/God is loving kindness and that God is merciful."

First, let's see the definition of some terms associated with the afterlife.

Sheol in the Hebrew Bible is a place of still darkness and the abode of the dead.

The name "**Hades**", Greek Aides (Greek does not have the letter H) "the Unseen", means god of the underworld, abode of the dead in Greek mythology.

The word "**Hades**" present in the Bible, is the Greek translation of Sheol; it is present only in the New Testament. Therefore, Sheol and Hades mean the same thing; Sheol used in Judaism and in the Old Testament, becomes Hades when translated into Greek, in the New Testament, that is, **the place where the dead or let's say, where the departed souls/spirits reside.**

Gehenna, also called Gehinnom, **abode of the damned in the afterlife** in Jewish and Christian eschatology, the doctrine of the end of times.

Jesus uses the word Gehenna to symbolise a place of torment but in reality, it was a real place, which existed in Christ's time; a valley outside Jerusalem called Valley of Hinnom where rubbish and any other dirt, for example, dead animals were thrown and continually burned. In Judaism, it came to symbolise a place where unrighteous souls are tormented or punished. The word "Gehenna" is translated as Hell in some Bibles.

In the New Testament, Jesus tells a parable/story regarding a rich man and a poor beggar, named Lazarus: (**Luke 16: 19-31);** in this particular parable, Jesus did not confirm that hell exists, he simply said that the rich man was tormented in Hades, however, if the rich man could see and communicate with Abraham and, although far off, it implies that Abraham must have been in in the same area, that is in Hades, but in the bliss area, while the rich man was in Hades but in the area of torment. Some Christians may interpret his parable is to mean, something else. If Jesus was using this parable to illustrate something, it was based on real situations, that is, something that really exists or could really exists as he described it and not fantasies.

See **Luke 16:23**; "And being in torments **in Hades**, he lifted up his eyes and saw Abraham far off, where? In Hades? In Heaven? and Lazarus in his bosom." Note: the rich man "sees" Abraham and Lazarus and "talks" to Abraham and also makes a request for Abraham to send Lazarus to him.

In your opinion, do you think Abraham and Lazarus were in Paradise?

Abraham informs the rich man that: *"between us and you a great chasm has been set in place so that those who want to go from here to you cannot, nor can anyone cross over from there to us."*

It is apparent that Hades is not all uniform, but there exist two different zones completely separated by a deep fissure, a chasm, however, both of these zones are present in Hades.

This means that when good and bad people die, they both go to Hades/Sheol, but to different zones. Souls of "Godly people" go to an area of Bliss in Hades and those of "Non-Godly people" go to an area of Torment, in Hades.

According to the Bible; Sheol has a "bad zone," a zone of torment, i.e. "hell" where the wicked go when they die and it also has a "good zone"/area of bliss, where the good people go when they die.

Note; some Bibles translate Sheol or Hades as "**hell**," this is because there is **also** a common belief that "Good People" go to Heaven when they die.

Note: **according to the Bible, no one goes to heaven when they die but to Sheol/Hades, where one dwells until the Day of Judgement.**

Examples of how the word Sheol is used in the Old Testament:

Genesis 37:35: All his sons and all his daughters rose up to comfort him, but he refused to be comforted and said, "No, I shall go down to Sheol, to my son, mourning. Here Abraham starts mourning when informed of his son's death, that is of Joseph's death, but Joseph had actually been sold into slavery.

In 1 Samuel 28:3-19; the "dead" Prophet, Samuel informs the king, Saul that: "The LORD will deliver both Israel and you into the hands of the Philistines, and tomorrow you and your sons will be with me," in Sheol. See explanation below under: Why is divination prohibited in the Bible?

In the Old Testament, the phrase: *"Went to rest with his ancestors,"* is frequently used, to refer to what happens when someone dies.

See **2 Samuel 7:12**: When your days are over and **you go to be with your ancestors,** I will raise up your offspring to succeed you, one of your own sons, and I will establish his kingdom. **Note: this is God talking to King David of Israel, through the prophet Nathan.**

1 Kings 14:31; Rehoboam **slept with his ancestors**, i.e. his spirit has passed on to join the other departed spirits, of his ancestors.

Judges 2:10; And **all that generation were gathered to their fathers**, i.e. Joshua's generation.

Matthew 18:8; *"If then, your hand or your foot makes you stumble, cut it off and throw it away from you. It is better for you to* *enter into life maimed or lame than to be thrown with two hands or two feet into **the everlasting fire.**"*

Note: **only the fire is: "everlasting", Jesus does not say that the sinner will burn in everlasting fire forever.**

From the book of Revelation, the sinners will be **destroyed in an everlasting fire.**

The only beings in the Bible that are said to be "tormented forever in a lake of fire," are the Devil and The Wild Beast and its prophets. See **Revelation 20:10**; And the Devil who was misleading them was hurled into the lake of fire and sulphur, where both the wild beast and the false prophet already were; and they will be tormented day and night forever and ever.

Rev: 20:12-13; And I saw the dead, the great and the small, standing before the throne, and scrolls were opened. But another scroll was opened; it is the scroll of life. The dead were judged out of those things written in the scrolls according to their deeds. **And the sea gave up the dead in it, and death and the Graves/Hades/Sheol** gave up the dead in them, and they were judged individually according to their deeds.

Please note: in Rev. 20: 14-15; then death and Hades were hurled into the lake of fire. This means the second death, the lake of fire. This verse means that the common grave: Hades or Sheol or Hell, will be destroyed **after the final** Universal Judgement.

Note: After the Universal judgement, all the evil doers will be destroyed, the people resurrected will live forever so Hell/Hades/Sheol will not serve any more, therefore, it will be destroyed.

Rev. 20:15; Note, the Lake of Fire, means a second death, that is these "sinners", **those not found in the Book of Life, and Sheol/Hades** will cease to exist, after a second "death".

See **Rev. 21:8**; But as for the cowards and those without faith and those who are disgusting in their filth and murderers and the sexually immoral and those practising spiritism and idolaters and all the liars, their portion will be in the lake that burns with fire and sulphur. This means the second death.

This means: "Sinners, will be destroyed and therefore, will not continue burning forever.

In the Old Testament, God destroys his enemies **immediately and rapidly**; see **Numbers Chapter 16** and, in Sodom and Gomorrah in **Genesis 19:24-25.**

Therefore, my conclusion on the existence of hell as a place of eternal torment, by the burning sinners in everlasting fire is: such a place does not exist for mankind. According to Revelation in the Bible, the evil people will be destroyed, through a lake that burns with fire and sulphur; they will have a second and final death; **they will cease to exist**.

False prophets

Jesus warned his disciples about false prophets: **Matthew 7:15-16**; *"Be on the watch for the false prophets who come to you in sheep's covering, but inside they are ravenous, (extremely hungry) wolves (extremely dangerous because they will "eat you up" i.e. they will destroy you). **by their fruits, you will recognize them."***

Reading the Bible gives you accurate knowledge of God so that you are able to benefit yourself and others. Bible knowledge helps you identify deception in religious matters, that is people who preach and practise falsehood in the name of Christianity or in the name of other religions and also from other false ideas, especially in politics. But the most important defence against false prophets is praying to God; He is accessible from every corner of the universe; He will illuminate your mind on what the truth is.

Please note: Most biblical figures did not have Bibles but relied solely on God for guidance.

Religious hierarchy or ranks

Jesus instructed his disciples not to accept titles of authority in religious matters: **Matthew 23: 8-11;** "*But you, do not you be called Rabbi, for one is your Teacher, and all of you are brothers; Moreover, do not call anyone on earth, your father, for ONE is your Father, the heavenly one. Neither be called leaders/instructors, for your leader/instructor is one, the Messiah. The greatest among you shall be your servant.*

With titles, you acquire privileges and authority over your fellow Christians. These Titles tend to generate pride and division, that is; they are a trap.

Jesus goes on to say in **Matthew 23:11-12;** "*But the greatest one among you must be your minister. Whoever exalts himself will be humbled, and whoever humbles himself will be exalted.*" This is a caution against someone considering themselves superior (for any reason) to their fellow Christians.

Mark 10:45; "*For even the Son of Man came, not to be ministered to, but to minister and to give his life as a ransom in exchange for many.*" Jesus says he came to serve and not to be served.

Paul and the other disciples of Jesus, address their fellow Christians as: "brothers." Jesus would like Christians to consider each other with equal affection; like brothers. This attitude and doing away with titles should eliminate rivalry in the Christian congregation.

The rivalry between Christian denominations

Luke 9: 49-50; In response, John said: "*Instructor, we saw someone expelling demons by using your name, and we tried to prevent him because he is not following with us.*" But Jesus said to him: "*Do not try to prevent him, for whoever is not against you is for you.*"

John 17: 20-21; "*I make request, not concerning these only, but also concerning those putting faith in me through their word, **so that they may all be one**, just as you, Father, are in union with me and I* *am in union with you, that they also may be in union with us, so that the world may believe that you sent me."*

In his last meal, Jesus made a point of praying for Christians, (*those putting faith in me through their, the apostles', word/preaching.* Therefore, it is Christ's wish that all Christians should be united, after all, they should all be following the **same teachings** of the one and only Jesus Christ.

There is no compulsion regarding religion

When Jesus sent out his disciples to preach, see **Luke 10: 1-12**; he told them, *"Wherever you enter into a house, say first: 'May this house have peace.' And if a friend of peace is there, your peace will rest upon him. But if there is not, it will return to you."*

But wherever you enter into a city and they do not receive you, go out into its main streets and say: *'We wipe off against you even the dust that sticks to our feet from your city. Nevertheless, know this: that the Kingdom of God has come near."*

Luke 9: 51-56; As the days were drawing near for him to be taken up, he resolutely set his face to go to Jerusalem. So, he sent messengers ahead of him. And they went and entered a village of Samaritans to make preparations for him. But they did not receive him, because he was determined to go to Jerusalem. When the disciples James and John saw this, they said: **"Lord, do you want us to call fire down from heaven and annihilate them?" But he (Jesus), turned and rebuked them**. So, they went to a different village.

Mark 5: 1-16, tells of an event where Jesus casts out an evil Spirit, called Legion, from a demonized man. This evil spirit, with permission from Jesus, transfers to a very large group of swine grazing nearby. Once Legion had transferred into the herd of swine, the herd rushed over the precipice into the sea and all the herd, about 2,000 of them, drowned. The herdsmen, who had been looking after these pigs, rushed into the city and reported the incident to the people, who then came out to where Jesus was.

They were very impressed to see the ex-demonized man dressed up and calmly seated, but they pleaded with Jesus to go away from their region, most probably due to the loss of their pigs. Jesus did not argue with or threaten these people, they were Gentiles, as Jews do not eat swine; he took the next boat and sailed away.

These people must have realized that he was a prophet, but clearly, were not interested in hearing the word of God.

Note: a pig is a domesticated swine.

The above events clearly show that there should be no forced preaching, to people who do not want to hear the word of God and consequently, there should be no forced conversions into the Christian faith.

Idle talk

Mathew 12:36: *"But I tell you that everyone will have to give account, on the Day of Judgment, for every empty/idle word they have spoken."* I was shocked to find this verse in the Bible, and then I thought about it and wondered: Why would anybody give idle talk? Who would be prepared to listen to idle talk? They too must be very bored.

It is my opinion that today, idle talk is very present in our society and media; which means that the public likes it or tolerates it because boredom is also very present in our society today. What is wrong with idle talk? I **believe it is a waste of time and time is precious**. I believe that such talk also shows spiritual emptiness, that is you do not have God in your heart. It is like one is not fully conscious of what comes out of their mouth. It is well known that idleness leads to sin; if one does not consciously monitor their thoughts and actions. Therefore, be aware of your free time and channel it into something constructive. Jesus was never idle.

Also, God is not wasteful because He is the most efficient being in the universe. What is the evidence of this efficiency? Look at any animal and study it; you will marvel to see how all parts of its body work in great harmony and how everything in its body serves for its existence, nothing is wasted.

Jesus's view on food

Jesus in "The Lord's Prayer," acknowledges that our food, a basic and daily necessity for our physical survival, comes from God; an act of loving care from Jehovah, because it is He who makes the plants grow; the primary source of food in all food chains and provides water, which is vital to life for all living creatures. This means that the food on our plates originates through God's vital energy.

See **Matthew 6: 9-11**; Our Father in the heavens; Let your name be sanctified; Let your kingdom come; Let your will take place; On earth as it is in heaven.

Give us this day our daily bread.

See **Mark 7: 14-23** "he (Jesus) then called the crowd to him and said**: listen to me, all of you, and understand the meaning. *"nothing from outside a man that enters into him can defile him; but the things that come out of a man are the things that defile him."***

Mark 7: 17-23; Now, when he had entered a house away from the crowd, his disciples began to question him about the illustration he had just made on food. So, he said to them: "Are you also without understanding like them? Are you not aware that nothing from outside that enters into a man can defile him, since it enters, not into his heart, but into his stomach, and it passes out into the sewer?"

He went on: "What comes out of a person is what defiles them, For it is from within, out of the hearts of men, that evil thoughts come: sexual immorality, thefts, murders, acts of adultery, greed, acts of wickedness, deceit, brazen conduct, an envious eye, blasphemy, haughtiness and unreasonableness. All these evils come from inside and defile a person."

This parable is interpreted to mean that, Jesus had declared all foods clean.

It is true that certain animals, if not well managed, for example, pigs, have a high rate of carrying parasites and therefore infecting people. They are therefore considered unclean in many cultures. Chickens eat everything a pig does but do not carry the parasites that a pig does, therefore, they are not considered unclean by most people, however, some people do. Should you get parasites from your food, it is your body that is infected and not your soul, however your health is very important; without it you can do little, therefore, take good care of it.

If the Food Safety Agencies of your country guarantees that high risk foods are safe for human consumption, I do not see why they should not be consumed.

As regards the consumption of alcohol, Jesus did not condemn it; in fact, the first of his miracles regarded converting water into wine at a wedding ceremony, where they had run out of wine; see **John 2: 1-11.** During his last meal with the apostles, wine was consumed at the table. See **Luke 22:18** *"For I tell you I will not drink again from the fruit of the vine until the kingdom of God comes."*

Drinking wine during meals is very normal, in fact, it is a tradition in many wine-producing countries. Wine consumption during meals was part of the Jewish way of life, in Christ's time, because, Israel is in the Mediterranean region, which is a wine-producing area. Wine helps digest food and hardly anyone gets drunk from drinking wine at the table.

If you observe a vine tree, you will note that it produces such a huge quantity of grapes, one cannot practically eat them all up. This is why since ancient times; man has made wine from grapes.

It is you who has the brains to decide how much and how frequently to consume alcohol, depending on various factors: age, sensitivity to alcohol, affordability of alcohol and climate. The production of high-grade alcohol like vodka or whiskey is common in areas which have extremely cold weather, for example, Russia, Scotland or the Alps; it is an important means to fight cold.

Alcohol does not think; it is a dead substance; it is you who has the brains to decide whether to make good or bad use of it.

Is there life after death; does man have a soul?

Did Jesus acknowledge life after death?

First of all, the resurrection of Jesus not only acknowledged but actually confirmed that life after death is a reality, it really exists. The more pressing question today is: does man have a soul and if he does, does it survive death? **Jesus was confronted with the same kinds of questions.**

Some Sadducees, Israelites who believed only in the Mosaic Law and who did not believe in life after death, confronted Jesus with queries about the existence of life after death. They wanted Jesus to tell them, if a woman had married her husband's brother, as was the tradition, due to the death of her husband; to whom would she belong to after resurrection? **See Matthew 22: 23-28.**

Jesus replied: **Matthew 22:29-30** "You are in error because you do not know the Scriptures or the power of God. At the resurrection people will neither marry nor be given in marriage; they will be like the angels in heaven.

Jesus further informed them that if God had told Moses; "*I am the God of Abraham, Isaac and Jacob,*" it meant that these three individuals were still in existence, although physically dead; "*He is not the God of the dead, but of the living. ...*" see: **Matthew 22: 31-32.**

In **Mathew 22: 36-38**; "*Teacher, which is the greatest commandment in the Law?*" He said to him: "*You must love Jehovah your God with your whole heart and with **your whole soul** and with* *your whole strength/vital force.*" Jesus was quoting **Deuteronomy 6: 5**; "*You must love Jehovah your God with all your heart and all **your soul** and all your strength*," written by the prophet Moses, who informs the Israelites that they must love God with all their being, that is with all the components that make them human beings.

From the above information, it is clear that: **the soul** is a component of every human being.

Matthew 10:28; And do not become fearful of those **who kill the body but cannot kill the soul**; rather, fear him who can **destroy both soul and body** in Gehenna. This means that the soul cannot be destroyed by man, but only by God.

The word "spirit" is sometimes used to represent the word "soul," expressing the immaterial nature of the soul; therefore, spirit and soul mean the same thing.

Note: The word soul is sometimes used to represent a human being, because without it, one dies; it is the essence of what gives life to a human being. See; **Joshua 11:11;** "*And they smote all the souls, who were therein... "They struck all the people who were in it."* They killed all the people in the city).

In Judaism, (Jesus practised Judaism), he therefore used the terms present in Judaism. The term "heart" was used to refer to where you felt your emotions and where you made decisions and where your desires originated from. For example:

Mark 7:21-22; For from inside, **out of the heart of men**, come injurious reasoning: sexual immorality, thefts, murders, acts of adultery, greed, acts of wickedness, deceit, brazen conduct, an envious eye, blasphemy, haughtiness, and unreasonableness.

Please note: When you die, your body, including all the components that make your body, your brain, your mind, your sense organs, your emotions etc. die. **A dead body does not perceive anything or express any sentiment.**

The soul survives death; however, this fact is highly contested today, even by some Christian Churches.

When Jesus raised the dead, he did not create new human beings, he simply called the soul of the deceased back into the dead body, because, God's power extends also into the invisible world.

Please note: The soul is not the same thing as the mind; the soul is immaterial but the mind is a functional part of the brain and therefore does not survive death.

The Bible confirms that man has a soul and it is immaterial **and** survives death.

Jesus explained what will be the signs of the conclusion of the system of things, at the end of the world.

Mathew 24:3-14: While he was sitting on the Mount of Olives, the disciples approached him privately, saying: "Tell us, when will these things be, and what will be the sign of your presence/your coming and the conclusion of the system of things/the coming of age?"

Jesus answered, "Watch out that no one misleads you. For many will come in my name, claiming, 'I am the Messiah,' and will deceive many. You will hear of wars and rumours of wars, but see to it that you are not alarmed. Such things must happen, but the end is still to come. Nation will rise against nation and kingdom against kingdom. There will be famines and earthquakes in various places. All these are but the beginning of pangs of pain/acute or sharp pains.

"Then you will be handed over to be persecuted and put to death, and **you will be hated by all nations because of me**. At that time many will turn away from the faith and will betray and hate each other, and many false prophets will appear and deceive many people. Because of the increase of wickedness, the love of most will grow cold, but the one who stands firm to the end will be saved. And this gospel of the kingdom will be preached in the whole world as a testimony to all nations, and then the end will come.

Please note: The Good News of the Kingdom will be preached in all the inhabited earth for a witness to all the nations, and then the end will come.

In line with God's eternal justice, at the conclusion of the system of things, "The Good News," will have been made accessible to every nation and all peoples; no one will be able to claim, that he has never heard of it.

From the description given above of the period before the end of times, mankind will be in a state of great suffering, there will be a lot of wickedness directed above all to practising Christians, and for this reason, Jehovah will have to intervene, to stop all that suffering and to wipe out all the evil, as He has always done, and will restore his righteousness, by installing his Kingdom.

Why is divination prohibited in the Bible?

Definition of divination: the practice of seeking knowledge of the future or the unknown by supernatural means.

What supernatural means are used for divination?

Sorcery: The use of black magic, that is invocation of evil spirits.

Spiritism: Communicating with the dead, done generally through a professional, a medium or a spirit medium, that is someone capable of communicating with the dead. The so-called "dead people" who communicate with the Mediums are actually evil spirits, because when a human being dies, he loses all capabilities associated with the body e.g. hearing, seeing, talking etc. and therefore, is not able to talk or communicate in any way.

Therefore, it is these evil spirits that communicate with the mediums and take on the form and voice of the dead person. See

1 Samuel 28:3-19. In this story, Saul the first king of the Israelites was at war with the Philistines. God chose him to govern Israel, but later God abandoned him because he refused to do what God had requested him.

1 Samuel 28:5-6: "When Saul saw the Philistine army, he was afraid; terror filled his heart. **He inquired of the Lord, but the Lord did not answer him** by dreams or Urim or prophets."

King Saul was desperate to find out the future outcome of his forthcoming battle with the Philistines. As Jehovah did not answer him, he decided to consult a Medium; something forbidden by Jehovah himself.

In the following biblical passage: **1 Samuel 28:3-19**, it is clear that the image the medium sees cannot be that of the real prophet Samuel, though she perceives it to be him because it resembles the Prophet Samuel in all ways. This is because, when the prophet Samuel lived, he was obedient to God and lived in harmony with God, up until his death. Therefore, if God Himself had refused to answer Saul's enquiries, there is no way the Prophet Samuel would have overruled it by answering Saul's enquiries; besides Saul was doing something prohibited by God, seeking counsel from a medium.

God's authority and protection are present in the visible and in the invisible world and continue to protect, even after death, those who live and die obedient to His Law. Therefore, in my opinion, God's protection over the Prophet Samuel was present even after his death and no evil spirit could have overcome Jehovah's power to make the Prophet Samuel be used by a Medium to foretell the future. Therefore, the image of the prophet Samuel visualized by the Medium, could not have been that of the real prophet; an evil spirit took up the form of the Prophet Samuel and communicated to the King Saul about the future events in battle with the Philistines.

Of all the Jewish prophets, why did Saul seek the prophet Samuel specifically? Saul had known the prophet, Samuel, before his death, in fact, it was him who had anointed him into his kingship; he also knew that God had previously communicated through Samuel, therefore, whatever the prophet Samuel said, must have been credible.

See Leviticus **19:31**; "*Do not turn to the spirit mediums and do not consult fortune-tellers so as to become unclean by them. I am Jehovah your God.*" See also: **Leviticus 20: 6, 27** and **Deuteronomy 18: 9-14**.

God has created man in such a way that he is not able to foresee the future, and God saw that it was good; so let us leave it at that.

It is also true that evil spirits, some evil spirits, have some supernatural powers and actually can foretell the future accurately. They use this particular supernatural power to entice mankind. See; **Mark 5: 11-17**, where Jesus allowed the evil spirits to enter into a herd of about 2,000 swine, the whole herd went mad, and rushed over the precipice into the sea; all of them drowned in the sea. It is evident that these particular evil spirits were extremely powerful, to be able to "infect" and control a herd of two thousand pigs.

See **Acts 16:16-34,** where the disciple Paul exorcises a spirit from a slave, who was also a fortune teller; from the moment the spirit left her, she lost the ability to foretell the future.

Why would anyone want to seek knowledge of the future, **or to know something hidden?** Is it not because of insecurity, which leads to wanting to be in control of all events in their own life? Another frequent cause for seeking services from mediums is vengeance, that is one would like to vindicate a particular, unresolved crime or find out if her husband, or if his wife, has a lover in order to harm them. Note: Christians are not supposed to commit revenge; see **Matthew 5:38-45.**

In divination, one fails to put faith in God; that He will protect them and their loved ones and save them from whatever situation they fear in their future. In divination, one resolves to take things into their own hands; using evil spirits, which **are actually subordinate to God and are his enemies.**

Anyone who uses mediums and evil spirits will come to rely on them **and not on God** and will be doing what God has forbidden.

Evil spirits do exist; Jesus confirmed it through the numerous exorcisms he performed. Jesus was able to cast out **all** evil spirits from "infected people" by simply ordering them to "get out" and they all did; they all acknowledged Jesus, as an authority; he being the Son of God.

The Devil will not tamper with anyone who has God in their heart. See **Job 1:9-12** and **Job 2:1-6**; the Devil cannot harm Job, without God's consent because Job is a God-fearing man and God protects him and all he has.

Anti-Semitism

Definition of anti-Semitic: Prejudice or hatred towards the Jewish People.

God chose the Jewish people to be a light to the world, through their prophets and Jesus Christ. It is God who decided that Jesus would be born a Jew.

I will quote Jesus Christ: **John 4:22**; *"You Samaritans worship what you do not know; we worship what we do know, for salvation is from the Jews."*

At the birth of Christianity, the Jews persecuted and killed Jewish Christian converts, that is the disciples of Jesus Christ, accusing them of blasphemy and heresy. Christians Jews and Christian gentiles (non-Jewish Christians), were also persecuted and killed throughout the Roman Empire, but generally, this persecution depended on various conditions of the local communities they lived in. Christianity, in its early years of existence, was not officially recognized by Rome.

When Christians were free from persecution, and in a position of power; in **February AD 313**, through the Edict of Milan, all hostilities against the Christian religion in the Roman Empire ceased and in **AD 380**, Christianity became the official religion of the Roman Empire. Christians then started to persecute, torture and kill Jews and coerce them into becoming Christians. This very unchristian behaviour clearly shows that the Christian Church of that particular period had become extremely corrupt and evil, for such things to happen.

In Europe over the centuries, with the support of and/or lack of protection from the authorities, Christian Churches and politicians, Jews have been persecuted horrendously; their homes and properties burnt down and/or vandalized. Such actions cannot be considered Christian in any way.

One of the frequent justifications used for these horrendous crimes was, among others, "Jews killed Christ." Why don't they say: thanks to the Jewish people, we have Jesus Christ and consequently, the Christian religion? Jesus Christ, his apostles and many of the early disciples were all Jews and it was through their preaching that the Christian religion was born.

The Jewish nation was honoured by the fact that God chose it to provide Jesus Christ and many prophets to humanity. Jesus Christ himself was a Jew; he never mistreated his own people, but preached to them and did numerous miracles among them. If you consider yourself a Christian, you should follow Christ's example.

It is important for Christians to read the Bible, but above all to pray, so that they can recognize and fight evil in their own Christian community and also to avoid being used by politicians, the clergy, false Christians and others; for non-Christian goals.

What did Jesus say about wealth?

I believe the parable of Lazarus the beggar and the rich man; (**Luke 16:19-31**), is concerned mainly with the cruel indifference of a man towards another fellow human being, more than the fact that he was rich. Being wealthy, it would have cost him nothing to give Lazarus a plate of food, leave alone what fell off his plate. This man breached outrageously the basics of Judaism and Christianity: "Love/treat your neighbour as yourself."

The parable of A certain Ruler, who wanted to know what he could do to inherit everlasting life, that is, the Kingdom of God. **Luke 18: 18-30, Mark 10: 17-31 and Matthew 19: 16- 30**

I really do not understand this parable. I do not understand why being rich makes it almost impossible to get Eternal Life. Although it is an enormous privilege to be a disciple of Jesus Christ, not everyone can or would like to be, a disciple. Does this mean that only Christ's disciples and "the not rich" people can go to heaven? Jesus seems satisfied when the rich man says, he has followed The Commandments since the days of his youth, but reacts to the fact that this man wants to be perfect or wants to be doubly sure, that he will get Eternal Life.

In Mark 10:21: "Jesus looked at him and loved him. This means he was a good man, for Jesus "to love him." "One thing you lack," he said. "Go sell everything you have and give to the poor, and you will have treasures in Heaven. Then come and follow me."

Eternal Life is very important, so what was wrong with the guy making sure that he gets it?

"It is easier for a camel to go through the eye of a needle than for someone who is rich to enter the kingdom of God."

Being rich has never been condemned before, in the Bible.

Christ concludes: "With God all things are possible," I believe, even a camel going through the eye of a needle.

I do not understand this parable, perhaps you will.

Sexual morality

Morality definition: principles concerning the distinction between right and wrong or good and bad behaviour, therefore immoral behaviour goes against the accepted concepts of what is right.

The sixth Commandment is: You shall not commit adultery.

Adultery is when one or more of the partners having consensual sexual intercourse is married to another person.

Fornication is sexual intercourse between two people not married to each other.

In Christ's time, fornication in Israel was very unlikely because all women were supposed to be under their father's protection until they married and no woman would have liked to dishonour her own father, due to love and respect for him, by engaging in fornication.

See **Deuteronomy 22: 20-21:** If, however, the charge is true and no proof of the young woman's virginity can be found, after marriage, she shall be **brought to the door of her father's house and there the men of her town shall stone her to death**. She has done an outrageous thing in Israel by being promiscuous while still in her father's house. You must purge the evil from among you.

Note: This Law confirms that sex was and is reserved only for a married couple.

The proof of virginity in ancient Israel was: **Deuteronomy 22:16-17**; Her father will say to the elders, "I gave my daughter in marriage to this man, but he dislikes her. Now he has slandered her and said, 'I did not find your daughter to be a virgin.' But here is the proof of my daughter's virginity. Then her parents shall display the cloth before the elders of the town." This cloth was laid on the bed of a newly married couple and was supposed to be soiled with blood after the couple's first night of marriage if the woman was a virgin.

The Laws on procreativity imply that the woman who had committed adultery must have been well-instructed by her family in the Law as regards sexual immorality; that is, she should have been well aware of the consequence of breaching this Law and this is why she is brought to the door of her father's house, to be stoned. She has deliberately disobeyed her own father or mother whoever was responsible for instructing her on the Law of God and also disobeyed God's Law.

Leviticus 20:10; "If a man commits adultery with another man's wife, with the wife of his neighbour, both the adulterer and the adulteress must be put to death."

Deuteronomy 22:13-30; Gives some rules and regulations of sexual behaviour in Judaism.

Note: Today it is a proved fact that the presence or absence of the hymen is not a reliable indicator of virginity or sexual experience, in fact, the study by Emans et al found that 19% of the sexually active postpubertal females had no visible abnormalities of the hymen, that is, they still had a hymen. Some women are born without a hymen, besides the use of menstrual tampons and menstrual cups could break the hymen. According to: www.healthify.nz; of date: 5 June 2020, some hymens are stretchier than others and will never split or bleed. It is impossible to tell by looking at a hymen whether you are a virgin or not.

Please note: Jesus talked very little about sexual morals, probably, because this was not an issue during his life time. It is my opinion that all Jewish women and men in ancient Israel and in Christ's lifetime were very well instructed in the Law on sexual morality and that breaching it led to capital punishment: by stoning.

In **John 8:1-11,** Jesus saved a woman from being stoned to death, accused of committing adultery.

I had often wondered why the Law on sexual morality was so brutal: **Deuteronomy 22: 20-21, Deuteronomy 22:23-24, Leviticus 20:10**, yet this brutality must be justified as God is the source of justice and righteousness.

If one knows very well because they had been instructed, that breaching a Law will lead to capital punishment, why would you dare breach it? Apparently, someone might prefer risking their own life than renouncing certain "romantic encounters" or it may be someone was drunk, when he or she broke the Law; whatever the reason, one should be fully aware of the consequences of their actions.

In Judaism, a child born through forbidden sexual practices, by the Torah, is called **a mamzer**, that is, an illegitimate child. A mamzer is forbidden under Torah law to marry anyone who is not a mamzer. He can only marry another mamzer or converts. The stigma of being a mamzer **lasts forever.**

Deuteronomy 23:2; "No one of illegitimate birth shall enter the assembly of the Lord; none of his descendants, even to the tenth generation, shall enter the assembly of the **Lord**.

What kind of woman, in the ancient and present-day Jewish community, could dare breach the Law on procreation and risk having an illegitimate child, thereby condemning her child and all his offspring to eternal hardship and discrimination, of being a mamzer?

It now makes sense why people and especially women, were given capital punishment in ancient Israel for breaching the Law regulating procreation.

The death of King David's illegitimate son now makes sense. See **2 Samuel 12:14-31**.

All women should be educated to view themselves as potential mothers; this is the most important role that a woman has in her life. As such, a potential mother should uphold the dignity and rights of her child at all times, **even before their birth**. Having an illicit affair means that, "a potential mother" forgets or ignores or is unaware of the rights of her child: to have a father and a right to live free of discrimination and condemnation, putting her own immediate sexual desire above the well-being of her own child. This is what is unacceptable.

Today women are encouraged by the Media, to be attractive, not with a goal of finding a husband, but to be sexually desired and therefore, to have some "romantic adventures"; it promotes illicit sex as "a pleasure to be consumed", just as one eats a pizza, as the social norm. The media however hardly ever mentions: pregnancy, contraception, abortions, sexually transmitted diseases, motherhood and marriage.

Young people should also be made well aware of the dangers of deception by the media: film scenes where couples jump "in and out of bed," using no contraception and with no consequences at all, is far from reality.

Many young people have been forced to move far from home, due to survival factors; work, education and careers and have had to postpone having children to a later age. All this adds up to making young people even more vulnerable to being misled, due to lack of support from their families and friends and the education system. This is why, in some cultures, people marry while still young and remain under the care of their parents, that is the man's or the woman's parents. This is because many young couples cannot yet maintain themselves financially and more so if they have children.

Many young people, who have no clear instructions on sexual morals or any laws and regulations regarding procreativity, are easy prey for the media.

Who in their right mind would risk getting pregnant, just for "fun"? The problem is many young people never really believe they can get pregnant until it happens, and then the seriousness of their actions hits them. Who is to blame?

This lack of morals and lack of education on procreativity, lack of clear instructions on the use of contraceptives, has been a source of constant suffering for young people and the society in general.

Today, all women from a certain age, and especially in the early reproductive years, when they are most vulnerable, should be well aware because they should be well instructed that **any** sexual relationship could lead to a pregnancy; they should also know that: **no method of contraception is 100% effective or reliable** and that use of contraceptives does not make extramarital affairs morally acceptable; they still breach the Law of God. However, the option of contraception should be made readily available for all women married and not married, as a lesser evil to abortion.

Also, young people, male and female should be made fully aware of the other risks involved in extramarital affairs, especially from unwanted pregnancies. See examples these risks below.

- Get an abortion, or attempt an abortion with tragic consequences.
- If pregnant, you could suffer shame, which could even lead to suicide.
- You might be forced to give up your baby (which you desire to keep), for adoption, because you cannot afford to maintain it or for social stigma associated with single mothers.
- You might be forced to keep an unwanted baby, due to abortions being unaffordable or illegal.
- In some countries, you could get a death penalty, if procreativity outside marriage is forbidden by law; also in some countries, your own family could kill you if they feel you have dishonoured them.

- In the last months of pregnancy and after giving birth, you can't fend for yourself; you are handicapped and have to be maintained by others. You and your child are extremely vulnerable.

- Unwanted pregnancy could make you so desperate as to kill or abandon your child, where someone can find it and therefore take care of it.

- Unwanted pregnancies could make you a single parent, which could be extremely difficult if you and your child do not get enough financial and psychological support.

- As a single parent, your child may be considered "illegitimate," and their progress in life may be hampered by harsh discriminatory barriers, depending on the society you live in.

Other risks of extramarital affairs are:

- You might get sexually transmitted diseases/STDs: HIV, Hepatitis B, Human Papilloma Virus etc. some of which are incurable, and some could be transmitted to your new-born child.

- You could suffer mental anguish or a mental disorder, when things go wrong in your relationships.

- If photographed or filmed, you could be bribed, blackmailed or defamed.

- Illegal sex could create dangerous enemies and one could even get murdered for it, especially if it involves a high-ranking individuals.

What has God's identity got to do with human procreation? God's Law gives man an insight into God's personality.

God, who is Our Loving Father, would like all children to be born and raised up in the best possible environment and aims to do this through his Law on procreation. This same Law also safeguards women from the consequences of extramarital affairs and aims to have pregnant women well cared for, in their families, when in such a delicate phase of their life. This same Law safeguards the society; any child branded as illegitimate or bastard or other names could become extremely hostile to his society; developing ant-social behaviour, develop violent behaviour towards women or become a hard-core criminal. This child is innocent; does the society have any right to persecute him in any way?

One should never forget that God's Law is for the benefit of man and not God. Trust in God's Law even if you do not agree with or understand it completely. Do not forget that God is the source of righteousness. Although one might initially disagree with it or it may seem extremely cruel, for example, the Law on morals regarding procreativity, if you reflect deeply on it, pray to God to illuminate your mind and do some research on it; you are bound to come to the conclusion that it is 100% correct.

Respecting religious morals on procreativity is the most effective and reasonable way of preventing all the misery and problems associated with extra-marital affairs; because you will be following God's law out of love and respect for God; acknowledging that God's law is for your own benefit.

If one finds it difficult to follow God's Law; young people, in fact, anyone, could get an infatuation or a short-lived obsessive intense love for someone, perhaps with someone married, then you should pray to God for support to overcome your sinful craving. Your own personal experience, when God responds to you, is what will confirm to you that God is real and alive and willing to help those who appeal to him.

See below, one of the most painful consequences of unregulated procreation.

Abortion

According to the World Health Organization, as of 25 Nov. 2021, around 73 million induced abortions take place worldwide each year. This corresponds to approximately **125,000 abortions per day**. Six out of 10 (61%) of all unintended pregnancies, end in induced abortion. These statistics exclude spontaneous abortions. **The major cause of women having abortions is unwanted pregnancy**.

Is abortion murder?

The major religions and many other minor religions affirm that; from the moment of conception, the embryo is a complete human being and therefore, abortion is forbidden; it is taken to be murder.

The constitutions that permit abortion, give the foetus a legal human status after birth, when it takes its first breath.

Embryo: is formed from conception to the **first eight to ten weeks** of pregnancy. It is about 3,5cm, weighs about 8 grams and **has all the major body organs formed.**

A foetus: the embryo becomes a foetus from eight to ten weeks of pregnancy until birth.

The length of pregnancy, when you are legally permitted to have an abortion varies enormously among different countries and among different states of the same country; from before eight weeks to up to 24 weeks of pregnancy. Then, when people with unintended pregnancies face barriers to attaining safe, timely, affordable, geographically reachable, respectful and non-discriminatory abortion, they often resort to unsafe abortion. According to World Health Organization, WHO, unsafe abortions account for 13.2% of all maternal deaths and almost all of them: 97% of them are in developing countries.

The fact is, if women are denied abortions by the government, many will still have the abortion at the risk of their own lives; this is how revolting and frightening an unwanted pregnancy can be to a woman.

If a government or society does not equip young people with a thorough education on procreation, i.e. the morals, rules and laws, risks and means of regulating it; right from an early age, this is equivalent to a very serious form of neglect and the society itself is complicit in young people getting unwanted pregnancies and should not deny them the right to have abortions.

This subject regarding human procreation is delicate and complex and needs to be addressed properly, with clear moral, legal and practical guidance.

Marriage

According to Jesus, marriage is indissoluble, except in the case of adultery.

Matthew 5:32; But I say to you that everyone who divorces his wife, **except on the ground of sexual immorality,** makes her commit adultery, and **whoever marries a divorced woman commits adultery**. Jesus confirms here that; **marriage is for life**, with divorce being permitted only due to unfaithfulness.

This means that, from the Christian point of view, marriage is taken to be a lifetime commitment.

This means that practising Christians should do a bit of research before/when they select their partner and for example, meet the family of their spouse and should take marriage very seriously, because before God, marriage is infrangible, for those who marry in church. I believe that, in all cultures, except modern man, marriage is always considered to be a lifetime commitment; I believe this is to safeguard the children born to the couple.

Homosexuality

From **the Bible, it is clear that homosexual practices are regarded as a sin,** this we cannot deny. Generally, the homosexual activity described in the Bible, was associated with pagan worship and moral degradation e.g. that of Sodom and Gomorrah, but Homosexual orientation or identity is not considered in the Bible; probably because it never existed.

See **Leviticus 18:22**; "You must not lie down with a male in the same way that you lie down with a woman. It is a detestable act.

Leviticus 20:13; 'If a man lies down with a male the same as one lies down with a woman, both of them have done a detestable thing. They should be put to death without fail. Their own blood is upon them."

People who are homosexuals or lesbians have a **diverse** sense of sexual identity or orientation from normal people. What I am saying is, they perceive themselves to be different from their biological sex, at every moment of their lives and do not become homosexuals or lesbians only in bed. Many of them say that they realised they were different from other people, right from childhood.

I do not believe we have fully understood what leads people to acquire these **LGBTQ/ (Lesbian, gay, bisexual, transgender and questioning) identities**. It could be the roles played by each individual parent in their upbringing; it could be genetic or it could be a hormonal issue.

I personally, have known two gay people, who in my opinion rejected their male identity and have a feminine identity. I noted that their gestures are very feminine. It is my opinion that the input they had from their upbringing in their own families might have led them unconsciously to acquire this identity. In one case, the mother was the most dominant figure in their family and the boy was very attached to the mother; this might have led the young boy to reject his masculine identity, which might have been unconsciously perceived as "a weakling." In the other gay man's family, the mother was "a saint" as she was the pillar of the family, despite physical and financial abuse from an alcoholic, "good-for-nothing husband." I believe this gay man acquired a negative perception of the male figure from his father and did not want to identify as such, so ended up acquiring, perhaps unconsciously, a female identity. Therefore, I would not exclude that certain relationships in the family might create, unconsciously, a sexual bias against your own biological sexual identity.

If someone feels they have been created in a certain manner, which does not harm anyone else, why should people go after them; persecuting them or even killing them? If God has not yet killed the LGBTQ people, why should anyone else kill them? Why should they not be left to live their lives just like anyone else; provided they do not try to recruit people, especially young people into being LGBTQ? It is also unacceptable the use of coercive therapies and other measures, to "cure" or change the sexual orientation of LGBTQ people. Laws should be made to protect this group of people, that is LGBTQ from persecution and murder by other non-LGBTQ people. Everyone should be left free to follow their nature.

These LGBTQ people are our sons and daughters and our brothers and sisters, in some cases our fathers and mothers and dear friends, part of our families and communities; besides many of them play very important roles in our communities. **Acceptance and inclusion** is what LGBTQ people have been fighting for, over the centuries.

In, many countries in the Western world, people with LGBTQ identities, have now gained acceptance in their communities and Laws have been made to protect them. Nowadays, the struggle for inclusion is an on-going issue and is bound to continue because, although their relationships have been accepted by many societies, these relationships are not perceived and accepted as normal.

The LGBTQ people know very well that they are considered "sinners" by many people and by many religions, for example, Christians, Jews and Muslims. Many LGBTQ people have been killed or have had extremely difficult lives in their own communities, once their "diverse sexuality" became public; this has lead the LGBTQ people to live their lives without revealing their sexual orientation. "**Coming out**" is when an LGBTQ person decides to make his sexual orientation public. If certain people believe they were created by God as LGBTQ and cannot change their nature, we should leave God alone to be their judge.

Forgiveness

Luke 17: 4; If your brother commits a sin, **rebuke him**, and **if he repents**, forgive him. Even if **he sins seven times a day** against you and he comes back to you seven times, saying, '**I repent**,' you must forgive him. Now if one really repents, how then could they continue to sin?

Matthew 23-24: Therefore if you bring your gift to the altar, and there remember that your brother has something against you, leave your gift there before the altar, and go your way. First be reconciled to your brother, and then come and offer your gift.

Matthew 18:15-20. In this sermon, Jesus advises people not to let themselves be offended by someone who does you wrong then refuses to apologize; just forget about them.

Jesus explains that the key to being forgiven is to repent, however, note that Jesus says that: "**if your brother commits a sin, rebuke him.**" If you care for someone, then you should rebuke them and show your disapproval when they do what is sinful or bad in your eyes; hopefully, this might make "The Sinner" reconsider their behaviour.

This shows that Christians **should always** seek to forgive **if the wrongdoer repents.** Sometimes those who offended you will not repent; it is not advisable to carry bad feelings against someone;

just try and remove them from your mind. Sometimes it might prove very difficult to forgive certain wrongs, but with God everything is possible.

A controversial and frequent query:

This question is generally addressed to the clergy: "*If God knew I would go to Hell, why did he bother creating me?*"

Answer: Even though God knows you will go to Hell, this does not change the fact that it is you, **yourself** who chose to go to Hell.

God has provided man with free will. This means that it is man who decides on his course of action; he himself is accountable for his decisions on whether to follow God's Law or not.

Now one might argue, why should God give me free will and then punish me for my decisions, if they are not in harmony with his Law? God has also informed man of the consequences of living according to his Law and living without considering God's Law. If God has given you free will, it is very obvious that he has also given you the capacity to reason, that is the capacity to consider and understand various options, the capacity to form judgements and your own opinion and then the capacity to select what is **beneficial** for you.

Note: Your judgement will need to be based on **accurate information** for you to make the correct decision and it is your responsibility to make sure that your decisions are based on accurate, that is, correct information.

If God says: "If you live according to my Law, this will lead you to eternal life" and "If you do not live according to my Law, this will lead you to extinction/destruction, and you will cease to exist." This is the word of God: it is a fact; it is the truth. It is now up to man to decide; to make an informed conscious decision, of his own free will, on what option he prefers, but obviously after verifying that the options he has to choose from are accurate. One might decide to ignore God's Law and live as freely as they wish, without care for anything and to hell with eternal life and everything else. **Now who is to blame for the consequence of such decisions?**

The nature of God is that He knows the **past, the present and the future but this does not make Him responsible for your decisions.**

Fear of God

Previously, I found the phrases: "You should fear God" and "You should love God" contradictory. However, it is now clear that the phrase, "Fear God" does not mean the unpleasant feeling one gets when one senses danger, instead it means that we should acknowledge God's authority over us and all creation.

Generally, you "fear" your father and mother, in that you acknowledge their authority over you and would not like to do something that offends them. This is similar to what the Bible means when it says: "Fear God." The word "fear" in the Bible is translated from the Hebrew word, "Yir-ah" which means "awe" and "submission."

God is: "Our Father" in that He takes care of us, why should anyone seek offend him deliberately?

Salvation: being saved in Christianity

I feel that I should mention the word, Salvation; a word very present in many Christian churches today. **Salvation in Christianity** means redemption, deliverance and rescue from sin and its consequences, that is damnation and eternal death.

How does salvation take place?

Generally speaking, salvation is a gift from God, an act of goodwill, due to God's desire to save someone from sin and consequently from damnation, always taking into account that, all this is accomplished, due to the sacrifice of His Son Jesus Christ.

However, from what I have heard and seen, some people seem to get fulminated by some supernatural power, (the Holy Spirit), and they suddenly become overwhelmed and very emotional. They say that they suddenly realise, they have constantly sinned against God, their Major Benefactor and have failed to appreciate the fact that Jesus Christ sacrificed his life for them. They become filled with remorse and vow not to go back to their previous life of being a sinner. They acknowledge that it is by the grace of God, an unmerited favour; that they have been saved from sin and eternal damnation and this is why they say: "I am saved."

From that moment onwards, the saved person is transformed spiritually and resolves not to go back to their former sinful lives.

There are numerous examples in the Old Testament, where God sends out prophets to request the Israelites to turn back to Him, to avoid Him destroying them, because they had broken their Covenant with Him and had opted to practise evil.

A particular example is narrated in the book of Jonah in the Old Testament of the Bible, but in this case, God sent an Israelite prophet, Jonah, to a non-Israelite community, (which had made no covenant with Him) in the Assyrian city of Nineveh. The message was that impending destruction was scheduled due to their evil practices. God destroyed in the ancient world and continues to destroy evil today, wherever it is present and when it reaches a certain level.

Jonah had little sympathy for the Assyrians and would have preferred their destruction, so instead of going to Nineveh as God had requested him to do, he ran away and ended up being swallowed by a whale. Then Jonah prayed to Jehovah his God from the belly of this fish. After three days in the belly of the whale, Jehovah commanded the whale and it vomited Jonah out onto dry land; he eventually went to Nineveh. The people of Nineveh did repent, and were spared from destruction; however, they must have retaken up their sinful way of life, because, eventually, Nineveh was destroyed.

Examples of success in relying on God

This principle of reliance on God has been followed with great success by many people in desperate conditions; these people have come to believe firmly in God, because really, it is your personal experience with God, that shapes how you perceive Him. Here are some examples:

Myself

Example: I sometimes misplace my house keys, just when I am about to go out and I get quite distressed because, generally, I do this when I am going out for something important. Then it hits me; God surely knows where my keys are; why don't I ask him for help? I say a little prayer and guess what? After my prayer, I always find my keys, I have never failed to find them.

Alcoholics Anonymous, AA

Alcoholics Anonymous, AA, is an international organization, which was founded in 1935, in Ohio, USA, by two men who were ex-alcoholics: Bill Wilson and Dr Bob Smith.

Alcoholics Anonymous is formed specifically by ex-alcoholics with the aim of giving mutual aid and fellowship to alcoholics. It is dedicated to abstinence-based recovery from alcoholism, through its spiritually inclined Twelve Step program. AA is non-professional, non-denominational, as well as apolitical and unaffiliated.

Members of Alcoholics Anonymous use a Twelve Step Program, whose main principle is that of relying on God's help to maintain their abstinence and relying on mutual fellowship to support each other, in all ways possible, to achieve a **definite cure for intractable, chronic alcoholism.**

The term anonymous means not identifiable, especially not identifiable by name. In Alcoholics Anonymous, anonymity is provided for all members, which protects them from being identified as alcoholics, a safeguard often of special importance to newcomers. Because its founders and first members were recovering alcoholics themselves, they knew from their own experience how ashamed most alcoholics are about their drinking and how fearful they are of public exposure.

The term "anonymous" also means that AA members should not reveal to others, any information shared during AA meetings.

According to the Alcoholics Anonymous programme, the first thing an alcoholic needs to do is acknowledge his absolute failure in resolving his alcoholism and put himself totally in the hands of God and request help. Many alcoholics who have been successful in curing their addiction, through the AA association, reported having had a spiritual encounter with God which left them feeling quite different, more positive and inspired, and confident that they would make it to free themselves from alcohol.

One vows complete abstinence from alcohol and to follow a spiritually inclined Twelve Step Recovery Program. This cure has to be maintained by constant prayer, whereby one seeks through prayer and meditation to improve their conscious contact with God as you personally perceive Him, praying only for knowledge of His will for you and for the power to carry that out that will. **Complete abstinence from alcohol and fellowship, are obligatory**, whereby one does community work with other members of Alcoholics Anonymous, which regards mainly supporting other alcoholics or ex-alcoholics and their families. All members of the AA are ex-alcoholics who have overcome their chronic alcoholism and the remaining members are those striving to overcome their dependence on alcohol. This is a huge advantage for AA because the members really understand what alcoholism really is and therefore, are in a very good position to help other alcoholics overcome their addiction to alcohol.

The health issues associated with chronic alcoholism are so severe that generally, the initial part of recovery involves medical support in a hospital, for the alcoholic through nutrition, vitamins and iron supplements etc. before starting the Alcoholics Anonymous therapy, in full swing. There is no rehab centre or detox centre for alcoholism in the world or even medication for alcoholism, **with more success than** the therapy followed by Alcoholics Anonymous, that of relying on God for support.

Alcoholics Anonymous is the most effective treatment for abstinence from alcohol in the world, as confirmed by the most recent research by Keith Humphrey, PhD Professor of Psychiatry and Behavioural Sciences, and two collaborators of Stanford School of Medicine (2020/23) and other research studies. Alcoholics Anonymous has now become an international organization with branches all over the world. **Today it is present in over 180 countries. It is open to all who wish to abstain from alcohol and is free of charge**.

If a serious addiction to alcohol can be cured through trust in God and prayer, why not drug addiction or other forms of addiction? In fact, this Twelve Step recovery programme of Alcoholics Anonymous is currently being followed to cure other types of addictions: drug addiction, compulsive gambling, sex addiction and overeating.

I once heard on the radio, an ex-heroin addict claim to have been permanently cured by God; addiction to heroin is incurable. The programme on the radio was discussing how best to treat drug addicts, but they didn't follow up on how this particular man had been cured by God; most probably they did not believe in what he had said.

Psychiatry

The mind is called psyche in Greek and the study of diseases relating to the psyche is called psychiatry, when the study is done by doctors in medicine but it is called when done as a speciality, by those not of the medical profession.

Today the mind is defined as a collection of mental processes: perception, thought, memory, attention etc. essential for the proper and conscious functioning of the individual, which leads to discernment and being able to make proper judgement. It is not known exactly where the mind's multiple functions are located inside the brain, but when any of its components do not function well, this becomes visible in the person's behaviour, perception, thought or mobility. The state of consciousness, that of being aware, and the state of unconsciousness are also functional parts of the mind.

Please note: The soul is not the same thing as the mind; the soul is immaterial, but the mind is a functional part of the brain and therefore subject to death.

Cognition is a mental process of knowing or **being aware of,** derived from the Latin "con" that is "with" and "gnosco," "know," the word "gnosco" has a Greek origin: "I know" or "I perceive."

This process of cognition involves acquiring knowledge through senses and experiences, and **understanding this knowledge** through thought, reasoning, imagination, intuition, memory etc.

In Psychiatry, disorders like anxiety, panic attacks and depression are increasingly present in our society today. They create a lot of suffering for the sick people and their families, but sometimes their communities could also be affected. Psychiatric diseases place a huge economic burden on the healthcare systems, worldwide.

The burden of disease, definition: the negative impact of disease in a society in terms of financial cost, morbidity and mortality.

The treatment of many psychiatric disorders, for example, those mentioned above, is based mainly on medication and psychotherapy. Medication is given mainly to control the symptoms but does not cure these diseases. If these diseases are not identified early and therefore not treated early, they tend to become chronic and may degenerate into more severe psychiatric disorders. Although deemed incurable, combined treatment using medicine and a skilled psychotherapist could eventually cure some people.

If a sick person identifies himself or herself as: "a believer," that is they believe in God, why not benefit from your faith? These diseases could be cured definitely through faith and prayer; God can do it.

Case 1: A certain mother of two had a husband who had a very dangerous job. Lately, this lady had started thinking of what might happen to her and her kids, if her husband died on the job. Eventually, this became an obsession, to the point that she required medicine to calm her anxiety. A God-fearing professional had a talk with this lady and informed her that she was correct; there was a real possibility that her husband could die at work, but there was also a possibility that he could survive until he was eligible for his pension. Why then was this lady so fixed on the idea that her husband might die?

It is natural for us to take issues regarding our security very seriously because our safety and survival depend on them. Generally, before you go to sleep, you control to see your doors and windows are shut and take other security measures. The same thing in life, it is normal to try and ensure that anything that endangers your life and that of your loved ones, is taken care of by getting rid of it or decreasing its potential to harm anyone. However, one cannot get rid of all the diverse risks in your life, you could reduce them, but you cannot get rid of them all, completely; because you cannot foresee the future and really do not know what lies ahead in life. For this reason, one has to admit that risk is always present and is a part of life.

This is where a disease like anxiety creeps in; one starts to feel extremely vulnerable to a particular type of risk present in their life or to worry that a loved one could be at risk of something terrible. This state of "lack of control," of something perceived to be dangerous to your well-being, or to that of your loved ones, is what generates anxiety. Anxiety could also come from other factors, such as fear of not being able to pass your exams.

The above lady, whose husband did a dangerous job, was made to note that her husband could also die in his own home, through an accident or could get hit by a car just outside their house; also she too could die; who then would take care of her kids? This lady had to acknowledge that, bad things do happen but one cannot foresee them because as a human being, you cannot foresee the future. Why then should one waste their time worrying over something which they have absolutely no control over? This lady had to acknowledge her limits; that she cannot foresee and therefore cannot manage future risks because she is human. She was made to note that practically no one is able to foresee the future and therefore, everyone has to live with some risk; it is part of life.

On enquiring if she believed in any God, she said she did; she was a Christian. On enquiring if she was really convinced that God was all-powerful, knew all the future and had full control of the future, she said she believed it. So, it was suggested that it would be wise if she prayed for God's protection, as God is all-powerful and all-knowing and she could rest assured, if she had faith in God, that she would be fully protected whatever bad event happened to her or her loved ones, in the future. She was advised to learn to live her faith; to rely on God, as He is really the one who takes care of us; He is Our Heavenly Father; that said, he is also The Sovereign Lord of the Universe, and nothing is impossible for him.

Following this suggestion, this lady changed her attitude to life and did not need any more medication for anxiety; she got her life back from worrying. She later admitted that, whenever negative thoughts came into her mind, she would say a prayer and get on with it.

The medical definition of trauma is:

• A physical trauma is a big blow to your body, which may result in severe damage to your body. For example, a fall from a ladder, resulting in quite a large quantity of blood collecting under your skin, or even a broken arm.

• Trauma is also used to define "an emotional blow", a psychological trauma, which really is a deeply disturbing and emotional experience. For example: if someone survives an earthquake physically unharmed, they might suffer serious emotional trauma, from this experience and might refuse to go back inside buildings, if they had witnessed some buildings collapsing and people being killed and/or injured.

Panic Attack

Case Two: Panic Attack

A Panic Attack is a psychiatric/ mental disorder, which involves someone having intense fear, out of the blue, which is without any apparent cause for alarm. This huge surge of paralysing fear repeats sporadically, without any warning.

Generally, these Panic Attacks start after one has survived a terrible event in their life. Such events could be:

- A terrible train crash, resulting in the death of some people.
- Experiencing a robbery with violence, where you lose something precious or suffer great financial damage.
- Experiencing war and witnessing extreme brutality or you perpetrating very brutal actions on others, under orders.
- Rape or attempted rape.
- A terrorist attack or a hijack.
- The sudden death of someone very close to you, especially in your presence.

These horrendous experiences could create huge emotive/psychological scars due to how deeply you felt the events, accompanied by your incapacity to intervene in any way at that particular moment.

Our minds are made in such an effective way, that sometimes when one suffers a huge and ugly emotive/psychological trauma, your mind eliminates it from your consciousness **temporarily**, to protect you from being overwhelmed by your emotions. This means that the memory of your terrible experience goes blank.

In your activities of daily life, all will be normal until the memory of this particular event emerges from your subconscious; then you will get a flashback, a sudden vivid memory of a past event, whereby you will re-live that horrendous moment of "your forgotten horrible experience."

A Panic Attack starts when you start having a flashback, because you will be transported back to "your forgotten horrible experience" and will re-live the traumatic episode in all its colours, sounds, images, emotions and sensations, including the paralysing fear or anxiety you felt when it happened. Your body's reaction when you are having a Panic Attack will be that of extreme panic or extreme anxiety, dry mouth, increased heart rate, lack of breath, sweat etc.,

Generally, something that acutely reminds you of that particular horrible event triggers your memory making it emerge from your subconscious. For example, if you were involved in a terrorist attack and one of the terrorists had on a blue shirt, if you meet a man wearing a blue shirt, this fact will bring back vivid memories of that particular terrorist attack, provoking a full-swing Panic Attack.

The people near you will notice that you are suddenly acting strangely and also that you are very distressed; usually, someone will call for a doctor. The doctor might give you medication that will calm you down for the time being and might refer you to a psychiatrist, however, episodes of these Panic Attacks, tend to re-occur.

I must say that anyone who suffers a Panic Attack could put themself and others in great danger when having the Panic Attack. This is because one has an altered state of mind and is not fully conscious of their actions. One is capable of doing things like pulling the stop chain of a moving train, trying to open a door of a moving train or car or jumping off a moving bus or suddenly crossing a road full of traffic without taking the necessary precautions etc.

These Panic Attacks will keep coming back, making you and those near you very distressed, until you address the terrible experience you had. Generally, one needs help to get over these Panic Attacks.

Family, friends, physiotherapists, psychiatrists and your own strength are essential in helping you overcome the Panic Attack. One needs to go through these flashbacks by consciously reviewing them, slowly and in detail, with the support of someone whom you trusts, who will comfort and support you and serve as a connection to "a real, safe and present environment." Eventually, when you are finally cured, you will manage to consciously remember the distressing event that occurred, without going into a panic.

Feeling safe is especially important in curing a Panic Attack because the distressing experience that happened leaves the person concerned feeling very vulnerable. One is bound to ask themselves: "What if this happens again?"

This is where one's faith comes in; one has to cultivate getting in touch with God in their daily life. If you believe in God, then you should know that God is always present and will take care of you, if you pray for His protection and trust in Him. This should bring comfort and security into your life, as no one can take better care of you than Your Heavenly Father, who is also The Sovereign Lord of the Universe.

Major depressive disorder (MDD) chronic depression, clinical depression, major unipolar depression

All the above "Depressions" refer to the same psychiatric disease or disorder or the same mental disease or disorder. This is a real and serious psychiatric, mental illness and not just a one-off feeling of sadness, but something that is constantly present both night and day. It must last continually for at least two weeks, for it to be of any clinical relevance. Generally, an episode of Chronic Depression, if left untreated, will last for six to twelve months or more. Major Depression Disorder, are also called Unipolar Major Depression; this term differentiates it from the Depression present in bipolar disorders.

A point of information on bipolar disorder:

In Bipolar disorder, one alternates between depression and a manic episode. While in the maniac episode, one **loses touch with reality and** is in a state of elation, feeling extremely happy and overconfident in everything they do; they perceive themselves to be a kind of genius in everything. In this maniac phase, one could ruin themselves financially, due to wrong investments or due to overspending; one could have short-lived romantic adventures because they believe themselves to be irresistible to the opposite sex, also one could do very dangerous things, risking other people's lives. Here is an example, when in a maniac phase, a bipolar person has an inflated believe in his capabilities and if he works with dangerous machines, he might ignore some safety rules, endangering all those handling these machines. In this maniac state, one sleeps little, because he feels full of energy and with less need to sleep.

In Bi-polar disorder, this state of elation is followed by a change of mood to one of depression, where one feels so miserable and incompetent and would just like to disappear.

Let's continue with Major Depressive Disorders ...

In psychiatry and psychology, the term **affect** is used to define the immediate emotive state of a person; that is how you feel. Diseases that affect how one feels are referred to as Affective Disorders; Major Depressive Disorder is an **Affective Disorder**.

Major Depression Disorder is a chronic recurrent disease and if left untreated, about 50% of depressed people will have one or more recurrent episodes.

According to the World Health Organization (WHO), Major Depression Disorder is the most common type of mental illness in the world, followed by anxiety disorders.

Today in the Western World, Major Depression is one of the leading causes of disability, whereby one ends up being maintained by family, friends or the government. Furthermore, your relationship with your friends and family may become quite difficult; they no longer understand you because you seem to have acquired a negative and difficult personality overnight.

Major Depression affects how you feel. Your perception of life becomes 100% negative, in that you are not able to perceive anything good or positive anymore. You also feel that you do not have the will to do anything; all your past hobbies will cease to interest you. You will notice that nothing really gives you pleasure anymore/ **anhedonia**. You start finding life very difficult to live; when you wake up in the morning, you will find that there is nothing to look forward to, for that particular day. You will curse the state of your being alive and eventually, this lack of interest in anything will lead you to start contemplating committing suicide.

Major Depression is a disease that creeps into your existence, so that you can't tell with precision, exactly when you started feeling different, having a negative perception of almost everything.

Symptoms of Chronic Major Depression:

- **Your thoughts and perception are always negative**. Try hard as you can, you will never see any positive side in anything.

- **You have no will to do anything**; you simply exist but are not living. Try hard as you can, nothing really interests you and nothing gives you any pleasure/**anhedonia**. Your former interests are completely dead to you.

- **You are constantly in a state of irritation**, a kind of internal restlessness a kind of internal emotional distress.

- **Altered appetite**, too much or too little.

- **Frequent suicidal ideation:** you frequently consider suicide or have attempted to commit suicide.

- **Feelings of sadness, tearfulness, emptiness** or hopelessness, worthlessness or guilt, fixating/concentrating only on past failures or self-blame.

- **Disturbed sleep patterns**: either too much sleep or it is too short and superficial, in that when you awake, you feel like you have not slept.

- You could become extremely sensitive to cold, even in the summer.

- **Trouble thinking, concentrating**, making decisions and remembering things.

- Constant headache, which intensifies when you try to concentrate on something and which does not respond to medication.

- **Psychomotor retardation**: slowing down of your mental and physical capacity whereby one suffers tiredness and lack of energy so that even small tasks take extra effort.

According to the Diagnostic and Statistical Manual of Mental Disorders, 5th Edition (**DSM-5**), which is the standard classification of psychiatric disorders used by The American Psychiatrist Association (**APS**); an individual **must have five or more** of the above-mentioned symptoms, the ones containing capital letters, **of which one must be** either depressed mood or **Anhedonia,** failure to find pleasure in anything and these symptoms should be causing social or occupational impairment.

Complications of Major Depression

Individuals with Major Depressive Disorder (MDD) are at a high risk of developing comorbid anxiety disorders and substance use disorders, which further increases their risk of suicide. Depression can aggravate medical comorbidities such as diabetes, hypertension, chronic obstructive pulmonary disease, and coronary artery disease. Depressed individuals are at high risk of developing self-destructive behaviour as a coping mechanism. MDD is often very debilitating if left untreated. **(NCBI Bookshelf 559078)**

One should exclude the presence of a major depressive disorder in children and adolescents who present with a persistent irritable mood or anxiety.

What causes Clinical Depression/Major Depressive Disorder?

In certain circumstances, depression could be a side effect of some types of medication or a hormonal imbalance. It could occur postpartum because there is a big hormonal change immediately after giving birth. It is said that drugs and alcohol could also lead to depression; perhaps it might have been a non-diagnosed depression that leads someone to use drugs or drink alcohol excessively in the first place. Hereditary factors have been shown to play an important role in Chronic Depression, but if the negative experiences or other causes are absent, these particular people would not get depressed, however, their genetic composition makes them more sensitive and therefore, more susceptible to negative events and consequently more likely to suffer Depression.

Some examples of causes of Major/Chronic/Clinical Depression:

- Constant failure in achieving something, which is very important to you. For example, failure to graduate and failing exams.

- Prolonged abuse, especially in childhood.

- Bereavement of someone very close to you.

- A sequence of recent negative events in your life.

- Redundancy and or failure to find employment, especially if you are a man and have kids to maintain; men seem more affected than women.

- A chronic debilitating disease, e.g., Parkinson's disease.

The main cause of Major Chronic Depression is repeated negative experiences, or just one major bad experience, from which one feels there is no escape; a hopeless, helpless situation. The huge stress generated by this sense of defeat ends up affecting your mental state, which makes it difficult for you to function normally in your activities of daily life.

Many people suffering from Major Depression do not know for sure if they are actually sick; they realise that they are feeling different, but many do not know why. Until recently, mental diseases were and are still largely unknown to the public but, nowadays, they have become much more frequent at all levels of society. In the last few years, various campaigns have been launched in the Western World, to make the public aware of mental health illnesses and to fight the stigma associated with them. Today, almost all medical schools in the world teach psychiatry as part of their medical syllabus.

Chronic depression/Major depression could be quite difficult to diagnose, because it regards how you feel and if you do not tell the doctor your feelings unless he has had previous experiences with such mental health issues or he knows you and can note some unusual changes, this important disease could escape his attention. Most depressed people will consult their doctor for physical symptoms like lack of sleep but will not talk about their permanent state of misery.

Depression is, "a very private disease," in that the people who have it do not talk about it to their friends or family; perhaps the sick person does not know exactly what is ailing him or her. This is why the public and especially the medical profession should be well acquainted with the symptoms of Depression.

I must say that people with untreated depression could also be very dangerous and there are many people who have lived with undiagnosed Chronic Depression for years. If people suffering from Chronic Depression have a grudge against someone, colleagues, their boss etc. or against a certain group of people in their society, or any other persons, they might end up shooting them or executing a mass shooting because their state of depression makes them more sensitive to negative feelings, more than other people; also they don't mind being shot at, as their life is not important to them; actually, they frequently end up shooting themselves and committing suicide.

Studies suggest that depressed people are much more likely to harm others or themselves; 5-6 times more than non-depressed people; (Swedish study of Feb. 26/2015). This means that if left untreated, people suffering from Major Depression could be very dangerous.

About 10% to 15% of chronically depressed people commit suicide.

Studies show that the earlier you diagnose chronic depression and the earlier you start treatment, the better the outcome of the disease.

Officially, there is no permanent cure for Major Depression Disorder. It is an on-going disease with variable outcomes even when treated. The success in curing depression is affected by various things, for example, the presence or not of other diseases, the level of support available, the level of functioning before the onset of the disease, etc.

An episode of untreated Major Depressive Disorder could last from 6 to 12 months, but here also there is a lot of individual variability.

The main treatment for major depression today is:

Medication:

Selective serotonin reuptake inhibitors/SSRIs and Serotonin and norepinephrine reuptake inhibitors/SNRIs, Serotonin Modulators, **TCAs,** MAOIs, Mood Stabilizers and Anti-Psychotics. Generally, **these medications aim at modifying or increasing serotonin and/or Dopamine** two neurotransmitters present in the brain, which are responsible for "feel good mood." Serotonin in particular is said to "increase happiness," and is used to treat depression and anxiety.

Psychotherapy:

Cognitive-behavioural therapy and Interpersonal Therapy. **Electroconvulsive Therapy** is for more severe depression; various procedures involving measured electrical stimulation of the brain or nerves may prove very effective in stabilizing very seriously ill patients by reducing or eliminating their symptoms.

It has been observed that some people, about 10-30%, are resistant to conventional anti-depressants. Today there are various clinical trials worldwide, for various substances aimed at eventually treating these drug-resistant patients.

The anti-depressant medication, when effective, removes the severe symptoms, making the person feel normal. Sometimes one has to try out different medications to get the one that works best for them. When chronically depressed people respond to their medication, they feel normal; they then realise that actually, they had been seriously sick. Medication is very important because, when effective, it stabilises a person and makes it easier to tackle the underlying issues that first led to depression, if this is possible.

It is important to educate the patient and his family about Major Depressive Disorder and also to inform them that it is one of the most common mental illnesses; this will make them feel less isolated and less stigmatized, in dealing with this disease which is likely to give a better outcome.

Although the emotional state of all depressed people is one of hidden suffering, many depressed people still have their reasoning capacity intact and they are bound to start wondering, "Why is it that my perception of everything is so negative? This perception cannot be correct." This might prompt someone to seek answers and eventually to seek treatment; sometimes your friends and or family might note your change in body weight; either you are grossly underweight or grossly overweight and insist on your seeing a doctor.

In the school syllabus we learn about germs, hygiene and diseases of the physical body but diseases of the mind, that is, Mental Health is not taught. This has now become a necessity, due to the rapid increase of mental disorders/diseases at all levels of society and also because we are now better at identifying them.

Many depressed people will continue taking their anti-depressant medication for a very long time, however, in some patients, their anti-depressant medication may actually stop working and their chronic depression symptoms will return. If anti-depressants are taken for long periods, at some point, most people get tired of taking them and will therefore stop taking them; however, there is always a risk of becoming ill again. If you decide to try and stop taking your anti-depressant medication, first it is advisable to inform your doctor so that someone is aware of you being at risk; also, it is advisable to scale down your medication, gradually.

Officially there is no permanent cure for depression; if not under any treatment, it tends to reoccur periodically and for longer periods.

Anti-depressant medication may help tackle and perhaps, solve some important problems related to depression, because it stabilizes you, in that you now feel normal; it removes many of the symptoms, such as negative thinking, lack of sleep or too much sleep, lack of concentration. If you are a student, you may now be able to concentrate, study and pass your exams, but other problems that led to depression might persist, even after one starts taking medication, for example, the presence of chronic diseases, however, one is able to deal with them better. The anti-depressant medication also has some side effects, which decrease over time.

One could also succeed in overcoming certain underlying problems, if one learns to re-consider them from a different and positive point of view, which will also change how one behaves in response to certain situations, in other words, cognitive behavioural therapy (CBT). However, to be honest, some problems have no positive point of view, for example, child sexual exploitation.

This is where prayers and faith become an important part of treatment. If one has faith and **full trust in God** and acknowledges that God is able to cure them, a permanent cure is possible. You might not get cured the first time you pray, but if you persist in prayer, and seek God's support constantly, you will surely get cured.

More than twenty years ago, I suffered from depression for a long time before I self-diagnosed myself. One of the main issues that prompted me to consider the possibility of being sick was when I encountered my friends, a family member or anyone I knew, they would all swear that I was sick. They all said that I was extremely thin, but I had always been quite thin, so I refused to believe them. Eventually, I noted that all my trousers had become extra-large; I also noted that I had become extremely sensitive to cold; I had to wear warm socks in the summer! It was then that I became convinced that I might be sick and sought to understand what disease I had.

I used to eat a lot, I could see someone eyeing my breakfast, quite impressed by its size, but surprisingly I was losing weight. I went to see my doctor to rule out Diabetes, but all the results turned out to be negative. I had a constant headache that was unresponsive to painkillers, so I did a scan of my neck and brain to rule out problems of circulation there, but the scans were negative. So, I decided to try and find out all by myself, what was ailing me. Luckily, I was a medical student. I listed all my very evident symptoms such as lack of sleep, loss of weight, constant headache, lack of concentration etc. and all the diseases associated with them. It was then that I noticed that one particular disease was positive for all my symptoms: Chronic Depression. I then read about this particular disease and to my surprise, it described my disease perfectly, even the strange symptoms, which I was not fully aware of before, like **anhedonia**, a lack of interest in almost everything.

Once I had understood my problem, I went to look for medication. In those days I had a sceptical attitude towards taking medication, but to my pleasant surprise, the medication prescribed, a Tricyclic Anti-depressant called Amitriptyline, worked overnight. For the first time in over six months, I slept deeply and felt rested in the morning. Before, I would wake up very early in the morning; I noted my eyes were always dry and I had a sensation like I had not actually slept. My other symptoms were also eliminated or very reduced, but had also some side effects, however, the benefits far outweighed them.

This was my first personal experience with a psychiatric illness; it confirmed that these diseases are real and could be very debilitating and this has permitted me to help other people suffering from psychiatric disorders.

I took medication for a long while and then I got tired of taking it and stopped. At that particular time, I was in my personal search for God. I had requested God to give me a sign that He was real and alive and I kept looking out for this particular sign. One day, I woke up and realised that I no longer had any Depression; I was completely cured and have not had this illness again for over twenty years. My cure for depression was the sign that God gave to me, to show me that He is real and alive.

Note: I had not prayed for a cure for my depression, it was a gift from God, and at the time was not aware of any cures by faith.

I personally have witnessed all the above three listed psychiatric illnesses, anxiety, panic attack and chronic depression completely cured, through faith and prayer. There are many other mental diseases, which I have not mentioned here, that are also curable through prayer; no disease is incurable to God.

One does not need to be seriously sick in order to request God's supernatural healing powers; if you are feeling low, unwell, worried, stressed, inclined to sin, or defeated, please get in touch with your Heavenly Father. It is only after resolving your numerous problems that you will acknowledge that God is real and has mighty, positive power and that He is worthy of worship.

Is the use of faith to cure psychiatric disorders legal?

In psychiatry today, the use of religion and spirituality for the treatment of psychiatric disorders is contentious and is banned in many countries. However, research so far shows that religion has a very important role to play in the treatment and management of psychiatric disorders. Psychiatrists, who are atheists, should not be involved in these, "faith cures."

I do not understand, what is disputable about the use of religion as a means of cure in psychiatry because it is not the psychiatrist who cures the patient, it is God. If the psychiatrist believes in God, the only thing a psychiatrist should do is to make known to the patient, if they are believers in God, of this possibility and suggest that the patient could seek a cure from God, if they have faith and confidence that God can cure them. The psychiatrist should make it clear to the patient, that he himself cannot guarantee them any cure from God, **this matter is personal between the patient and God and they should not feel obliged to seek any cure from God; it is up to the patient to decide, what to do after deep reflection and that the patient is not obliged to inform the psychiatrist of their decision.**

Giving the patient a brochure, informing them of the cures by faith and contacts of those who could explain it further to them, **if they are interested**, would make life easier for all, patients, psychiatrists, psychologists and others.

The psychiatrist should also give the patient the officially accepted treatment for their mental condition; this medication might make the patient more stable and therefore in a better position to evaluate their options.

Consent from the patient should always be sought when considering the use of religion for the treatment of mental illnesses; if it doesn't interest them, then do not go ahead with it. **Using faith as a means of cure is just another option, of which the patient is made aware of.**

Healthcare workers, including psychiatrists, psychologists, psychotherapists, nurses and others, are trained and obliged to always respect and be sensitive to the spiritual or religious beliefs and practices of their patients, **or the lack of them.**

The problem comes when psychiatrists who would like to suggest the use of religion as an alternative cure, are prohibited from doing so by some rules or regulations. Generally, there is a lack of legislation regarding "Cures by Faith" mainly because there is not enough research done to prove that these are real and effective. Legislation could be achieved only if the use of these

Cures by Faith is allowed and their outcome is recorded in research programmes.

This continued lack of legislation on the use of religion or spirituality as a therapeutic tool for treating mental illness, is a serious form of neglect, that of failing to act in the patient's interest.

Classification of mental/psychiatric illnesses

There are mainly two sources for classifying mental illnesses:

1. International Classification of Diseases/ICD, created by the World Health Organisation/WHO. It is updated every one to three years.

2. Diagnostic Statistical Manual/DSM 5th Edition, which is the American Psychiatrist Association's classification of psychiatrist disorders and is reviewed and updated, every five to seven years.

By consulting any of these classifications of mental illnesses, one could come to understand if they or someone else could be suffering from mental illness.

Note: The definition of specific mental disorders keeps changing with time; for example, homosexuality was classified as a mental disorder in the USA, by the Diagnostic and Statistical Manual of Mental Disorders /DSM, up until 1973. From 1974 to 2013, homosexuality was described as: "Distress over one's sexual orientation." From 2013, sexual orientation, including homosexuality, was not classified anymore in the Diagnostic Statist Manual/DSM-5, (5th edition), used by the American Psychiatric Association to classify mental diseases or disorders; that is, it ceased to be considered a mental disorder and nowadays, is not considered a mental disease.

33

Psychedelics, new cures for drug addiction and mental disorders

There is a new and very promising treatment for severe psychiatric disease and addiction: psychedelics.

Psychedelics definition: These are **serotonergic hallucinogens** and are powerful psychoactive substances that alter perception, mood, affect and numerous **cognitive processes** and also expand your state of consciousness; that is, you perceive things that normally you are not able to. In addition, some psychedelics like Ibogaine, have **a dissociative action,** that is one perceives themselves to be detached from their own body and/or from their environment.

Please note: Dissociation could also occur "naturally," after suffering extreme psychological/ emotional trauma. A person in this dissociative state does not know who they are, they lose their sense of identity. This type of dissociation is a defence mechanism of the body's psyche or mind, to protect itself from more extreme suffering, by switching off or altering its state of perception, in order to escape a very painful reality. This condition could last from a few hours to some days.

In the Nervous System, a substance called Serotonin acts as a neurotransmitter, which is a substance that nerves use to communicate with each other. A low production of serotonin in the brain is thought to be one of the major causes of depression. The major anti-depressant medication, SSRIs/selective serotonin reuptake inhibitors and SNRIs/Serotonin and norepinephrine reuptake inhibitors, aim at increasing the level of serotonin and dopamine accessible to the brain nerves, by blocking or inhibiting selectively the nerve receptors responsible for their reabsorption, reuptake or removal from the synaptic cleft.

The term "Serotonergic" means that a substance has an affinity for Serotonin receptors on the brain's nerve cells and by binding to them, they stimulate the release of serotonin.

Note: The digestive tract makes 90% of the body's serotonin, identical to the brain serotonin, which actually originates from being secreted by gut bacteria. This hormone is involved in digestion, mood regulation and many other physiological and biological processes, creating the so-called Gut-Brain Axis. This is because this particular hormone and others that are made in the gut, influence the brain and therefore your mood. The gut is also called the Second Brain, as there is an extensive nervous system which regulates the gastrointestinal system, which in turn connects to the brain and influences it in various ways; it could also alert it when something is amiss. Have you heard the expression "gut feeling"? This is an instinctive emotional response, which alerts you when something is wrong; it should not be ignored, because surprisingly, most times, it turns out to be correct.

The origin of the use of most **psychedelics,** which are **plant extracts**, is ancient. Various indigenous peoples have used them **safely** for ritual and religious ceremonies, for hundreds of years. Most of these people have a reverence for these psychedelic substances. **When used by these indigenous peoples, they do not lead to dependence or addiction.**

In recent years, the study of psychedelics as alternatives for the treatment of severe mental illnesses and addiction has been reconsidered. In some countries, the use of psychedelic substances has been banned for a long time, due to their abuse as recreational drugs but right now, in many centres in the world, psychedelic substances are on clinical trials.

Below is a list of the most well-known psychedelics

- LSD (d-lysergic acid diethylamide), originally from Rye fungus.
- Psilocybin, from mushrooms grown in Mexico and South America.
- Peyote, from Mescaline, spineless, thornless cactus grown in Mexico.
- DMT (Dimethyltryptamine), occurs naturally in some Amazonian plants; species: Ayahuasca.
- Ibogaine: derived from roots of a West African shrub: Tabernanthe iboga. It has been used successfully by trained professionals to cure cocaine and heroin addiction in a very short period.

Please view below, some clinical trials and clinical use of psychedelics to cure mental disorders and addiction.

1. https://nyulangone.org/news/single-dose-hallucinogenic-drug-psilocybin

   A single dose of hallucinogen, psilocybin, relieves anxiety and depression in patients with advanced cancer.

2. https://ec.europa.eu.>horizon-magazine>psychedelics

   Check for: "Psychedelics paired with Therapy could help treat mental conditions" 24 Oct. 2022.

3. Can a hallucinogen from Africa cure addiction? BBC News (13 April 2012)

4. Psilocybin-assisted treatment for alcohol dependence: a proof-of-concept study - NIH

5. LSD "Helps alcoholics give up drinking." BBC 9 March 2012

6. LSD, a new treatment emerging from the past-PMC-NCBI

7. Dr Nikola Ognyenovitis and co-presenter "Jansen" Ibogaine

Are psychedelics drugs harmful?

It all depends on how you use them; like most substances, they could be very useful or very harmful, even lethal; it all depends on how you use them.

On the Google website, digit: "LSD ORIGIN ", then click on: "Apparently useless": The accidental discovery of LSD, (Under the Atlantic.com)

The above article is taken from an account of: Albert Hoffmann (a Sandoz lab researcher), who accidentally discovered one of the most powerful synthetic psychedelics: lysergic acid diethylamide/LSD. It is written by Tom Shroder.

At 4:20 in the afternoon of April 19, without informing anyone at Sandoz except his lab assistant, Hofmann dissolved **250 millionths of a gram** of lysergic acid diethylamide tartrate, the crystallized salt form of the compound, and drank it. He expected it to do absolutely nothing.

But just 40 minutes after that initial dose, he wrote the one and only entry in his lab journal:

17:00: *"Beginning dizziness, feeling of anxiety, visual distortions, symptoms of paralysis, desire to laugh."*

Note: In just 40 minutes, Mr Hoffmann felt he had lost complete control of his actions and perception, after ingesting an **infinitesimal dose: 250 millionths of a gram** of **pure** lysergic acid diethylamide/LSD.

You will discover, directly from the man who first isolated LSD, that this psychedelic, LSD **should be used in infinitesimal quantities**, a pinch of is just too much. With regard to artificially synthesized psychedelics, extra care in dosing is essential, specifically because they **are pure** i.e. they lack the natural "impurities", which modulate and dilute the psychedelic/drug.

View more information regarding the safe use of psychedelics, from the websites below.

- Synthetic drugs – Europol
- Hallucinogens Drug Facts – National Institute of Drug Abuse/NIDA
- adf.org.au/drug-facts

More information on the safe use of synthetic psychedelics.

Note: synthetic psychedelics and other substances such as synthetic heroin and synthetic cocaine are extremely dangerous, when commercialized as **recreational drugs, because most of them, such as cocaine are sold pure and are therefore very effective/powerful. However, it has become increasingly frequent for all forms of drugs to be sold in impure forms.** This trend is driven by the small drug dealers seeking to increase their profit margin by mixing the original pure drug with other chemical substances to increase the quantity ("cutting") of the drug they are selling, in order to gain additional profit from their sale.

The psychedelic recreational drugs, however, are marketed as small, very beautifully and colourfully designed pills; aimed to entice young people. They are very dangerous, and each such small pill could contain more than a lethal dose of the drug. **Please, do not get fooled into exchanging your life for a pill**. Do not fall under **peer pressure**; if someone is your friend, they should safeguard your life, unless they themselves are ignorant of the very dangerous properties of recreational drugs.

When a new recreational drug is officially made illegal, then, to evade prosecution, the illegal drug-manufacturing companies will start to produce something slightly different from the substance that has just been declared illegal. This new substance will never have been used before and therefore, no one knows the effects it has on man. **The illegal drug companies will put this new substance on the market, as "legal", because there is no law prohibiting its sale as yet.** When this new drug has killed enough people and has been brought to the attention of the drug regulators, then, after studying its effects, it will be declared illegal; and the cycle continues: another new "legal drug" will be invented. **The "legal drugs" are simply waiting to be made illegal; this means that all "legal drugs" are not safe.**

See NCBI's article on, "Coca: The History and Medical Significance of an Ancient Andean Tradition."

I quote the above article, under the heading of **Toxicity and Other Medical Concerns:** "The whole blood concentration of **pure cocaine** is almost 50 times greater after using the pure isolate in comparison to chewing whole coca."

Coca means a whole coca leaf of the cocaine-producing plant. Therefore, pure cocaine which is consumed in Europe and the USA, is extremely toxic, harmful and addictive. The American Indios who have used coca leaves for centuries, by chewing them, never get addicted to cocaine. The cocaine present in the coca leaf has "other plant impurities" which also have beneficial effects on the body and which also modulate the metabolism of cocaine, making it safe. These coca leaves have been used for centuries and are still used today in some South American countries, without any prosecution and their use is legal. The Indios have always perceived the cocaine or coca plant to be a gift from the gods because of the many benefits they derive from it. Coca leaves act as a very strong tonic for the whole body.

I have made a point of writing about Psychedelics because of the plight of addicts and other people with various psychiatric conditions, which are a source of great suffering for them, their families and society as a whole and with no definite solution. I hope the above information will help them resolve their problems permanently.

It is advisable also to watch an old documentary, (2005-2006): The Psychedelic Pioneers. It was produced in Canada and has among others; university researchers, psychologists, psychiatrists actors; one of them Abram Hoffer **discovered the cure for Schizophrenia**: See the book: Niacin The Real Story.

The Drug Enforcement Administration/DEA of the USA government has a lot of information on various types of drugs being marketed world-wide. Therefore, digit the drug's name, then hyphen then DEA, for example "Ecstasy-DEA" and search what you are looking for.

May I say that the plants, from which psychedelics are derived, were created by God and when used wisely, are for man's benefit?

In this booklet, I have tried to give accurate information about God, as best I can. I have heard many people say: Who really is God? Show me where God is. Why should I know God and of what use is he to me?

This booklet tries to answer these specific queries, by highlighting the qualities of God, that is His personality according to how he portrays Himself through his creations, in the Bible and according to how Jesus Christ defined Him. It is vital to have accurate knowledge of God in order to benefit yourself.

God Himself teaches man how to live **by instructing him through His Laws.** It is not surprising that the first of this Law, tells man to rely on Him **alone** "as a God," **because there is no other God but him**. That is, if you have any problems, let me be your first point of contact. Why? Because I am God, I care for man and nothing is impossible for me.

Now which individual would be so unwise, so ignorant or so self-conceited as to deliberately ignore making use of and hence benefitting from God and his very positive and infinite qualities, offered to him, **free of charge?**

Lastly, if one believes in God, their personal experience in relating to God is what really confirms to them, who God really is.